CASENOTE® Legal Briefs®

CRIMINAL PROCEDURE

Keyed to Courses Using

Saltzburg, Capra, and Gray's
American Criminal Procedure: Cases and Commentary
Twelfth Edition

Authored by: Publisher's Editorial Staff

ASPEN PUBLISHING

This publication is designed to provide accurate and authoritative information in regard to the subject matter covered. It is sold with the understanding that the publisher is not engaged in rendering legal, accounting, or other professional services. If legal advice or other expert assistance is required, the services of a competent professional person should be sought.

— From a Declaration of Principles adopted jointly by a Committee of the American Bar Association and a Committee of Publishers and Associates

To contact Customer Service, e-mail customer.service@aspenpublishing.com, call 1-800-950-5259, or mail correspondence to:

Aspen Publishing
Attn: Order Department
P.O. Box 990
Frederick, MD 21705

Printed in the United States of America.

1 2 3 4 5 6 7 8 9 0

ISBN 979-8-8861-4355-3

About Aspen Publishing

Aspen Publishing is a leading provider of educational content and digital learning solutions to law schools in the U.S. and around the world. Aspen provides best-in-class solutions for legal education through authoritative textbooks, written by renowned authors, and breakthrough products such as Connected eBooks, Connected Quizzing, and PracticePerfect.

The Aspen Casebook Series (famously known among law faculty and students as the "red and black" casebooks) encompasses hundreds of highly regarded textbooks in more than eighty disciplines, from large enrollment courses such as Torts and Contracts to emerging electives such as Sustainability and the Law of Policing. Study aids such as the *Examples & Explanations* and the *Emanuel Law Outlines* series, both highly popular collections, help law students master complex subject matter.

Major products, programs, and initiatives include:

- **Connected eBooks** are enhanced digital textbooks and study aids that come with a suite of online content and learning tools designed to maximize student success. Designed in collaboration with hundreds of faculty and students, the Connected eBook is a significant leap forward in the legal education learning tools available to students.
- **Connected Quizzing** is an easy-to-use formative assessment tool that tests law students' understanding and provides timely feedback to improve learning outcomes. Delivered through CasebookConnect.com, the learning platform already used by students to access their Aspen casebooks, Connected Quizzing is simple to implement and integrates seamlessly with law school course curricula.
- **PracticePerfect** is a visually engaging, interactive study aid to explain commonly encountered legal doctrines through easy-to-understand animated videos, illustrative examples, and numerous practice questions. Developed by a team of experts, PracticePerfect is the ideal study companion for today's law students.
- The **Aspen Learning Library** enables law schools to provide their students with access to the most popular study aids on the market across all of their courses. Available through an annual subscription, the online library consists of study aids in e-book, audio, and video formats with full text search, note-taking, and highlighting capabilities.
- Aspen's **Digital Bookshelf** is an institutional-level online education bookshelf, consolidating everything students and professors need to ensure success. This program ensures that every student has access to affordable course materials from day one.
- **Leading Edge** is a community centered on thinking differently about legal education and putting those thoughts into actionable strategies. At the core of the program is the Leading Edge Conference, an annual gathering of legal education thought leaders looking to pool ideas and identify promising directions of exploration.

Format for the Casenote® Legal Brief

Nature of Case: This section identifies the form of action (e.g., breach of contract, negligence, battery), the type of proceeding (e.g., demurrer, appeal from trial court's jury instructions) or the relief sought (e.g., damages, injunction, criminal sanctions).

Fact Summary: This is included to refresh your memory and can be used as a quick reminder of the facts.

Rule of Law: Summarizes the general principle of law that the case illustrates. It may be used for instant recall of the court's holding and for classroom discussion or home review.

Facts: This section contains all relevant facts of the case, including the contentions of the parties and the lower court holdings. It is written in a logical order to give you a clear understanding of the case. The plaintiff and defendant are identified by their proper names throughout and are always labeled with a (P) or (D).

Issue: The issue is a concise question that brings out the essence of the opinion as it relates to the section of the casebook in which the case appears. Both substantive and procedural issues are included if relevant to the decision.

Palsgraf v. Long Island R.R. Co.

Injured bystander (P) v. Railroad company (D)

N.Y. Ct. App., 248 N.Y. 339, 162 N.E. 99 (1928).

NATURE OF CASE: Appeal from judgment affirming verdict for plaintiff seeking damages for personal injury.

FACT SUMMARY: Helen Palsgraf (P) was injured on R.R.'s (D) train platform when R.R.'s (D) guard helped a passenger aboard a moving train, causing his package to fall on the tracks. The package contained fireworks which exploded, creating a shock that tipped a scale onto Palsgraf (P).

RULE OF LAW

The risk reasonably to be perceived defines the duty to be obeyed.

FACTS: Helen Palsgraf (P) purchased a ticket to Rockaway Beach from R.R. (D) and was waiting on the train platform. As she waited, two men ran to catch a train that was pulling out from the platform. The first man jumped aboard, but the second man, who appeared as if he might fall, was helped aboard by the guard on the train who had kept the door open so they could jump aboard. A guard on the platform also helped by pushing him onto the train. The man was carrying a package wrapped in newspaper. In the process, the man dropped his package, which fell on the tracks. The package contained fireworks and exploded. The shock of the explosion was apparently of great enough strength to tip over some scales at the other end of the platform, which fell on Palsgraf (P) and injured her. A jury awarded her damages, and R.R. (D) appealed.

ISSUE: Does the risk reasonably to be perceived define the duty to be obeyed?

HOLDING AND DECISION: (Cardozo, C.J.) Yes. The risk reasonably to be perceived defines the duty to be obeyed. If there is no foreseeable hazard to the injured party as the result of a seemingly innocent act, the act does not become a tort because it happened to be a wrong as to another. If the wrong was not willful, the plaintiff must show that the act as to her had such great and apparent possibilities of danger as to entitle her to protection. Negligence in the abstract is not enough upon which to base liability. Negligence is a relative concept, evolving out of the common law doctrine of trespass on the case. To establish liability, the defendant must owe a legal duty of reasonable care to the injured party. A cause of action in tort will lie where harm, though unintended, could have been averted or avoided by observance of such a duty. The scope of the duty is limited by the range of danger that a reasonable person could foresee. In this case, there was nothing to suggest from the appearance of the parcel or otherwise that the parcel contained fireworks. The guard could not reasonably have had any warning of a threat to Palsgraf (P), and R.R. (D) therefore cannot be held liable. Judgment is reversed in favor of R.R. (D).

DISSENT: (Andrews, J.) The concept that there is no negligence unless R.R. (D) owes a legal duty to take care as to Palsgraf (P) herself is too narrow. Everyone owes to the world at large the duty of refraining from those acts that may unreasonably threaten the safety of others. If the guard's action was negligent as to those nearby, it was also negligent as to those outside what might be termed the "danger zone." For Palsgraf (P) to recover, R.R.'s (D) negligence must have been the proximate cause of her injury, a question of fact for the jury.

ANALYSIS

The majority defined the limit of the defendant's liability in terms of the danger that a reasonable person in defendant's situation would have perceived. The dissent argued that the limitation should not be placed on liability, but rather on damages. Judge Andrews suggested that only injuries that would not have happened but for R.R.'s (D) negligence should be compensable. Both the majority and dissent recognized the policy-driven need to limit liability for negligent acts, seeking, in the words of Judge Andrews, to define a framework "that will be practical and in keeping with the general understanding of mankind." The Restatement (Second) of Torts has accepted Judge Cardozo's view.

Quicknotes

FORESEEABILITY A reasonable expectation that change is the probable result of certain acts or omissions.

NEGLIGENCE Conduct falling below the standard of care that a reasonable person would demonstrate under similar conditions.

PROXIMATE CAUSE The natural sequence of events without which an injury would not have been sustained.

Party ID: Quick identification of the relationship between the parties.

Concurrence/Dissent: All concurrences and dissents are briefed whenever they are included by the casebook author.

Analysis: This last paragraph gives you a broad understanding of where the case "fits in" with other cases in the section of the book and with the entire course. It is a hornbook-style discussion indicating whether the case is a majority or minority opinion and comparing the principal case with other cases in the casebook. It may also provide analysis from restatements, uniform codes, and law review articles.

Holding and Decision: This section offers a clear and in-depth discussion of the rule of the case and the court's rationale. It is written in easy-to-understand language and answers the issue presented by applying the law to the facts of the case. When relevant, it includes a thorough discussion of the exceptions to the case as listed by the court, any major cites to the other cases on point, and the names of the judges who wrote the decisions.

Quicknotes: Conveniently defines legal terms found in the case.

Note to Students

Aspen Publishing is proud to offer *Casenote® Legal Briefs*—continuing thirty years of publishing America's best-selling legal briefs.

Casenote® Legal Briefs are designed to help you save time when briefing assigned cases. Organized under convenient headings, they show you how to abstract the basic facts and holdings from the text of the actual opinions handed down by the courts. Used as part of a rigorous study regimen, they can help you spend more time analyzing and critiquing points of law than on copying bits and pieces of judicial opinions into your notebook or outline.

Casenote® Legal Briefs should never be used as a substitute for assigned casebook readings. They work best when read as a follow-up to reviewing the underlying opinions themselves. Students who try to avoid reading and digesting the judicial opinions in their casebooks or online sources will end up shortchanging themselves in the long run. The ability to absorb, critique, and restate the dynamic and complex elements of case law decisions is crucial to your success in law school and beyond. It cannot be developed vicariously.

In addition to *Casenote® Legal Briefs*, Aspen Publishing offers the following study aids:

- *Casenote® Legal Briefs*
- *Emanuel® Law Outlines*
- Emanuel® *Law in a Flash Flash Cards*
- Emanuel® *CrunchTime® Series*

Each of these series is designed to provide you with easy-to-understand explanations of complex points of law. Each volume offers guidance on the principles of legal analysis and, consulted regularly, will hone your ability to spot relevant issues. We have titles that will help you prepare for class, prepare for your exams, and enhance your general comprehension of the law along the way.

To find out more about our law school tools for success, visit us at *www.AspenPublishing.com* or e-mail us at *customer.service@aspenpublishing.com.* We'll be happy to assist you.

How to Brief a Case

A. Decide on a Format and Stick to It

Structure is essential to a good brief. It enables you to arrange systematically the related parts that are scattered throughout most cases, thus making manageable and understandable what might otherwise seem to be an endless and unfathomable sea of information. There are, of course, an unlimited number of formats that can be utilized. However, it is best to find one that suits your needs and stick to it. Consistency breeds both efficiency and the security that when called upon you will know where to look in your brief for the information you are asked to give.

Any format, as long as it presents the essential elements of a case in an organized fashion, can be used. Experience, however, has led *Casenote® Legal Briefs* to develop and utilize the following format because of its logical flow and universal applicability.

NATURE OF CASE: This is a brief statement of the legal character and procedural status of the case (e.g., "Appeal of a burglary conviction").

There are many different alternatives open to a litigant dissatisfied with a court ruling. The key to determining which one has been used is to discover *who is asking this court for what.*

This first entry in the brief should be kept as *short as possible.* Use the court's terminology if you understand it. But since jurisdictions vary as to the titles of pleadings, the best entry is the one that addresses who wants what in this proceeding, not the one that sounds most like the court's language.

RULE OF LAW: A statement of the general principle of law that the case illustrates (e.g., "An acceptance that varies any term of the offer is considered a rejection and counteroffer").

Determining the rule of law of a case is a procedure similar to determining the issue of the case. Avoid being fooled by red herrings; there may be a few rules of law mentioned in the case excerpt, but usually only one is *the* rule with which the casebook editor is concerned. The techniques used to locate the issue, described below, may also be utilized to find the rule of law. Generally, your best guide is simply the chapter heading. It is a clue to the point the casebook editor seeks to make and should be kept in mind when reading every case in the respective section.

FACTS: A synopsis of only the essential facts of the case, i.e., those bearing upon or leading up to the issue.

The facts entry should be a short statement of the events and transactions that led one party to initiate legal proceedings against another in the first place. While some cases conveniently state the salient facts at the beginning of the decision, in other instances they will have to be culled from hiding places throughout the text, even from concurring and dissenting opinions. Some of the "facts" will often be in dispute and should be so noted. Conflicting evidence may be briefly pointed up. "Hard" facts must be included. Both must be *relevant* in order to be listed in the facts entry. It is impossible to tell what is relevant until the entire case is read, as the ultimate determination of the rights and liabilities of the parties may turn on something buried deep in the opinion.

Generally, the facts entry should not be longer than three to five *short* sentences.

It is often helpful to identify the role played by a party in a given context. For example, in a construction contract case the identification of a party as the "contractor" or "builder" alleviates the need to tell that that party was the one who was supposed to have built the house.

It is always helpful, and a good general practice, to identify the "plaintiff" and the "defendant." This may seem elementary and uncomplicated, but, especially in view of the creative editing practiced by some casebook editors, it is sometimes a difficult or even impossible task. Bear in mind that the *party presently* seeking something from this court may not be the plaintiff, and that sometimes only the cross-claim of a defendant is treated in the excerpt. Confusing or misaligning the parties can ruin your analysis and understanding of the case.

ISSUE: A statement of the general legal question answered by or illustrated in the case. For clarity, the issue is best put in the form of a question capable of a "yes" or "no" answer. In reality, the issue is simply the Rule of Law put in the form of a question (e.g., "May an offer be accepted by performance?").

The major problem presented in discerning what is *the* issue in the case is that an opinion usually purports to raise and answer several questions. However, except for rare cases, only one such question is really the issue in the case. Collateral issues not necessary to the resolution of the matter in controversy are handled by the court by language known as *"obiter dictum"* or merely *"dictum."* While dicta may be included later in the brief, they have no place under the issue heading.

To find the issue, ask *who wants what* and then go on to ask *why did that party succeed or fail in getting it.* Once this is determined, the "why" should be turned into a question.

The complexity of the issues in the cases will vary, but in all cases a single-sentence question should sum up the issue. *In a few cases,* there will be two, or even more rarely, three issues of equal importance to the resolution of the case. Each should be expressed in a single-sentence question.

Since many issues are resolved by a court in coming to a final disposition of a case, the casebook editor will reproduce the portion of the opinion containing the issue or issues most relevant to the area of law under scrutiny. A noted law professor gave this advice: "Close the book; look at the title on the cover." Chances are, if it is Property, you need not concern yourself with whether, for example, the federal government's treatment of the plaintiff's land really raises a federal question sufficient to support jurisdiction on this ground in federal court.

The same rule applies to chapter headings designating sub-areas within the subjects. They tip you off as to what the text is designed to teach. The cases are arranged in a casebook to show a progression or development of the law, so that the preceding cases may also help.

It is also most important to remember to *read the notes and questions* at the end of a case to determine what the editors wanted you to have gleaned from it.

HOLDING AND DECISION: This section should succinctly explain the rationale of the court in arriving at its decision. In capsulizing the "reasoning" of the court, it should always include an application of the general rule or rules of law to the specific facts of the case. Hidden justifications come to light in this entry: the reasons for the state of the law, the public policies, the biases and prejudices, those considerations that influence the justices' thinking and, ultimately, the outcome of the case. At the end, there should be a short indication of thedisposition or procedural resolution of the case (e.g., "Decision of the trial court for Mr. Smith (P) reversed").

The foregoing format is designed to help you "digest" the reams of case material with which you will be faced in your law school career. Once mastered by practice, it will place at your fingertips the information the authors of your casebooks have sought to impart to you in case-by-case illustration and analysis.

B. Be as Economical as Possible in Briefing Cases

Once armed with a format that encourages succinctness, it is as important to be economical with regard to the time spent on the actual reading of the case as it is to be economical in the writing of the brief itself. This does not mean "skimming" a case. Rather, it means reading the case with an "eye" trained to recognize into which "section" of your brief a particular passage or line fits and having a system for quickly and precisely marking the case so that the passages fitting any one particular part of the brief can be easily identified and brought together in a concise and accurate manner when the brief is actually written.

It is of no use to simply repeat everything in the opinion of the court; record only enough information to trigger your recollection of what the court said. Nevertheless, an accurate statement of the "law of the case," i.e., the legal principle applied to the facts, is absolutely essential to class preparation and to learning the law under the case method.

To that end, it is important to develop a "shorthand" that you can use to make marginal notations. These notations will tell you at a glance in which section of the brief you will be placing that particular passage or portion of the opinion.

Some students prefer to underline all the salient portions of the opinion (with a pencil or colored underliner marker), making marginal notations as they go along. Others prefer the color-coded method of underlining, utilizing different colors of markers to underline the salient portions of the case, each separate color being used to represent a different section of the brief. For example, blue underlining could be used for passages relating to the rule of law, yellow for those relating to the issue, and green for those relating to the holding and decision, etc. While it has its advocates, thecolor-coded method can be confusing and time-consuming (all that time spent on changing colored markers). Furthermore, it can interfere with the continuity and concentration many students deem essential to the reading of a case for maximum comprehension. In the end, however, it is a matter of personal preference and style. Just remember, whatever method you use, underlining must be used sparingly or its value is lost.

If you take the marginal notation route, an efficient and easy method is to go along underlining the key portions of the case and placing in the margin alongside them the following "markers" to indicate where a particular passage or line "belongs" in the brief you will write:

N	(NATURE OF CASE)
RL	(RULE OF LAW)
I	(ISSUE)
HL	(HOLDING AND DECISION, relates to the RULE OF LAW behind the decision)
HR	(HOLDING AND DECISION, gives the RATIONALE or reasoning behind the decision)
HA	(HOLDING AND DECISION, applies the general principle(s) of law to the facts of the case to arrive at the decision)

Remember that a particular passage may well contain information necessary to more than one part of your brief, in which case you simply note that in the margin. If you are using the color-coded underlining method instead of marginal notation, simply make asterisks or checks in the margin next to the passage in question in the colors that indicate the additional sections of the brief where it might be utilized.

The economy of utilizing "shorthand" in marking cases for briefing can be maintained in the actual brief writing process itself by utilizing "law student shorthand" within the brief. There are many commonly used words and phrases for which abbreviations can be substituted in your briefs (and in your class notes also). You can develop abbreviations that are personal to you and which will save you a lot of time. A reference list of briefing abbreviations can be found on page x of this book.

C. Use Both the Briefing Process and the Brief as a Learning Tool

Now that you have a format and the tools for briefing cases efficiently, the most important thing is to make the time spent in briefing profitable to you and to make the most advantageous use of the briefs you create. Of course, the briefs are invaluable for classroom reference when you are called upon to explain or analyze a particular case. However, they are also useful in reviewing for exams. A quick glance at the fact summary should bring the case to mind, and a rereading of the rule of law should enable you to go over the underlying legal concept in your mind, how it was applied in that particular case, and how it might apply in other factual settings.

As to the value to be derived from engaging in the briefing process itself, there is an immediate benefit that arises from being forced to sift through the essential facts and reasoning from the court's opinion and to succinctly express them in your own words in your brief. The process ensures that you understand the case and the point that it illustrates, and that means you will be ready to absorb further analysis and information brought forth in class. It also ensures you will have something to say when called upon in class. The briefing process helps develop a mental agility for getting to the *gist* of a case and for identifying, expounding on, and applying the legal concepts and issues found there. The briefing process is the mental process on which you must rely in taking law school examinations; it is also the mental process upon which lawyers rely in serving their clients and in making a living.

Abbreviations for Briefs

acceptance	acp
affirmed	aff
answer	ans
assumption of risk	a/r
attorney	atty
beyond a reasonable doubt	b/r/d
bona fide purchaser	BFP
breach of contract	br/k
cause of action	c/a
common law	c/l
Constitution	Con
constitutional	con
contract	K
contributory negligence	c/n
cross	x
cross-complaint	x/c
cross-examination	x/ex
cruel and unusual punishment	c/u/p
defendant	D
dismissed	dis
double jeopardy	d/j
due process	d/p
equal protection	e/p
equity	eq
evidence	ev
exclude	exc
exclusionary rule	exc/r
felony	f/n
freedom of speech	f/s
good faith	g/f
habeas corpus	h/c
hearsay	hr
husband	H
injunction	inj
in loco parentis	ILP
inter vivos	I/v
joint tenancy	j/t
judgment	judgt
jurisdiction	jur
last clear chance	LCC
long-arm statute	LAS
majority view	maj
meeting of minds	MOM
minority view	min
Miranda rule	Mir/r
Miranda warnings	Mir/w
negligence	neg
notice	ntc
nuisance	nus
obligation	ob
obscene	obs
offer	O
offeree	OE
offeror	OR
ordinance	ord
pain and suffering	p/s
parol evidence	p/e
plaintiff	P
prima facie	p/f
probable cause	p/c
proximate cause	px/c
real property	r/p
reasonable doubt	r/d
reasonable man	r/m
rebuttable presumption	rb/p
remanded	rem
res ipsa loquitur	RIL
respondeat superior	r/s
Restatement	RS
reversed	rev
Rule Against Perpetuities	RAP
search and seizure	s/s
search warrant	s/w
self-defense	s/d
specific performance	s/p
statute	S
statute of frauds	S/F
statute of limitations	S/L
summary judgment	s/j
tenancy at will	t/w
tenancy in common	t/c
tenant	t
third party	TP
third party beneficiary	TPB
transferred intent	TI
unconscionable	uncon
unconstitutional	unconst
undue influence	u/e
Uniform Commercial Code	UCC
unilateral	uni
vendee	VE
vendor	VR
versus	v
void for vagueness	VFV
weight of authority	w/a
weight of the evidence	w/e
wife	W
with	w/
within	w/i
without	w/o
without prejudice	w/o/p
wrongful death	wr/d

Table of Cases

CHAPTER 1

Basic Principles

Quick Reference Rules of Law

Duncan v. Louisiana

Defendant convicted of simple battery (D) v. State (P)

391 U.S. 145 (1968)

NATURE OF CASE: Appeal from conviction for battery.

FACT SUMMARY: Duncan (D) contended the Sixth Amendment right to jury trial applied to the states through the Due Process Clause of the Fourteenth Amendment.

RULE OF LAW

A right guaranteed by the Sixth Amendment that is fundamental to the American scheme of justice applies to the states through the Fourteenth Amendment.

FACTS: Duncan (D) was charged with battery by the state of Louisiana (P). He demanded and was refused a trial by jury and was convicted by the court. He appealed, contending the Sixth Amendment right to jury trial applied to the states through the Due Process Clause of the Fourteenth Amendment. He contended the failure to honor his request for a jury trial denied him liberty without due process of law.

ISSUE: Does a right guaranteed by the Sixth Amendment that is fundamental to the American scheme of justice apply to the states through the Fourteenth Amendment?

HOLDING AND DECISION: (White, J.) Yes. A right guaranteed by the Sixth Amendment that is fundamental to the American scheme of justice applies to the states through the Fourteenth Amendment. The jury trial, in cases wherein that right would be available in a federal court, is fundamental to the scheme of American justice. Thus Duncan (D) was denied due process and his conviction cannot stand. Reversed.

CONCURRENCE: (Black, J.) Although I will support the "selective incorporation" process applied here, I would like to emphasize that the Fourteenth Amendment is intended to make the "entire" Bill of Rights applicable to the states. The words "No state shall make or enforce any law which shall abridge the privileges or immunities of citizens of the United States" clearly express this intention. There is no more precious "privilege" than that to claim the protections of the Bill of Rights.

DISSENT: (Harlan, J.) The Fourteenth Amendment requires that state procedures be fundamentally fair. It does not impose nationwide uniformity in such procedures. The Court's opinion, based on the concept of such uniformity, is a misinterpretation of the Amendment.

ANALYSIS

The United States Supreme Court has adopted several tests to be used in determining what rights guaranteed by the Bill of Rights apply to the several states through the Due Process Clause of the Fourteenth Amendment. In *Powell v. Alabama*, 287 U.S. 45 (1932), the test was whether the right was a fundamental principle of liberty. In *Gideon v. Wainwright*, 372 U.S. 335 (1963), the test followed was whether the right was essential to a fair trial.

Quicknotes

FOURTEENTH AMENDMENT Declares that no state shall make or enforce any law that shall abridge the privileges and immunities of citizens of the United States; no state shall deny to any person within its jurisdiction the equal protection of the laws.

RIGHT TO JURY TRIAL The right guaranteed by the Sixth Amendment to the federal Constitution that in all criminal prosecutions the accused has a right to a trial by an impartial jury of the state and district in which the crime was allegedly committed.

SIXTH AMENDMENT Provides the right to a speedy and public trial by impartial jury, the right to be informed of the accusation, the right to confront witnesses, and the right to have the assistance of counsel in all criminal prosecutions.

Teague v. Lane

Convicted felon (P) v. Government (D)

489 U.S. 288 (1989)

NATURE OF CASE: Review of denial of habeas corpus petition following conviction for attempted murder.

FACT SUMMARY: After Teague (P), a Black man, was convicted of attempted murder, he sought to overturn his conviction on collateral review based upon the prosecutor's exclusion of Black people from the jury.

RULE OF LAW

In general, new constitutional rules are not retroactively applicable to cases on collateral review.

FACTS: Teague (P), a Black man, was convicted by an all-White jury of attempted murder and armed robbery. During jury selection, the prosecutor used all of his peremptory challenges to exclude Black people in the jury. On appeal, Teague (P) argued unsuccessfully that the prosecutor's use of peremptory challenges denied him the right to be tried by a jury that was a fair cross-section of the community. Teague (P) then filed a habeas corpus writ, which was rejected by the district and appellate courts. Teague (P) petitioned the Supreme Court for review.

ISSUE: In general, are new constitutional rules retroactively applicable to cases on collateral review?

HOLDING AND DECISION: (O'Connor, J.) No. In general, new constitutional rules are not retroactively applicable to cases on collateral review. When a new constitutional requirement for criminal procedure is applied to the defendant, justice requires that it apply to all similarly situated defendants. Therefore, the initial question that must be determined is whether the constitutional rule sought by Teague (P) would be applied retroactively. A case announces a new rule when the result was not dictated by precedent existing at the time the defendant's conviction was final. New constitutional rules for criminal procedures have not been treated uniformly for retroactivity in the past. In *Griffith v. Kentucky*, 479 U.S. 314 (1987), we rejected the old process and adopted the approach advocated by Justice Harlan. According to this approach, new rules must be applied to all similar cases pending on direct review. However, for cases on collateral review, generally there is no retroactive application of rules. This is consistent with the purpose behind habeas corpus, which acknowledges the importance of finality to the justice system. Otherwise, convictions could never be considered final since new constitutional commands might arise even though the state faithfully applied the existing law at the time of the trial. The only exceptions to the general rule of non-retroactivity are where the new rule places certain private individual contact beyond the power of authorities or if the new procedure is central to an accurate determination of guilt. In the instant case, Teague (P) brought his appeal on collateral review. Therefore, the new rule he seeks, requiring a fair cross-section on the petit jury, will not be applied retroactively unless it meets one of the exceptions. Since the absence of a fair cross-section on the jury itself does not undermine the fundamental fairness of a conviction, it does not qualify as an exception. Because the proposed rule cannot be applied retroactively, it would be unfair to apply it solely to Teague (P) in this case. Accordingly, the Court will not determine the merits of proposed rule. Affirmed.

CONCURRENCE: (Stevens, J.) The Court should adopt Justice Harlan's analysis of retroactivity but should not modify it by limiting the second fundamental fairness exception solely to those new procedures deemed by the Court to be "watershed" or "bedrock."

DISSENT: (Brennan, J.) The majority opinion will prevent the resolution of substantial constitutional questions that were previously addressed on habeas claims. Even though a favorable decision might result in some inequality of treatment for convicted defendants, it is better that a faulty conviction be rectified for at least one defendant than to have all defendants suffer a wrong.

ANALYSIS

Justice O'Connor's opinion was joined by only a plurality in this case, but subsequently, a majority of the Court adopted the position. When a rule is not "new," it is completely retroactive under the Harlan-O'Connor approach. However, as Justice Brennan pointed out, the majority's definition of a new rule was very broad and the exceptions to non-retroactivity were extremely narrow.

Quicknotes

ATTEMPTED MURDER An intent to commit murder plus an action taken toward commission of the crime, falling short of completion.

HABEAS CORPUS COLLATERAL REVIEW An independent review of whether a prisoner is being lawfully imprisoned.

CHAPTER 2

Searches and Seizures of Persons and Things

Quick Reference Rules of Law

Olmstead v. United States

Convicted liquor bootlegger (D) v. Federal government (P)

277 U.S. 438 (1928)

NATURE OF CASE: Appeal from affirmance of conviction of conspiracy to violate the National Prohibition Act by unlawfully possessing, transporting, importing, and selling intoxicating liquors.

FACT SUMMARY: Olmstead (D) was convicted of conspiracy to violate the National Prohibition Act by, inter alia, unlawfully possessing, transporting, importing, and selling intoxicating liquors. The evidence against Olmstead (D) was largely obtained through the wiretapping by federal agents of private telephone conversations Olmstead (D) had with others. Olmstead (D) contended that the wiretaps, which had not been obtained with a warrant, were unconstitutional searches or seizures under the Fourth Amendment.

RULE OF LAW

A warrantless wiretap by the government of a private telephone conversation is not an unconstitutional search or seizure under the Fourth Amendment.

FACTS: Over a period of many months, wiretaps by federal agents of private telephone conversations Olmstead (D) had with others revealed that Olmstead (D) and others were engaged in a very large enterprise for importing, transporting, possessing, and selling liquor—which, at the time, was unlawful under the National Prohibition Act. The wiretaps, which were not made pursuant to a warrant, were made without trespassing on Olmstead's (D) property, by inserting wires into the regular phone wires in places not controlled or owned by Olmstead (D). Olmstead (D), who was convicted in federal district court of conspiracy to violate the National Prohibition Act, appealed on the ground that the warrantless wiretaps were unconstitutional searches or seizures under the Fourth Amendment. The Ninth Circuit Court of Appeals affirmed, and the United States Supreme Court granted certiorari.

ISSUE: Is a warrantless wiretap by the government of a private telephone conversation an unconstitutional search or seizure under the Fourth Amendment?

HOLDING AND DECISION: (Taft, C.J.) No. A warrantless wiretap by the government of a private telephone conversation is not an unconstitutional search or seizure under the Fourth Amendment. The Fourth Amendment expressly provides that its purpose is to protect the "right of the people to be secure in their persons, houses, papers, and effects, against unreasonable searches and seizures" by the government absent probable cause and a warrant. The Court's precedents have emphasized that the Fourth Amendment is directed at the misuse of governmental force and compulsion. Thus, although a warrantless stealthy search of an individual's office and the taking away of personal papers has been held to violate the Fourth Amendment, here the telephone conversations were made voluntarily, and were merely overheard secretly. Thus, no property rights were infringed, and nothing material was searched or seized. Additionally, this is not like the case where a government official warrantlessly rifles through a sealed letter in the mail, given that the letter is the sender's "papers" and "effects," which are in the government's custody and protection. In that case, the government official's conduct constitutes an unreasonable search and seizure. Here, however, the government does not have custody of telephone messages in the same way it has custody over mailed, sealed letters. Here, the evidence was obtained by the federal agents using their sense of hearing only—there was no unlawful entry of property, and nothing material was searched or seized. Thus, the Fourth Amendment's language cannot be expanded to include telephone wires, reaching to the whole world from the defendant's house or office. The intervening wires used for a wiretap are not part of the defendant's house or office, any more than are the highways along which the telephone wires are stretched. The Amendment's language is limited to "houses, persons, papers, and effects," and that language cannot be stretched to encompass telephone conversations, nor can the words "search and seizure" be stretched to encompass hearing or sight. For these reasons, the challenged wiretaps did not amount to a search or seizure within the Fourth Amendment's meaning. [Affirmed.]

DISSENT: (Brandeis, J.) The Constitution must be interpreted to accommodate modern conditions to keep its principles vital. "In the application of a Constitution, therefore, our contemplation cannot be only of what has been but of what may be." Otherwise, its general principles will have little value and will become "impotent and lifeless formulas." When the Fourth and Fifth Amendments were adopted, the evils they were intended to address were simple; government could directly effect self-incrimination only through force and violence via torture. Government could take a person's private possessions and papers only through breaking and entering. Since that time, however, subtler and more far-reaching means of invading privacy have become available to the

Continued on next page.

government. "Discovery and invention have made it possible for the government, by means far more effective than stretching upon the rack, to obtain disclosure in court of what is whispered in the closet." Merely because conditions change, discoveries are made, and technology advances, the Constitution does not stop affording protections against the types of evils it was designed to shield. If a sealed letter is protected from tampering by the amendments, a telephone conversation should likewise be protected from interception, because the evil incident to invasion of the privacy of the telephone is far greater than that involved in tampering with the mails. That is because whenever a telephone line is tapped, the privacy of the persons at both ends of the line is invaded, and all conversations between those persons, regarding any subject, even if proper, confidential, and privileged, may be overheard. In other words, wiretapping can be a great instrument of tyranny and oppression. Because the Constitution's makers sought to secure conditions favorable to the pursuit of happiness, they sought to protect Americans in their beliefs, their thoughts, their emotions, and their sensations. They conferred, as against the government, the right to be let alone—the most comprehensive of rights and the right most valued by civilized people. To protect that right, every unjustifiable intrusion by the government on the privacy of the individual, regardless the means employed, must be deemed a violation of the Fourth Amendment. In the case at bar, it is immaterial where the physical connection with the telephone wires leading into Olmstead's (D) premises was made, and it is also immaterial that the intrusion was made to aid law enforcement. "Experience should teach us to be most on our guard to protect liberty when the government's purposes are beneficent. Men born to freedom are naturally alert to repel invasion of their liberty by evil-minded rulers. The greatest dangers to liberty lurk in insidious encroachment by men of zeal, well-meaning but without understanding." For the preservation of decency, security, and liberty, government officials must act in ways that citizens are commanded to act, since, in a government of laws, the existence of the government will be imperiled if it fails to observe the law scrupulously. "If the government becomes a lawbreaker, it breeds contempt for law; it invites every man to become a law unto himself; it invites anarchy." Therefore, government should not be allowed break the law in the name of enforcing the law.

DISSENT: (Holmes, J.) Because the wiretap challenged by Olmstead (D) violated state law, any evidence obtained from the wiretap must be excluded at trial.

DISSENT: (Butler, J.) The safeguards of the Fourth Amendment extend against all evils that are comparable to the evils identified by the ordinary meaning of its words. Therefore, whether a certain act is covered by the Amendment depends on a correct understanding of the facts involved. Here, telephone communications belong to the parties between whom they are made, and, during the transmission of telephone communications, the exclusive use of the wire belongs to the persons served by it. Wiretapping, therefore, involves interference with the wire while being used, and the tapping of the wires and listening in by government officers literally constitutes a search for evidence.

DISSENT: (Stone, J.) The opinions of the other dissenting Justices are correct.

ANALYSIS

Olmstead was overruled by *Katz v. United States,* 389 U.S. 347 (1967), which expanded the Fourth Amendment's search and seizure protections from "persons, houses, papers, and effects", as written in the Constitution, to any areas where a person has a "reasonable expectation of privacy." This "reasonable expectation of privacy" standard, known as the *Katz* test, is still used by courts to address technological advances that create new questions about cultural privacy norms and unconstitutional government intrusions on privacy. Likewise, Justice Brandeis's dissent in *Olmstead* is of continuing importance to the evolution of the Court's privacy jurisprudence, and the "right to be left alone" that Justice Brandeis articulated has formed the basis of several influential contemporary Court opinions.

Quicknotes

FIFTH AMENDMENT Provides that no person shall be compelled to serve as a witness against him- or herself, be subject to trial for the same offense twice, or be deprived of life, liberty, or property without due process of law.

FOURTH AMENDMENT Provides that persons be secure as to their person and private belongings against unreasonable searches and seizures.

Katz v. United States

Convicted felon (D) v. Federal government (P)

389 U.S. 347 (1967)

NATURE OF CASE: Appeal from criminal conviction for transmitting betting information over the phone.

FACT SUMMARY: Katz (D) was arrested for transmitting wagering information by telephone to another state. At his trial the Government (P) introduced recordings of his telephone conversations. To make the recordings, a listening and recording device was attached to the outside of a phone booth.

RULE OF LAW

The Fourth Amendment protects a person from search and seizure if, under the circumstances, he or she has a justifiable expectation of privacy, regardless of whether an actual physical trespass occurred.

FACTS: Katz (D) was arrested and convicted for transmitting betting information by telephone to another state in violation of a federal statute. At his trial, the Government (P) introduced recordings of phone conversations Katz (D) had had. These recordings were made by attaching a recording and listening device to the outside of a phone booth from which Katz (D) made calls. There was no search warrant. The Government (P) used this device only after its investigation indicated that the phone booth was being used to transmit such information, and the Government (P) recorded only conversations that Katz (D) personally had. Katz (D) was convicted, the federal Court of Appeals in California affirmed, and he appealed.

ISSUE: Does the Fourth Amendment protect a person from search and seizure if, under the circumstances, he or she has a justifiable expectation of privacy, regardless of whether an actual physical trespass occurred?

HOLDING AND DECISION: (Stewart, J.) Yes. The Fourth Amendment protects a person from search and seizure if, under the circumstances, he or she has a justifiable expectation of privacy, regardless of whether an actual physical trespass occurred. Whatever a person knowingly exposes to the public, even in his or her own home, is therefore not protected by the Fourth Amendment; but what a person keeps private, even in a public place, may be protected. Earlier cases stated surveillance without a trespass or seizure of a material object is outside of the Fourth Amendment, and now these cases must be overturned. Even though the phone booth was a public place and there was no physical trespass (the device was on the outside of the booth), there was a search because the Government (P) violated the privacy upon which Katz (D) justifiably relied. There is also a seizure, even though no tangible property was taken, because the recording of a statement overheard, even if there is no trespass, is a seizure. The remaining question, then, is whether the Government (P) complied with the constitutional standards of the Fourth Amendment. Although the Government (P) reasonably believed that the phone booth was being illegally used, and its search and seizure was carefully limited both in scope and duration, the action cannot be upheld because there was no search warrant issued. A search warrant is a safeguard in several ways: a neutral magistrate, on the basis of information presented to him or her, can determine whether a warrant should issue; the search warrant carefully limits the scope of the search; and, the government must report back on the evidence it finds. Without such safeguards, even if the search was in fact reasonable, it cannot be upheld. Reversed.

CONCURRENCE: (Harlan, J.) In order to be protected by the Fourth Amendment a person must have an actual, subjective expectation of privacy and, also, that expectation of privacy must be reasonable.

DISSENT: (Black, J.) When the Fourth Amendment was adopted, eavesdropping was a common practice, and if the framers of the Constitution wished to limit that procedure, they would have used appropriate language. This case, then, goes against the plain meaning of the Fourth Amendment, which was solely aimed at limiting the practice of breaking into buildings and seizing tangible property. Therefore, wiretapping, which is a form of eavesdropping, is not subject to the Fourth Amendment.

ANALYSIS

Katz rejects the old rule that held there was no search unless there was a physical trespass and substitutes a new rule based on the defendant's expectation of privacy. One facet of this privacy concept is the place involved – for example, if, unlike Katz (D), the defendant had engaged in conversation in a public place that was audible to others, there would be no search within the meaning of the Fourth Amendment. Also, the privacy concept turns on the action of the defendant. If Katz (D) had engaged in a loud conversation, even in his own home, that was audible to a person standing outside of defendant's door, there would be no search

Continued on next page.

since the conversation was exposed by the defendant to the public.

Quicknotes

EXPECTATION OF PRIVACY Requirement that in order to invoke the Fourth Amendment's protection against unreasonable searches and seizures, the individual must have a reasonable expectation of privacy in respect to the location searched or thing seized.

United States v. Jones

Federal government (P) v. Individual (D)

565 U.S. 400 (2012)

NATURE OF CASE: Appeal from intermediate appellate court decision in favor of the defendant.

FACT SUMMARY: Government agents installed a Global Positioning System tracking device on the undercarriage of a vehicle owned by Jones (D), who was suspected of trafficking in narcotics, and then monitored the vehicle's movements for a period of 28 days.

RULE OF LAW

The government's installation of a Global Positioning System device on an individual's vehicle, and the government's use of the device to track the location of that vehicle, constitutes a search under the Fourth Amendment.

FACTS: Government agents installed a Global Positioning System (GPS) tracking device on the undercarriage of Jones's (D) vehicle for a period of 28 days. The device was able to track the location of the vehicle to within 50 feet. The district court judge denied Jones's (D) motion to suppress the GPS evidence and a jury convicted him. The Court of Appeals for the D.C. Circuit then reversed, finding that the evidence obtained by the use of the GPS device without a warrant violated the Fourth Amendment. The Government (P) appealed to the United States Supreme Court.

ISSUE: Does the government's installation of a Global Positioning System device on an individual's vehicle, and the government's use of the device to track the location of that vehicle, constitute a search under the Fourth Amendment?

HOLDING AND DECISION: (Scalia, J.) Yes. The government's installation of a Global Positioning System device on an individual's vehicle, and the government's use of the device to track the location of that vehicle, constitutes a search under the Fourth Amendment. The Government (P) argues that no search occurred because Jones (D) had no reasonable expectation of privacy in the area of the vehicle accessed by government agents or in the location of the vehicle on public roads. However, this case need not be analyzed on the reasonable expectation of privacy theory. Instead, the government's physical trespass in the form of attaching a device to one's vehicle constitutes the search. One's private vehicle is protected by the Fourth Amendment's prohibition of unreasonable searches of one's "person, houses, papers, and effects." The more general unreasonable expectation of privacy theory did not replace the original trespass to property theory of unreasonable searches. Rather, it is supplemental to the original understanding of the Fourth Amendment. It is enough for this case to focus narrowly upon the government's trespass upon Jones's (D) "effects," i.e., his vehicle, to find that a search occurred. Affirmed.

CONCURRENCE: (Sotomayor, J.) The government's physical invasion of Jones's (D) personal property constituted a search. However, this Court may need to utilize the more general reasonable expectation of privacy theory in other cases because many forms of electronic surveillance do not include a physical intrusion.

CONCURRENCE: (Alito, J.) The Court should have analyzed this under the broader reasonable expectation of privacy theory rather than the simple trespass to property theory. Reliance on the narrow trespass theory will not provide any guidance to law enforcement for those surveillance cases where there is no physical intrusion. The majority's decision unnecessarily avoids the more important issue of the legality of the use of Global Positioning System (GPS) devices for long-term tracking. If such long-term tracking can be somehow accomplished in the future without having to attach a device on the vehicle, this opinion will offer no guidance. The result is also incongruous. If law enforcement uses police vehicles or helicopters to track a vehicle for a long period of time, that will not result in a Fourth Amendment violation, but attaching a GPS device to the car will. The best solutions to all of these new search and seizure issues arising from technological advances should be devised and enacted by federal or state legislatures.

ANALYSIS

While the judgment in this case was unanimous, the United States Supreme Court was split 5-4 on how to analyze the use of the Global Positioning System tracking device. The federal agents' intrusion upon the personal property of Jones (D) was the significant factor in this case. As the concurring justices note, however, the issue remains undecided on how far law enforcement can go with electronic or even Internet searches that do not include a physical intrusion.

Quicknotes

FOURTH AMENDMENT Provides that persons be secure as to their person and private belongings against unreasonable searches and seizures.

SEARCH AND SEIZURE An inspection conducted in order to obtain evidence to be utilized for the prosecution of a crime and the subsequent taking of such evidence.

Florida v. Jardines

State (P) v. Marijuana grower (D)

569 U.S. 1 (2013)

NATURE OF CASE: Review of Fourth Amendment search criminal case.

FACT SUMMARY: Detective Douglas Bartelt brought his trained drug-sniffing dog to the home of Joelis Jardines (D). As Bartelt and the dog approached Jardines's home, the dog alerted to the scent of marijuana with the strongest source of the odor at the base of the front door.

RULE OF LAW

The curtilage is part of a private home for Fourth Amendment purposes and it is impermissible to enter the curtilage with a trained police dog for search purposes without express or implied permission from the homeowner.

FACTS: Miami-Dade Police Department Detective William Pedraja observed Joelis Jardines's (D) home on a tip Jardines (D) was growing marijuana inside the home. Pedraja could not see into the home because the blinds were drawn. Detective Douglas Bartelt and his trained drug-sniffing dog approached the home. Bartelt kept the dog on a six-foot leash because the dog acted erratically when searching. As Bartelt approached Jardines's (D) home, the dog apparently sensed an odor he was trained to detect and he began "bracketing" and "spinning" around while on the leash. The dog then located the strongest source of the odor and sat at the base of the front door. Bartelt then returned with the dog to the car, informed Pedraja of the positive alert for narcotics, and Pedraja obtained a warrant to search the residence. At the time of the search, Jardines (D) attempted to flee and was arrested. The search revealed marijuana plants and Jardines (D) was charged with trafficking in cannabis.

ISSUE: Is the curtilage part of a private home for Fourth Amendment purposes and is it impermissible to enter the curtilage with a trained police dog for search purposes without express or implied permission from the homeowner?

HOLDING AND DECISION: (Scalia, J.) Yes. The curtilage is part of a private home for Fourth Amendment purposes and it is impermissible to enter the curtilage with a trained police dog for search purposes without express or implied permission from the homeowner. The home is first among equals for Fourth Amendment purposes. A person's right to retreat to his or her home would have very little practical value if the state's agents could search side yards and porches for evidence with impunity. There is no doubt here the detectives entered the curtilage, which is the area immediately surrounding and associated with the home. The issue then becomes whether the intrusion into a constitutionally protected area occurred with leave from Jardines (D). It did not. The habits of the country may provide an implicit license to a visitor to approach a home. A front door knocker allows for "solicitors, hawkers and peddlers of all kinds." Officers can knock on a front door and speak with the homeowner. There is no customary invitation for a trained police dog to explore the area looking for incriminating evidence. The State (P) relies on this Court's cases finding the subjective intent of the officer is irrelevant. Those cases, however, deal with objectively reasonable searches, so the officer's real reason for the search does not vitiate the objective reasonableness. Here, the objective basis for the officers' behavior was to conduct a search and no one believes they had license to do so. The Court need not consider whether the officers violated Jardines's (D) expectation of privacy under *Katz v. United States*, 389 U.S. 347 (1967), because the officers conducted a search by physically intruding on Jardines's (D) property. *Katz's* reasonable-expectations test adds to, not substitutes for, the property-based understanding of the Fourth Amendment. [Decision not stated in the excerpt.]

CONCURRENCE: (Kagan, J.) The Court could have arrived at the same decision by considering Jardines's (D) privacy interests. Privacy expectations are heightened in the home and surrounding area and it was an invasion of Jardines's (D) privacy for them to invade those expectations when searching with a trained canine assistant.

DISSENT: (Alito, J.) The Court's decision relies on trespass law that is nowhere to be found in Anglo-American jurisprudence. The majority finds Bartelt committed a trespass when he engaged in an otherwise lawful visit to Jardines's (D) home but brought his dog, Franky. Trespass law provides no support for such a holding. The police are permitted to "knock and talk." They are permitted to see, hear, and smell what can be detected from their lawful vantage point. The Court states Bartelt had the objective purpose of conducting a search. There is no meaningful way to distinguish between the objective purpose of a "knock and talk" and what occurred here. The dog is the difference here. There is not a single case that holds a visitor commits a trespass when accompanied by

Continued on next page.

a dog on a leash. The Court's trespass rule today is a newly struck counterfeit.

ANALYSIS

The United States Supreme Court's decision was a narrow one involving drug-sniffing dogs, but technological advancements continue to change state agencies' ability to collect evidence. The Court acknowledges officers may approach a private residence for the purpose of speaking with a resident and may even gather evidence from that "knock and talk." In the future, officers may have technological advances providing a greater ability to see, hear, and smell. The Court may have to reconsider what constitutes an impermissible intrusion resulting in an impermissible search.

Quicknotes

CURTILAGE The area immediately surrounding a dwelling.

Carpenter v. United States

Convicted robber (D) v. Federal government (P)

138 S. Ct. 2206 (2018)

NATURE OF CASE: Appeal by convicted robber from affirmance of denial of motion to suppress cellular phone routing data, known as cell-site location information, obtained without a warrant.

FACT SUMMARY: Carpenter (D), who was convicted of several counts of robbery, contended that cellular phone routing data, known as cell-site location information, that the Federal Bureau of Investigation obtained without a warrant and that showed that his cell phone was near robbery locations at the time the robberies occurred, should have been suppressed on the grounds that the Government's (P) seizure of that data without a warrant supported by probable cause violated the Fourth Amendment.

RULE OF LAW

An individual has a legitimate expectation of privacy in the record of his or her physical movements as captured through cell-site location information (CSLI), so that the government must generally obtain a search warrant supported by probable cause before acquiring CSLI.

FACTS: Each time a cell phone connects to a cell site, it generates a time-stamped record known as cell-site location information (CSLI). Wireless carriers collect and store this information for their own business purposes. After the Federal Bureau of Investigation (FBI) identified the cell phone numbers of several robbery suspects, prosecutors were granted court orders to obtain the suspects' cell phone records under the Stored Communications Act. Wireless carriers produced CSLI for Carpenter's (D) phone, and the Government (P) was able to obtain 12,898 location points cataloging Carpenter's (D) movements over 127 days—an average of 101 data points per day. Carpenter (D) moved to suppress the data, arguing that the Government's (P) seizure of the records without obtaining a warrant supported by probable cause violated the Fourth Amendment. The district court denied the motion, and prosecutors used the records at trial to show that Carpenter's (D) phone was near four of the robbery locations at the time those robberies occurred. Carpenter (D) was convicted. The court of appeals affirmed, holding that Carpenter (D) lacked a reasonable expectation of privacy in the location information collected by the FBI because he had shared that information with his wireless carriers. The United States Supreme Court granted certiorari.

ISSUE: Does an individual have a legitimate expectation of privacy in the record of his or her physical movements as captured through cell-site location information (CSLI), so that the government must generally obtain a search warrant supported by probable cause before acquiring CSLI?

HOLDING AND DECISION: (Roberts, C.J.) Yes. An individual has a legitimate expectation of privacy in the record of his or her physical movements as captured through cell-site location information (CSLI), so that the government must generally obtain a search warrant supported by probable cause before acquiring CSLI. The location information obtained from Carpenter's (D) wireless carriers was the product of a search. A person does not surrender all Fourth Amendment protection by venturing into the public sphere. To the contrary, the Court has recognized that what one seeks to preserve as private, even in an area accessible to the public, may be constitutionally protected, and that individuals have a reasonable expectation of privacy in the whole of their physical movements. Thus, when an individual seeks to preserve something as private, and his or her expectation of privacy is one that society is prepared to recognize as reasonable, official intrusion into that sphere generally qualifies as a search and requires a warrant supported by probable cause. Allowing Government (P) access to cell-site records—which "hold for many Americans the 'privacies of life'" [*Riley v. California*, 573 U.S. 373 (2014)]—contravenes that expectation, since the time-stamped data provides an intimate window into a person's life, revealing not only his or her particular movements, but through them his or her familial, political, professional, religious, and sexual associations. Moreover, cell phone tracking is remarkably easy, cheap, and efficient compared to traditional investigative tools, and, with just the click of a button, the Government (P) can access each carrier's deep repository of historical location information at practically no expense. Cell-site records raise great privacy concerns, given that cell phones have become almost a "feature of human anatomy" [*Riley*, 573 U.S. 373 (2014) (slip op., at 9)], in that individuals carry their phones with them at all times, beyond public thoroughfares and into private residences, doctor's offices, political headquarters, and other potentially revealing locales. Accordingly, when the Government (P) tracks the location of a cell phone it achieves near perfect surveillance, as if it had attached an ankle monitor to the phone's user, and it can do so retrospectively to retrace a person's whereabouts,

Continued on next page.

subject only to the five-year retention policies of most wireless carriers. Critically, location information is continually logged for all 400 million devices in the United States, not just those belonging to persons who might happen to come under investigation, so the tracking capacity of CSLI runs against everyone. Additionally, the precision of such information is rapidly increasing. For these reasons when the Government (P) accessed CSLI from the wireless carriers, it invaded Carpenter's (D) reasonable expectation of privacy in the whole of his physical movements and was a search. Therefore, the Government (P) must generally obtain a warrant supported by probable cause before acquiring CSLI records. Nonetheless, as with other searches, case-specific exceptions may support a warrantless search of an individual's cell-site records under certain circumstances. One well-recognized exception applies when the exigencies of the situation make the needs of law enforcement so compelling that a warrantless search is objectively reasonable under the Fourth Amendment. Such exigencies include the need to pursue a fleeing suspect, protect individuals who are threatened with imminent harm, or prevent the imminent destruction of evidence. Absent such exigencies, the Government (P) will have to obtain a warrant, and merely because CSLI is gathered by a third party will not render it less deserving of Fourth Amendment protection. Reversed.

DISSENT: (Kennedy, J.) First, cell-site location information (CSLI) is not nearly as precise as the majority asserts it is, and it only reveals a person's location generally, within an area of between a dozen to several hundred city blocks. Second, the majority errs in finding that precedent establishes that an individual has an expectation of privacy in the sum of the individual's whereabouts, and that CSLI records therefore implicate greater privacy interests than financial or telephone records. In fact, the opposite is true, since a person's movements are not particularly private. The Court previously held that when an individual travels over the public streets, he or she voluntarily conveys to anyone who wants to look the fact that he or she was traveling over particular roads in a particular direction, the fact of whatever stops he or she made, and the fact of his or her final destination. Today expectations of privacy in one's location are, if anything, even less reasonable. Millions of Americans choose to share their location daily, whether by using a variety of location-based services on their phones, or by sharing their location with friends and the public at large via social media.

DISSENT: (Thomas, J.) The reasonable expectation of privacy test has no place in Fourth Amendment analysis and involves prohibited judicial policymaking.

DISSENT: (Alito, J.) The Court's approach fractures Fourth Amendment principles by ignoring the basic distinction between an actual search (dispatching law enforcement officers to enter private premises and root through private papers and effects) and an order merely requiring a party to look through its own records and produce specified documents, as well as by allowing a defendant to object to the search of a third party's property. The order at issue was akin to a *subpoena duces tecum*, and these traditionally have not been considered "searches." They have been a part of the common law in both civil and criminal cases and are closely associated with grand juries. These routine methods for the government to obtain documents were not what the Founders had in mind when they prohibited unreasonable searches or seizures. Instead, the Founders sought to limit the degree of invasiveness when the government sought to obtain information or evidence; they did not intend to regulate courts' use of compulsory process. A *subpoena duces tecum* permits a subpoenaed individual to conduct the search for the relevant documents him- or herself, without law enforcement officers entering the individual's home or rooting through his or her papers and effects. As a result, subpoenas avoid the many incidental invasions of privacy that necessarily accompany any actual search. It was the invasions of privacy—which, although incidental, could often be extremely intrusive and damaging—that led to the adoption of the Fourth Amendment. Although *subpoenas duces tecum* and other forms of compulsory document production currently are evaluated under the Fourth Amendment, a reasonableness standard that is less demanding than the requirements for a warrant is used. Thus, even if the majority is correct that the Government (P) searched Carpenter (D), such a search under contemporary precedents should be considered a figurative or constructive search that does not require probable cause, but only that the request not be overbroad or too indefinite, as long as it is relevant. Here, the Government (P) met that standard, since the Stored Communications Act allows a court to issue an order such as the one at bar only if the Government (P) has offered specific and articulable facts showing that are reasonable grounds to believe that the records sought are relevant and material to an ongoing criminal investigation. Thus, the majority ignores centuries of precedent and practice when it asserts that it has never held that the Government (P) may subpoena third parties for records in which a suspect has a reasonable expectation of privacy. Moreover, even if the Fourth Amendment permitted someone to object to the subpoena of a third party's records, the majority cannot explain why that individual should be entitled to greater Fourth Amendment protection than the party actually being subpoenaed. Accordingly, the majority's decision has the potential to damage, if not destroy, the utility of subpoenas. For example, grand juries that have compelled the production of evidence to be able to determine the

Continued on next page.

need for probable cause will no longer be able to do so, because they will be required to show a need for probable cause to obtain such evidence, which could lead to investigations sputtering out at their inception. The majority's second significant error is its holding that a defendant has a Fourth Amendment right to object to the search of a third-party's property. Such an interpretation is supported neither by the Amendment's language, nor by precedent. Here, Carpenter (D) had no meaningful control over the cell-site records and no property interests therein; only the cell service providers did. Thus, the majority creates a revolutionary change in Fourth Amendment doctrine. The majority's holding, for example, could necessitate the showing of probable cause for all *subpoenas duces tecum* or other orders compelling production, and individuals will be able to claim a protected Fourth Amendment interest in any sensitive personal information about them that is collected and owned by third parties. The Stored Communication Act already restricts the misuse of cell-site records, and, if Americans believe its protections do not go far enough, the proper channel for strengthening those protections is Congress, not the courts. This is particularly true since the Fourth Amendment applies only to government actors, and some of the greatest threats to individual privacy may come from private companies that collect and sometimes misuse vast quantities of data about all Americans.

DISSENT: (Gorsuch, J.) The Court, in deciding this case, should have taken a more traditional Fourth Amendment approach to the issues raised here, rather than relying on a reasonable expectation of privacy approach. A person's cell-site data could qualify as his or her papers or effects under existing law. Although the carrier holds the information, the relevant statute (47 U.S.C. § 222) provides that a customer's cell-site location information (CSLI) is customer proprietary network information (CPNI) and gives customers certain rights to control use of and access to CPNI about themselves. Carriers are statutorily forbidden to use, disclose, or permit access to individually identifiable CPNI without the customer's consent, except as needed to provide the customer's telecommunications services. The statute also requires the carrier to disclose CPNI upon affirmative written request by the customer, to any person designated by the customer. Congress even afforded customers a private cause of action for damages against carriers who violate the Act's terms. Plainly, customers have substantial legal interests in this information, including at least some right to include, exclude, and control its use. Those interests might even rise to the level of a property right. Ostensibly, Carpenter (D) could have vindicated his Fourth Amendment rights by invoking the law of property or any analogies to the common law, but instead only relied on "reasonable expectations" arguments. Accordingly, Carpenter (D) may have forfeited his most promising line of argument.

ANALYSIS

As the Court in this case notes, a request for cell-site location information (CSLI) lies at the intersection of two lines of cases. The first addresses a person's expectation of privacy in his or her physical location and movements. Prior to this case, the Court held, in *United States v. Jones,* 565 U.S. 400 (2012), that warrantless Global Positioning System monitoring of a suspect's vehicle through a tracking device violated the Fourth Amendment, not only because of the Government's (P) physical trespass of the vehicle, but also because of the suspect's related privacy expectations. In the second line of cases, the Court has held that a person has no legitimate expectation of privacy in information he or she voluntarily turns over to third parties, even if the information is revealed on the assumption that it will be used only for a limited purpose. Thus, the Government (P) is typically free to obtain such information from the recipient without triggering Fourth Amendment protections. This third-party doctrine has been applied to bank records and to records of landline telephone companies. In this case, the Court declined to extend this doctrine, given what it found are the unique characteristics of cell phone location records, i.e., the ability to infallibly chronicle a person's location for years. Thus, whether the Government (P) uses its own surveillance technology or leverages the technology of a wireless carrier, an individual maintains a legitimate expectation of privacy in the record of his or her physical movements as captured through CSLI. Nonetheless, the Court's decision in *Carpenter* is a narrow one, and does not disturb the third-party doctrine or call into question conventional surveillance techniques and tools, such as security cameras. Nor does the decision address other business records that might incidentally reveal location information, or other collection techniques involving foreign affairs or national security.

Quicknotes

EXPECTATION OF PRIVACY Requirement that in order to invoke the Fourth Amendment's protection against unreasonable searches and seizures, the individual must have a reasonable expectation of privacy in respect to the location searched or thing seized.

FOURTH AMENDMENT Provides that persons be secure as to their person and private belongings against unreasonable searches and seizures.

PROBABLE CAUSE A reasonable basis for believing that a crime has been committed.

SUBPOENA DUCES TECUM A court mandate compelling the production of documents under a witness's control.

Torres v. Madrid

Individual injured by police (P) v. Police officer (D)

141 S.Ct. 989 (2021)

NATURE OF CASE: Appeal from affirmance of summary judgment in action brought under 42 U.S.C. § 1983 for damages resulting from alleged excessive police force.

FACT SUMMARY: State police officers Janice Madrid (Madrid) (D) and Richard Williamson (Williamson) (D) (collectively, "officers" (D)) arrived at an apartment complex to execute an arrest warrant and approached Roxanne Torres (Torres) (P). The officers (D) attempted to speak with Torres (P) as she drove away because she believed the officers (D) were carjackers. The officers (D) fired their service pistols to stop Torres (P), striking her twice. Torres (P) subsequently brought suit against the officers (D) under 42 U.S.C. § 1983 for damages, contending that that the officers (D) used excessive force against her and that the shooting constituted an unreasonable seizure under the Fourth Amendment.

RULE OF LAW

The application of physical force by a government agent to the body of a person with the intent to restrain is a seizure for Fourth Amendment purposes even if the person does not submit and is not subdued.

FACTS: State police officers Janice Madrid (Madrid) (D) and Richard Williamson (Williamson) (D) (collectively, "officers" (D)) arrived at an apartment complex to execute an arrest warrant and approached Roxanne Torres (Torres) (P), then standing near a Toyota FJ Cruiser. Although they determined that Torres (P) was not the target of the warrant, the officers (D) attempted to speak with her as she got into the driver's seat. Believing the officers (D) to be carjackers, Torres (P) hit the gas pedal to escape. The officers (D) fired their service pistols 13 times to stop Torres (P), striking her twice. Torres (P), who managed to escape and receive care at a hospital, subsequently brought suit against the officers (D) under 42 U.S.C. § 1983 for damages, contending that the officers (D) used excessive force against her and that the shooting constituted an unreasonable seizure under the Fourth Amendment. Affirming the District Court's grant of summary judgment to the officers (D), the Tenth Circuit Court of Appeals held that a suspect's continued flight after being shot by police negates a Fourth Amendment excessive-force claim. The United States Supreme Court granted certiorari.

ISSUE: Is the application of physical force by a government agent to the body of a person with the intent to restrain a seizure for Fourth Amendment purposes even if the person does not submit and is not subdued?

HOLDING AND DECISION: (Roberts, C.J.) Yes. The application of physical force by a government agent to the body of a person with the intent to restrain is a seizure for Fourth Amendment purposes even if the person does not submit and is not subdued. The Fourth Amendment protects "[t]he right of the people to be secure in their persons, houses, papers, and effects, against unreasonable searches and seizures." In *California v. Hodari D.*, 499 U.S. 621 (1991), the Court explained that common-law arrests are Fourth Amendment seizures, and that the common law considered the application of physical force to the body of a person with the intent to restrain to be an arrest—not an attempted arrest—even if the person does not yield and escapes. A review of the pertinent English and American decisions confirms that the slightest touching—or laying of hands—was a constructive detention that would complete the arrest. The analysis does not change merely because the officers (D) used force from a distance to restrain Torres (P). The required touching of the defendant's body can be as readily accomplished by a bullet as by the end of a finger. However, not every physical contact between a government employee and a member of the public is a Fourth Amendment seizure. A seizure requires the use of force with intent to restrain. Accidental force does not qualify, nor does force intentionally applied for some other purpose. The appropriate inquiry is whether the challenged conduct objectively manifests an intent to restrain. Thus, the test does not depend on either the subjective motivation of the officer or the subjective perception of the suspect. Finally, a seizure by force lasts only as long as the application of force unless the suspect submits. Applying these principles to the facts viewed in the light most favorable to Torres (P), the officers' (D) shooting applied physical force to her body and objectively manifested an intent to restrain her from driving away. Therefore, the officers (D) seized Torres (P) for the instant that the bullets struck her. Of course, a seizure is just the first step in the analysis. The Fourth Amendment does not forbid all or even most seizures—only unreasonable ones. Thus, the case is remanded to address questions regarding the reasonableness of the seizure, the damages caused by the seizure, and the officers' (D) entitlement to qualified immunity. [Vacated and remanded.]

Continued on next page.

DISSENT: (Gorsuch, J.) The majority holds that a criminal suspect can be simultaneously seized and roaming at large. The majority's view, that a Fourth Amendment "seizure" takes place whenever an officer "merely touches" a suspect, even if the suspect refuses to stop, evades capture, and is never to be seen again, is as mistaken as it is novel. Until now, a Fourth Amendment "seizure" has required taking possession of someone or something. To reach its contrary judgment, the majority must conflate a seizure with its attempt and confuse an arrest with a battery.

ANALYSIS

The Court took this case to resolve a split among the circuits, whereby some lower courts held that a "mere touch" constitutes a Fourth Amendment "seizure," whereas others, adhered to the view that the word "seizure" means "taking possession." The Court explained that this split occurred because courts were not careful to distinguish between seizures by control and seizures by force, and that each type of seizure enjoys a separate common-law pedigree. Unlike a seizure by force, a seizure by acquisition of control involves either voluntary submission to a show of authority or the termination of freedom of movement. The requirement of control or submission never extended to seizures by force, however, because, as the common-law courts recognized, any such requirement of control would be difficult to apply in cases involving the application of force. For example, at a basic level, it will often be unclear when an officer succeeds in gaining control over a struggling suspect, and courts would have to puzzle over whether an officer exercised control when the officer grabbed a suspect, when the officer tackled the suspect, or only when the officer secured handcuffs on the suspect. In cases involving seizures by force, the common law avoided such line-drawing problems by clearly fixing the moment of the seizure at the moment of touch.

Quicknotes

FOURTH AMENDMENT Provides that persons be secure as to their person and private belongings against unreasonable searches and seizures.

QUALIFIED IMMUNITY An affirmative defense relieving officials from civil liability for the performance of activities within their discretion so long as such conduct is not in violation of an individual's rights pursuant to law as determined by a reasonable person standard.

United States v. Drayton

Federal government (P) v. Drug possessor (D)

536 U.S. 194 (2002)

NATURE OF CASE: Appeal by Government (P) from suppression of drug evidence.

FACT SUMMARY: When a police officer conducted a pat-down search of his person during a "bus sweep," Christopher Drayton (D) argued that any purported consent he may have given was vitiated in the absence of some positive indication that consent could have been refused.

RULE OF LAW

Law enforcement officers do not violate the Fourth Amendment prohibition of unreasonable searches merely by approaching individuals on the street or in other public places and putting questions to them if they are willing to listen.

FACTS: Christopher Drayton (D) was traveling on a Greyhound bus. As part of a routine drug and weapons interdiction effort, police officers, dressed in plain clothes and with concealed weapons but visible badges, entered the bus and randomly asked passengers, "Do you mind if I check your bags?" and "Do you mind if I check your person?" When Officer Lang asked Drayton (D) if he minded to a search of his baggy pants, Drayton (D) responded by lifting his hands about eight inches from his legs, and Lang conducted a pat-down search, found bundles of cocaine, and arrested Drayton (D). Drayton (D) was charged with drug crimes, and the federal district court denied his motion to suppress the drugs on the ground the entire procedure was a consensual encounter. The Court of Appeals for the Eleventh Circuit reversed, and the Government (P) appealed.

ISSUE: Do law enforcement officers violate the Fourth Amendment prohibition of unreasonable searches merely by approaching individuals on the street or in other public places and putting questions to them if they are willing to listen?

HOLDING AND DECISION: (Kennedy, J.) No. Law enforcement officers do not violate the Fourth Amendment prohibition of unreasonable searches merely by approaching individuals on the street or in other public places and putting questions to them if they are willing to listen. Even when law enforcement officers have no basis for suspecting a particular individual, they may pose questions, ask for identification, and request consent to search luggage—provided they do not induce cooperation by coercive means. If a reasonable person would feel free to terminate the encounter, as here, then he or she has not been seized. Here, the officers gave the passengers no reason to believe that they were required to answer the officers' questions. When Officer Lang approached Drayton (D), he did not brandish a weapon or make any intimidating movements. He left the aisle free so that Drayton (D) could exit. He spoke to passengers one by one and in a polite, quiet voice. Nothing he said would suggest to a reasonable person that he or she was barred from leaving the bus or otherwise terminating the encounter. There was no application of force, no intimidating movement, no overwhelming show of force, no blockage of exits, no command, not even an authoritative tone of voice. It is beyond question that had this encounter occurred on the street, it would be constitutional. The fact that an encounter takes place on a bus does not on its own transform standard police questioning of citizens into an illegal seizure. Furthermore, even the presence of a holstered firearm is unlikely to contribute to the coerciveness of the encounter absent active brandishing of the weapon. Reversed.

DISSENT: (Souter, J.) Although anyone who travels by air today clearly submits to searches of the person and luggage as a condition of boarding the aircraft, the commonplace precautions of air travel have not, thus far, been justified for ground transportation. There is therefore "an air of unreality" about the majority's explanation that bus passengers consent to searches of their luggage to enhance their own safety and the safety of those around them. Furthermore, a police officer who is certain to get his or her way has no need to shout.

ANALYSIS

In *Drayton*, the United States Supreme Court notes that although Officer Lang did not inform Drayton (D) of his right to refuse the search, he did request permission to search and that the totality of the circumstances indicated that the consent was voluntary, hence the search was admissible. In a society based on law, said the Court, the concept of agreement and consent should be given "a weight and dignity of its own."

Quicknotes

TOTALITY OF THE CIRCUMSTANCES TEST Standard that focuses on all the circumstances of a particular case, instead of individual factors.

Johnson v. United States

Convicted drug user (D) v. Federal government (P)

333 U.S. 10 (1948)

NATURE OF CASE: Appeal from a conviction for violation of federal narcotic laws.

FACT SUMMARY: Johnson (D) claimed that the police needed a warrant to search her room after they smelled burning opium outside the door.

RULE OF LAW

The Fourth Amendment requires that police officers obtain a warrant from a neutral and detached magistrate before searching a person's living quarters.

FACTS: Seattle detective Belland received information from a confidential informer that persons were smoking opium in the Europe Hotel. Officers went to the hotel and smelled burning opium outside Johnson's (D) room. Johnson (D) opened the door when Belland identified himself. Belland told Johnson (D) to consider herself under arrest because they were going to search the room. The search turned up incriminating evidence and Johnson (D) was subsequently convicted. Johnson (D) then challenged the validity of the search.

ISSUE: Does the Fourth Amendment require that police officers obtain a warrant from a neutral and detached magistrate before searching a person's living quarters?

HOLDING AND DECISION: (Jackson, J.) Yes. The Fourth Amendment requires that police officers obtain a warrant from a neutral and detached magistrate before searching a person's living quarters. At the time the officers entered Johnson's (D) room, they had evidence that a judge may have found to constitute probable cause for a search. However, the inferences that can be drawn from such evidence must be made by neutral magistrates rather than officers engaged in the often competitive enterprise of ferreting out crime. Exactly when privacy rights must yield to a search must be decided by a judicial officer rather than a police officer unless exceptional circumstances are present, such as a fleeing suspect. In the present case, the officers did not present any reason that a search warrant could not be obtained. Therefore, the search violated Johnson's (D) Fourth Amendment rights and the resulting evidence should have been suppressed. Reversed.

ANALYSIS

Probable cause is the minimal amount of proof necessary to allow a search. It must be established by persons who are willing to swear to the truth of their statements. Thus, they are made accountable for these representations.

Quicknotes

FOURTH AMENDMENT Provides that persons be secure as to their person and private belongings against unreasonable searches and seizures.

PROBABLE CAUSE A reasonable basis for believing that a crime has been committed.

Spinelli v. United States

Convicted gambler (D) v. Federal government (P)

393 U.S. 410 (1969)

NATURE OF CASE: Appeal from conviction of violation of gambling statutes.

FACT SUMMARY: Spinelli (D) was convicted upon evidence seized with a search warrant. The search warrant was issued based upon an affidavit containing a statement from an anonymous informer and information from agents of the Federal Bureau of Investigation (FBI) agents.

RULE OF LAW

If an affidavit to obtain a search warrant is based upon an informer's tip (i.e., hearsay), then the affidavit must state why the informer is "reliable" and the "underlying circumstances" from which the informer drew his or her conclusions, so as to enable an independent magistrate to conclude that the informer's information provides probable cause for the search.

FACTS: Spinelli (D) was convicted of violation of gambling statutes based upon evidence seized by the Federal Bureau of Investigation (FBI) under a search warrant. The FBI obtained this warrant based upon an affidavit containing the following information: (1) the FBI had been informed by a reliable informer that Spinelli (D) was using two specific telephones to conduct gambling operations; (2) that Spinelli (D) had been seen entering the apartment in which these two telephones were located; and (3) that Spinelli (D) had a reputation as a gambler. Upon conviction, and affirmance of that conviction by the court of appeals, Spinelli (D) brought a petition of certiorari to the United States Supreme Court challenging the constitutionality of the issuance of the search warrant.

ISSUE: If an affidavit to obtain a search warrant is based upon an informer's tip (i.e., hearsay), then must the affidavit state why the informer is "reliable" and the "underlying circumstances" from which the informer drew his or her conclusions, so as to enable an independent magistrate to conclude that the informer's information provides probable cause for the search?

HOLDING AND DECISION: (Harlan, J.) Yes. If an affidavit to obtain a search warrant is based upon an informer's tip (i.e., hearsay), then the affidavit must state why the informer is "reliable" and the "underlying circumstances" from which the informer drew his or her conclusions, so as to enable an independent magistrate to conclude that the informer's information provides probable cause for the search. Of course, in the absence of a statement detailing how the informer's tip was gathered, a search warrant may still issue if (1) the tip describes the accused's criminal activity in such detail (Draper) that a magistrate may conclude that it was gained in a reliable manner, or (2) there is sufficient independent corroboration of criminal activity in the affidavit so that a magistrate may conclude that there is probable cause that a crime is being committed. Here, first, the tip is insufficient for the issuance of a warrant. The affidavit states neither why the informer was considered reliable nor how the informer obtained his or her information. Second, there is no sufficient corroboration of the tip. The fact that Spinelli (D) entered an apartment with two telephones contains no suggestion of criminal activity by itself, and the fact that Spinelli (D) is known as a gambler is only "suspicion" entitled to no weight. Judgment below reversed.

DISSENT: (Black, J.) The Court in this case sets a standard of proof requisite to the finding of probable cause to issue a warrant that far exceeds any reasonable interpretation of the constitutional requirements.

DISSENT: (Fortas, J.) A policeman's affidavit is entitled to a commonsense evaluation, as the majority itself recognizes. The requirements imposed by the rule today require such an affidavit to be judged according to form, like an entry in an essay contest.

ANALYSIS

This case illustrates the two-pronged *Aguilar* test, *Aguilar v. Texas*, 378 U.S. 108 (1964), applicable to affidavits for search warrants based upon hearsay. And *Harris v. U.S.*, 403 U.S. 573 (1971), further specified a situation in which a search warrant may be issued on the basis of hearsay. In *Harris*, a warrant was upheld based upon hearsay because the affidavit contained sufficient information to allow the magistrate to determine that there was probable cause for a search warrant. The affidavit contained (1) the informer's "personal and recent observations" of the accused's criminal activity; (2) the informer's statement, which was against his own penal interest; and (3) the fact that the officer himself had certain knowledge of the accused's background consistent with the illegal activity alleged. Note, finally, that police do not have to reveal the identity of their informer on a hearing on the issue of probable cause, although

Continued on next page.

they must do so when it is material at trial to establish guilt or innocence.

Quicknotes

PROBABLE CAUSE A reasonable basis for believing that a crime has been committed.

Illinois v. Gates

State (P) v. Convicted drug dealer (D)

462 U.S. 213 (1983)

NATURE OF CASE: Appeal from order to suppress evidence.

FACT SUMMARY: After the Bloomingdale, Illinois, police received an anonymous tip revealing the trip Lance Gates (D) and his wife (D) would be making to Florida would be to pick up drugs and describing their modus operandi, a search warrant was issued and drugs were seized from their car and home when the couple returned to Bloomingdale.

RULE OF LAW

A magistrate may issue a search warrant if the "totality of the circumstances" presented in the affidavit indicates probable cause for the search, even if the "veracity" and "basis of knowledge" factors of the two-pronged test of *Aguilar v. State of Texas*, 378 U.S. 108 (1964), and *Spinelli v. United States*, 393 U.S. 410 (1969), cannot be satisfied.

FACTS: The Bloomingdale, Illinois, police received an anonymous letter stating that Lance Gates (D) and his wife (D) were drug dealers and describing in detail a drug run they were to make to Florida. Detective Mader verified some elements of the tip and arranged for surveillance of a flight to Florida by the Drug Enforcement Administration (DEA). DEA agents watched the Gateses (D) in Florida until they drove off in the direction of Illinois. The DEA report to Mader confirmed many elements of the tip, and on the basis of the letter, Mader's research, and the DEA report, Mader swore out an affidavit and a county magistrate issued a search warrant for the car and home of the Gateses (D). When the Gateses (D) arrived home, about 36 hours after Mr. Gates's (D) flight to Florida, Bloomingdale police searched their car and home, finding marijuana, weapons, and other contraband. The trial court suppressed the evidence, and a state appeals court affirmed. The Illinois Supreme Court affirmed suppression of the evidence, holding that under the two-pronged test of *Aguilar* and *Spinelli* there was no probable cause for the warrant. The "veracity" prong was not satisfied because there was no basis for concluding the anonymous letter writer was credible and law enforcement officers had only corroborated "innocent" details of the tip. The "basis of knowledge" prong was also not satisfied because there was no indication of the means by which the tipster acquired the information in the letter. Illinois (P) appealed to the United States Supreme Court.

ISSUE: May a magistrate issue a search warrant if the "totality of the circumstances" presented in the affidavit indicates probable cause for the search, even if the "veracity" and "basis of knowledge" factors of the two-pronged test of *Aguilar* and *Spinelli* cannot be satisfied?

HOLDING AND DECISION: (Rehnquist, J.) Yes. A magistrate may issue a search warrant if the "totality of the circumstances" presented in the affidavit indicates probable cause for the search, even if the "veracity" and "basis of knowledge" factors of the two-pronged test of *Aguilar* and *Spinelli* cannot be satisfied. The "veracity" and "basis of knowledge" factors of the two-pronged test of *Aguilar* and *Spinelli* are highly relevant but are not separate and necessary elements of probable cause. Probable cause for a warrant is a practical, nontechnical consideration that is most often made by non-lawyers, so the rigid two-pronged test is not appropriate. The "totality of the circumstances" test permits balancing of all relevant factors and allows a deficiency in one factor to be overcome by a strong showing as to other indicia of reliability. The "totality of the circumstances" test serves the public by allowing police to rely on anonymous tips that frequently lead to the solution of otherwise unsolvable crimes, while at the same time still requiring an affidavit to contain more than merely conclusory statements as to the basis for finding probable cause. Applying the "totality of the circumstances" test to this case, corroboration by Mader and the DEA of major portions of the tipster's detailed predictions of highly suspicious behavior by the Gateses (D) provided probable cause for the warrant. Reversed.

CONCURRENCE: (White, J.) The evidence should not be suppressed since the police reasonably believed they were acting lawfully. However, the two-pronged test should not be overruled. Under the Court's "totality of the circumstances" test magistrates could dilute the probable cause standard by issuing warrants based on purely conclusory statements of honest citizens or previously reliable informants.

DISSENT: (Brennan, J.) The two-pronged test should not be abandoned. The two-pronged test requires police to provide crucial information to the magistrate and provides a structure to aid the magistrate in making the probable cause determination. With this information and a structure by which to process it, the magistrate can be an independent arbiter of probable cause and will not issue a warrant based on anything less than information acquired in a reliable way by an honest or credible person.

Continued on next page.

DISSENT: (Stevens, J.) The discrepancies between the tipster's predictions and Detective Mader's information made the conduct of the Gateses (D) seem less unusual and less probative of criminal activity. The anonymity of the tipster, the material mistake in the tip, and the fact that law enforcement corroborated only innocent activities, lead to the conclusion that there was no probable cause for the warrant.

ANALYSIS

The two-pronged test, still the rule in many jurisdictions, often required corroboration of information to establish the veracity of the informant. A major effect of *Gates* has been to weaken this requirement. A police informant whom the police have found reliable is now likely to be considered credible with minimal corroboration of information. See *United States v. Warner*, 894 F.2d 957 (8th Cir. 1990). Moreover, the trend is to consider an ordinary citizen who reports a crime almost presumptively credible, and corroboration of their information is unnecessary. See *United States v. Decoteau*, 932 F.2d 1205 (7th Cir. 1991).

Quicknotes

TOTALITY OF THE CIRCUMSTANCES TEST Standard that focuses on all the circumstances of a particular case, instead of individual factors.

Maryland v. Pringle

State (P) v. Convicted drug possessor (D)

540 U.S. 366 (2003)

NATURE OF CASE: Appeal by state from reversal of conviction for cocaine possession.

FACT SUMMARY: When Pringle (D) was arrested for cocaine possession when he was a front-seat passenger in a vehicle and the cocaine was found in the back seat, he argued that he did not have sufficient possession of the cocaine to show probable cause for his arrest. Hence, any confession resulting from such arrest would be invalid.

RULE OF LAW

The passenger of a vehicle, even if separated from the drugs, has sufficient constructive possession of drugs located in the vehicle to give rise to probable cause for the passenger's arrest.

FACTS: A police officer stopped an automobile for speeding. There were three occupants in the car. Pringle (D) was the front-seat passenger. When the driver opened the glove compartment to get the registration, the officer observed a large amount of rolled-up cash. The driver consented to a vehicle search, which yielded $763 from the glove compartment and cocaine from behind the back-seat armrest. Pringle (D) and both other occupants were arrested. Pringle (D) waived his *Miranda* rights and confessed the cocaine belonged to him. The trial court denied Pringle's (D) motion to suppress the confession as fruit of an illegal arrest, holding the officer had probable cause for the arrest. Pringle (D) was convicted of cocaine possession; however, the court of appeals in Maryland reversed, holding that the mere finding of cocaine in the back armrest when Pringle (D) was simply a passenger in the front seat failed to establish probable cause to arrest Pringle (D) for possession. Maryland (P) appealed.

ISSUE: Does the passenger of a vehicle, even if separated from the drugs, have sufficient constructive possession of drugs located in the vehicle to give rise to probable cause for the passenger's arrest?

HOLDING AND DECISION: (Rehnquist, C.J.) Yes. The passenger of a vehicle, even if separated from the drugs, has sufficient constructive possession of drugs located in the vehicle to give rise to probable cause for the passenger's arrest. Maryland law authorizes police officers to execute warrantless arrests, inter alia, for felonies committed in an officer's presence or where the officer has probable cause to believe a felony has been, or is being, committed. Here, the officer, upon recovering the plastic bags of cocaine, had probable cause to believe a felony had been committed. As to whether there was probable cause to believe Pringle (D) had committed that crime, Maryland law defines "possession" as the exercise of actual or constructive dominion over a thing by one or more persons. The probable cause standard is incapable of precise definition or quantification into percentages because it deals with probabilities and depends on the totality of the circumstances. In the instant case, Pringle (D) was one of three men riding in the car in the early morning hours when a large amount of rolled-up cash and five baggies of cocaine were found. The cocaine was "accessible" to all three of the occupants, including Pringle (D). It was an entirely reasonable inference from these facts that any or all three of the occupants had knowledge of, and exercised dominion and control over, the cocaine. Thus, a reasonable officer could conclude there was probable cause to believe Pringle (D) committed the crime of possession of cocaine, either solely or jointly. Reversed.

ANALYSIS

As the United States Supreme Court makes clear in *Pringle*, the probable cause standard is a practical, nontechnical conception that deals with the factual and practical considerations of everyday life on which reasonable and prudent persons, "not legal technicians," act. Probable cause is a "fluid concept" – turning on the assessment of probabilities in particular factual contexts, not readily, or even usually, reduced to a neat set of legal rules.

Quicknotes

PROBABLE CAUSE A reasonable basis for believing that a crime has been committed.

Warden v. Hayden

State (P) v. Convicted robber (D)

387 U.S. 294 (1967)

NATURE OF CASE: Appeal from conviction for armed robbery.

FACT SUMMARY: Hayden's (D) personal items were seized from his home during a search and introduced as evidence at his trial.

RULE OF LAW

The Fourth Amendment allows all types of evidence to be seized pursuant to a valid search.

FACTS: Hayden's (D) home was searched without a warrant, but the search was justified by exigent circumstances. Items of his clothing (cap, jacket, and trousers) were seized during the search and were admitted at his trial for armed robbery. Hayden (D) was convicted and then appealed, claiming that the Fourth Amendment prohibited the seizure of items that were mere evidence rather than the instrumentalities of crime. The Court of Appeals for the Fourth Circuit agreed with Hayden (D) and the State (P) appealed to the United States Supreme Court.

ISSUE: Does the Fourth Amendment allow all types of evidence to be seized pursuant to a valid search?

HOLDING AND DECISION: (Brennan, J.) Yes. The Fourth Amendment allows all types of evidence to be seized pursuant to a valid search. Previously, this Court has supported a distinction between items that were "mere evidence" from instrumentalities, fruits of crime, or contraband. This rule was based on the premise that the right to search for and seize property depended on the assertion of the government of a superior interest. The purpose of apprehending and convicting criminals was not considered sufficient. Thus, stolen property and contraband were subject to seizure, but other items were not. This premise that property interests control the right of governmental searches has subsequently been discredited. The Fourth Amendment is designed to protect privacy, and a search directed at purely evidentiary objects is no more intrusive than one for instrumentalities of crime. The "mere evidence" limitation has also spawned exceptions so numerous that there has been extreme confusion. As long as requirements of the Fourth Amendment are followed, i.e., probable cause and the intervention of a neutral and detached magistrate, there is no viable reason for maintaining the "mere evidence" limitation. Accordingly, Hayden's (D) personal items were properly seized. The Court of Appeals is reversed.

DISSENT: (Douglas, J.) The personal effects of an individual are sacrosanct from the prying eyes of the government.

ANALYSIS

The majority decision noted the practical problems implicit in distinguishing between mere evidence and instrumentalities of crime. Moreover, nothing in the language of the Fourth Amendment supports the distinction. It should be noted, however, that without the mere evidence limitation it is much easier for the government to meet the particularity requirement for a warrant.

Quicknotes

FOURTH AMENDMENT Provides that persons be secure as to their person and private belongings against unreasonable searches and seizures.

Andresen v. Maryland

Convicted criminal (D) v. State (P)

427 U.S. 463 (1976)

NATURE OF CASE: Appeal from conviction for fraud.

FACT SUMMARY: Andresen (D) contended that evidence of crimes other than those under which he was suspected of acting could not be seized under a warrant seeking evidence of the enumerated crimes.

RULE OF LAW

Evidence of crimes that relate to or are relevant to proving the crime under which a warrant is issued may be validly seized under the warrant.

FACTS: Andresen (D), an attorney, was suspected of committing the crime of false pretenses with respect to the sale of a particular lot of real property. A search warrant was issued that described in great detail the evidence sought and included a phrase allowing for the seizure of all other evidence of crime. A search was conducted of two of his premises and evidence relating to the sale of the particular lot as well as evidence of other transactions was seized and was used to convict him. Andresen (D) appealed on the basis that the warrant was unreasonably broad in that it allowed for the seizure of "mere evidence" not directly pertaining to the particular lot involved. The state appellate court upheld the conviction, and the United States Supreme Court granted certiorari.

ISSUE: May evidence of other crimes that relate to or are relevant to proving the crime under which a warrant be validly seized under the warrant?

HOLDING AND DECISION: (Blackmun, J.) Yes. Evidence of crimes that relate to or are relevant to proving the crime under which a warrant is issued may be validly seized under the warrant. The evidence seized that did not directly relate to the subject lot was relevant to prove Andresen's (D) complex real estate scheme. Thus, it was properly seized under the warrant. Affirmed.

DISSENT: (Brennan, J.) The statement in the warrant authorizing the seizure of evidence relevant to crimes not listed rendered the warrant a general warrant and therefore invalid under the Fourth Amendment.

ANALYSIS

This case laid the groundwork for the latter case of *Zurcher v. Stanford Daily*, 436 U.S. 547 (1978). That case squarely addressed the issue of the propriety of issuing a search warrant for premises owned by an innocent third party to seize evidence not specifically enumerated in the warrant. *Zurcher* has been roundly criticized as giving police too much leeway in their ability to search.

Quicknotes

FOURTH AMENDMENT Provides that persons be secure as to their person and private belongings against unreasonable searches and seizures.

United States v. Watson

Federal government (P) v. Convicted thief (D)

423 U.S. 411 (1976)

NATURE OF CASE: Appeal from conviction for possession of stolen mail.

FACT SUMMARY: Watson (D) contended his arrest was not valid as it was not made pursuant to an arrest warrant.

RULE OF LAW

Officials may make valid arrests based on probable cause without a warrant.

FACTS: Watson (D) was arrested after he was placed under surveillance by a postal official for possession of stolen mail. The official acted on information from an informant who had supplied reliable information in the past. Watson (D) challenged the legality of the arrest on the basis that no warrant had been issued. The trial court upheld the arrest, and the Ninth Circuit Court of Appeals reversed. The United States Supreme Court granted certiorari.

ISSUE: May officials make valid arrests based on probable cause without a warrant?

HOLDING AND DECISION: (White, J.) Yes. Officials may make valid arrests based on probable cause without a warrant. The Fourth Amendment did not change or modify the ancient common-law rule that police officers may make warrantless arrests where probable cause exists. Because there is no constitutional barrier, the Court here must look to the statute. The postal regulations empower inspectors to arrest suspects when they have probable cause to believe the postal laws have been violated. Such arrests may occur with or without arrest warrants. Therefore, because there clearly was probable cause to arrest, the arrest was valid. Reversed.

CONCURRENCE: (Powell, J.) A law enforcement officer is constitutionally empowered to make warrantless searches in public places even where there was adequate opportunity to obtain a warrant.

DISSENT: (Marshall, J.) Arrests should be subject to the same warrant requirements as searches.

ANALYSIS

This case illustrates the common-law rule that warrantless arrests are acceptable upon an articulable showing of probable cause. Arrest warrants generally are required only in the absence of hot pursuit and when the arrest is to be made in the suspect's home. Warrantless arrests, therefore, are the rule rather than the exception.

Quicknotes

FOURTH AMENDMENT Provides that persons be secure as to their person and private belongings against unreasonable searches and seizures.

PROBABLE CAUSE A reasonable basis for believing that a crime has been committed.

Terry v. Ohio

Convicted felon (D) v. State (P)

392 U.S. 1 (1968)

NATURE OF CASE: Appeal from a conviction of carrying a concealed weapon.

FACT SUMMARY: Terry (D) was stopped and patted down for weapons by an officer who thought Terry (D) was casing a store.

RULE OF LAW

Where a police officer observes unusual conduct that leads him or her reasonably to conclude in light of his or her experience that criminal activity may be afoot and that the persons with whom he or she is dealing may be armed and presently dangerous, the officer is entitled for the protection of him- or herself and others in the area to conduct a carefully limited search of the outer clothing of such persons in an attempt to discover weapons that might be used to assault him or her.

FACTS: Terry (D) was apparently casing a store. He and two men hovered about a street corner for an extended period of time, pausing to stare in the same store window roughly a dozen times. A police officer seized Terry (D) and patted him down for weapons. A concealed weapon was found. Terry (D) was arrested and subsequently convicted after the court denied Terry's (D) motion to suppress. The court of appeals affirmed. The Ohio Supreme Court dismissed the appeal on the ground that no substantial constitutional question was involved. The United States Supreme Court granted certiorari to determine the admissibility of the revolver into evidence under the Fourth Amendment.

ISSUE: Where a police officer observes unusual conduct that leads him or her reasonably to conclude in light of his or her experience that criminal activity may be afoot and that the persons with whom he or she is dealing may be armed and presently dangerous, is the officer entitled for the protection of him- or herself and others in the area to conduct a carefully limited search of the outer clothing of such persons in an attempt to discover weapons that might be used to assault him or her?

HOLDING AND DECISION: (Warren, C.J.) Yes. Where a police officer observes unusual conduct that leads him or her reasonably to conclude in light of his or her experience that criminal activity may be afoot and that the persons with whom he or she is dealing may be armed and presently dangerous, the officer is entitled, for the protection of him- or herself and others in the area, to conduct a carefully limited search of the outer clothing of such persons in an attempt to discover weapons that might be used to assault him or her. Here, the officer seized Terry (D) and subjected him to a search of his outer clothing. The officer had observed Terry (D) and two other men hover about a street corner for an extended period of time, and stare into a store window roughly a dozen times. These were suspicious circumstances that would justify the officer's turning his attention to Terry (D). Moreover, under the facts, a reasonably prudent person would have been warranted in believing that Terry (D) was armed and thus presented a threat to the officer's safety while he was investigating his suspicious behavior. The revolver seized from Terry (D) was properly admitted into evidence against him. Affirmed.

CONCURRENCE: (Harlan, J.) There are a few gaps in the decision of the Court, although its ultimate conclusion is sound. If a frisk is to be justified in order to protect the officer, the officer must first have constitutional grounds to make a forcible "stop" (i.e., reasonable suspicion). But a limited frisk incident to such a lawful stop requires no additional justification. There is no reason why an officer should risk a bullet by first questioning the suspect.

CONCURRENCE: (White, J.) There is no need for interrogation during an investigative stop before the officer frisks the suspect. Although an officer may question the suspect briefly when a temporary detention is justified by a fear for the officer's and others' safety, a protective frisk for weapons is justified regardless of whether any questions are answered.

DISSENT: (Douglas, J.) A search and seizure cannot be justified by Fourth Amendment standards unless there is "probable cause" to believe that a crime has been committed or is about to be committed. Here, however, since there was no "probable cause" for the issuance of a warrant, the court's holding allows police greater freedom to search and seize than even a judge could authorize.

ANALYSIS

The following is required for a stop and frisk in the *Terry* situation: (1) there is a reasonable belief that there may be criminal activity; (2) there is a reasonable belief that the detainees are dangerous; (3) after the officer announces who he or she is to the suspect and, after some questions, the officer is not convinced that the suspect is not dangerous; and (4) if the above

Continued on next page.

are present, a pat-down may be made (Hill, Criminal Procedure, at 79).

Quicknotes

PROBABLE CAUSE A reasonable basis for believing that a crime has been committed.

REASONABLE BELIEF A reasonable basis for believing that a crime is being or has been committed.

***TERRY* STOP** A search of a person suspected of intending to commit a crime that is conducted by patting down the clothes of the person; the search must be limited to the reason for which the individual was lawfully stopped.

Kansas v. Glover

State (P) v. Vehicle driver charged as habitual violator (D)

140 S. Ct. 1183 (2020)

NATURE OF CASE: Appeal from reversal of decision reversing grant of motion to suppress evidence obtained after traffic stop in prosecution of a vehicle driver as a habitual violator.

FACT SUMMARY: A deputy sheriff ran a license plate check on a pickup truck, discovering that the truck belonged to Charles Glover, Jr. (Glover) (D) and that Glover's (D) driver's license had been revoked. The deputy pulled the truck over because he assumed that Glover (D) was driving impermissibly. Glover (D), who was in fact driving and who was subsequently charged with driving as a habitual violator, moved to suppress all evidence from the stop, claiming that the deputy lacked reasonable suspicion for the stop, in violation of the Fourth Amendment.

RULE OF LAW

When a law enforcement officer lacks information negating an inference that the owner of a vehicle is driving the vehicle, an investigative traffic stop made after running the vehicle's license plate and learning that the registered owner's driver's license has been revoked is reasonable under the Fourth Amendment.

FACTS: Deputy Mark Mehrer (Deputy Mehrer), a Kansas (P) law enforcement officer, ran a license plate check on a pickup truck, and discovered that the truck belonged to Charles Glover, Jr. (Glover) (D) and that Glover's (D) driver's license had been revoked. Based solely on that information, Deputy Mehrer pulled the truck over. Deputy Mehrer did not observe any traffic infractions and did not attempt to identify the truck's driver. Once the vehicle was stopped, Deputy Mehrer was able to identify Glover (D) as the driver, and then charged Glover (D) with driving as a habitual violator. Glover (D) filed a motion to suppress all evidence seized during the stop, claiming that Deputy Mehrer lacked reasonable suspicion for the seizure, and, therefore, violated the Fourth Amendment. The state's trial court granted the motion. The state's intermediate appellate court reversed, concluding that the facts gave rise to a reasonable suspicion. The Kansas Supreme Court reversed, finding that Deputy Mehrer did not have reasonable suspicion because his inference that Glover (D) was behind the wheel amounted to "only a hunch" that Glover (D) was engaging in criminal activity, and that this "hunch" involved "applying and stacking unstated assumptions that are unreasonable without further factual basis," namely, that "the registered owner was likely the primary driver of the vehicle" and that "the owner will likely disregard the suspension or revocation order and continue to drive." The United States Supreme Court granted certiorari.

ISSUE: When a law enforcement officer lacks information negating an inference that the owner of a vehicle is driving the vehicle, is an investigative traffic stop made after running the vehicle's license plate and learning that the registered owner's driver's license has been revoked reasonable under the Fourth Amendment?

HOLDING AND DECISION: (Thomas, J.) Yes. When a law enforcement officer lacks information negating an inference that the owner of a vehicle is driving the vehicle, an investigative traffic stop made after running the vehicle's license plate and learning that the registered owner's driver's license has been revoked is reasonable under the Fourth Amendment. Under the Court's precedents, a law enforcement officer may initiate a brief investigative traffic stop when the officer has a particularized and objective basis to suspect legal wrongdoing. The level of suspicion required is less than that necessary for probable cause and depends on considerations of everyday life on which reasonable and prudent people act. The reasonable-suspicion standard thus permits officers to make commonsense judgments and inferences about human behavior. Here, Deputy Mehrer's commonsense inference that the owner of a vehicle was likely the vehicle's driver provided more than reasonable suspicion to initiate the stop. Such an inference is not made unreasonable merely because a vehicle's driver is not always its registered owner or because Glover (D) had a revoked license. Though common sense suffices to justify the officer's inference, empirical studies demonstrate that drivers with suspended or revoked licenses frequently continue to drive. Moreover, Kansas' (P) license-revocation scheme, which covers drivers who have already demonstrated a disregard for the law or are categorically unfit to drive, reinforces the reasonableness of the inference that an individual with a revoked license will continue to drive. Glover's (D) counterarguments are unpersuasive. Glover (D) argues that Deputy Mehrer's inference was unreasonable because it was not grounded in his law enforcement training or experience. Such a requirement, however, is inconsistent with this Court's Fourth Amendment jurisprudence. It would also place the burden on police officers to justify their inferences by referring to training materials or experience, and it would

Continued on next page.

foreclose their ability to rely on common sense obtained outside of their work duties. Glover's (D) argument that Kansas's (D) view would permit officers to base reasonable suspicion exclusively on probabilities also carries little force. Officers, like jurors, may rely on probabilities in the reasonable suspicion context. Moreover, the deputy here did more than that: He combined facts obtained from a database and commonsense judgments to form a reasonable suspicion that a specific individual was potentially engaged in specific criminal activity. The scope of this holding is narrow. The reasonable suspicion standard takes into account the totality of the circumstances. Although the presence of additional facts might dispel reasonable suspicion, here Deputy Mehrer possessed no information sufficient to rebut the reasonable inference that Glover (D) was driving his own truck with a revoked license. [Reversed and remanded.]

CONCURRENCE: (Kagan, J.) In this case, Deputy Mehrer had reasonable suspicion to stop Glover's (D) truck. First, as a matter of common sense, it is reasonable to suspect that a vehicle's registered owner is driving the vehicle. Although it is not similarly a matter of common sense that a vehicle's registered owner whose license is revoked will flout the law and drive the vehicle on pain of criminal penalties, such an inference is reasonable for a Kansas (P) law officer because Kansas (P) almost never revokes a license except for serious or repeated driving offenses. Thus, Deputy Mehrer had information about the registered owner's proclivity to break driving laws. Because a person with a revoked license in Kansas (P) has already shown a willingness to flout driving restrictions, that fact gives rise to a reasonable inference that such a person will drive without a license—at least often enough to warrant an investigatory stop. No such inference would be warranted, however, if Kansas (P) had barred Glover (D) from driving on a ground that provided no similar evidence of his penchant for ignoring driving laws. For example, Kansas (P) suspends driving licenses for matters having nothing to do with road safety, such as not paying child support. In such a case, the inference that the driver has a history of disregarding driving rules would no longer apply. Even where, as here, that inference at first is deemed reasonable, the inference may be rebutted by a showing that an officer knew of additional facts, such as where an officer knows the registered owner of a vehicle is an elderly man but can see the driver is a young woman, or where there is more than one registered owner. There are many such fact-specific situations that could negate reasonable suspicion notwithstanding an initial license-revocation alert. Additionally, a defendant may challenge the reasonableness of an officer's suspicion by adducing statistical evidence regarding "hit rates," i.e., the frequency with which vehicle stops such as the one made by the officer in a given case lead to the discovery of unlicensed drivers behind the wheel. Defendants may question testifying officers about such information, and, in fact, an officer may have an individual hit rate that if low enough could itself negate reasonable suspicion. In other words, in fully litigated cases, the license-revocation alert does not (as it did here) end the inquiry, but serves as the first step in assessing the reasonableness of the officer's suspicion.

DISSENT: (Sotomayor, J.) Under the majority's approach, a state's burden of proving reasonable suspicion for a vehicle stop is impermissibly reduced when viewed against the Court's precedents in this area. The state, until now, needed to show more than a mere hunch; a police officer needed to explain rational inferences from particular facts as viewed from the lens of the officer's experience and training. The Court's reasonable-suspicion jurisprudence not only required an objective reasonable officer's assessment of the facts, but also required that a stop be individualized, meaning there is a suspicion that the particular person being stopped is engaged in wrongdoing, rather than a suspicion based on a class to which the person belongs. Moreover, the majority flips the burden of proof by permitting police officers to make roadside stops whenever they do not have information that negates an inference that a vehicle's unlicensed owner is its driver. In the case at bar, Deputy Mehrer never indicated he had any informed belief about the propensity of unlicensed drivers to operate vehicles in the area, let alone that he relied on such a belief when seizing Glover (D). The majority thus absolves officers from any responsibility to investigate the identity of a driver where feasible. Cases are replete with instances where officers have been able to do just that, or at least ascertain a driver's age and gender from afar. The majority gives officers free rein to stop a vehicle involved in no suspicious activity merely because the vehicle is registered to a person with a revoked license. Such a stop, then, is (impermissibly) based on a mere hunch about the driver's identity. With no basis in the record to presume that unlicensed drivers routinely continue driving, the majority endeavors to fill the gap with its own "common sense." However, simply labeling an inference "common sense" does not make it so. To the contrary, whether a driver is likely to be its unlicensed owner is not at all obvious. Also, contrary to the majority's assertion, the reasonable-suspicion inquiry does not accommodate the average person's intuition, but only permits reliance on a particular type of common sense—that of the reasonable officer, developed through the officer's experiences and training in law enforcement. Such specialized knowledge, including knowledge of a geographical area's inhabitants and their customs, leads to the types of inferences and deductions that the police are permitted to make. However, allowing judges to offer their own brand of common sense where a state's proffered justifications for a search come up short

Continued on next page.

shifts police work to the judiciary and, thereby, promotes broad, inflexible rules that overlook regional differences. Finally, the majority cites empirical studies to bolster its claim that its inferences are grounded in "common experience." However, those studies do no such thing, since the studies do not provide information regarding the percentage of vehicle owners with revoked licenses in Kansas (P) who continue to drive their cars, and that might ostensibly inform an officer's inferences about driver identity. To the contrary, permitting the state to rely on large-data studies demonstrates the danger of relying on generalized data because it permits law enforcement to make seizures without particularized suspicion of wrongdoing or observed violations of law. In other words, the majority paves "the road to finding reasonable suspicion on nothing more than a demographic profile." That has never been the law, and it never should be.

ANALYSIS

As this case demonstrates, reasonable suspicion is a less demanding standard than probable cause not only in the sense that reasonable suspicion can be established with information that is different in quantity or content than that required to establish probable cause, but also in the sense that reasonable suspicion can arise from information that is less reliable than that required to show probable cause. The "reasonable suspicion" necessary to justify a vehicle stop until *Glover* was dependent upon both the content of information possessed by police and its degree of reliability. The standard took into account the totality of the circumstances. Although a mere hunch cannot create reasonable suspicion, the level of suspicion the standard has required is considerably less than proof of wrongdoing by a preponderance of the evidence, and obviously less than is necessary for probable cause. Arguably, *Glover* has reduced even that standard to where the government no longer needs to articulate individualized suspicion in certain vehicle stop cases, but only needs to connect a suspect's demographic class (i.e., the class of vehicle owners whose licenses have been revoked) to an inference of wrongdoing, with nothing more.

Quicknotes

FOURTH AMENDMENT Provides that persons be secure as to their person and private belongings against unreasonable searches and seizures.

PROBABLE CAUSE A reasonable basis for believing that a crime has been committed.

REASONABLE SUSPICION That which would cause an ordinary prudent person under the circumstances to suspect that a crime has been committed based on specific and articulable facts.

Navarette v. California

Individual (D) v. State (P)

572 U.S. 393 (2014)

NATURE OF CASE: Appeal from the California Court of Appeal decision against the defendant.

FACT SUMMARY: After receiving a single, anonymous tip of erratic driving on the highway by Navarrette (D), the California Highway Patrol pulled Navarette (D) over and discovered 30 pounds of illegal marijuana in the vehicle.

RULE OF LAW

Reviewing the totality of the circumstances, a single, anonymous tip may be sufficiently reliable to support the reasonable suspicion required to make an investigatory stop of a vehicle.

FACTS: The California Highway Patrol received an anonymous tip from a driver that another vehicle had allegedly run her off the road. The caller provided the mile marker on the highway where the incident occurred, a description of the silver Ford pickup truck, and the license plate number. Approximately 18 minutes later, police caught up to the vehicle operated by Navarette (D). They followed him for five minutes. Navarette (D) did nothing else unusual during that time period. The police eventually pulled him over and located 30 pounds of marijuana in the vehicle. Prior to trial, Navarette (D) moved to suppress the evidence on the grounds the police did not have reasonable suspicion to pull him over. The court denied the motion. After his conviction, Navarette (D) appealed to the California Court of Appeal. That court upheld the denial of the motion to suppress and his conviction. Navarette (D) appealed to the United States Supreme Court.

ISSUE: Reviewing the totality of the circumstances, may a single, anonymous tip be sufficiently reliable to support the reasonable suspicion required to make an investigatory stop of a vehicle?

HOLDING AND DECISION: (Thomas, J.) Yes. Reviewing the totality of the circumstances, a single, anonymous tip may be sufficiently reliable to support the reasonable suspicion required to make an investigatory stop of a vehicle. The initial issue to be determined is whether the 911 call provided enough information to be reliable. Here, the call provided a specific vehicle description and a license plate number. In addition, the police located the vehicle some 19 miles down the highway. This was 18 minutes after the 911 call. These facts support the conclusion that the 911 call was made contemporaneously with the incident. This is not unlike the excited utterance exception to the hearsay rule in evidence. The statement is reliable because it was made close in time to the event. Also, 911 calls are recorded, and it is presumed callers are aware that potential false reports may be investigated and discovered. The second part of the analysis is whether the reliable tip creates reasonable suspicion that criminal activity is occurring. Not all allegations of erratic driving imply that a driver is impaired. Here, the 911 caller specifically alleged that Navarette (D) attempted to run her off the road. This type of conduct supports a belief that the driver was intoxicated. In addition, it is irrelevant that Navarette (D) did not drive erratically while the police followed him for five minutes. It is typical that drivers will drive more carefully while being followed by the police. Affirmed.

DISSENT: (Scalia, J.) The Court's decision unnecessarily limits our freedom of movement while operating a motor vehicle. The Court is essentially holding that an anonymous call about a single incident of erratic driving is enough to satisfy the reasonable suspicion standard to effectuate an investigatory stop. The Court incorrectly compares this 911 call to the hearsay exception of an excited utterance. Here, the 911 caller had ample time to observe the license plate number, bring their vehicle to a halt, and then call the police. This is plenty of time to embellish their account of the incident. In addition, the allegation of one incident of erratic driving is not enough to provide reasonable suspicion that Navarette (D) was driving while impaired. Most incidents of such driving are not due to intoxication. Moreover, the unremarkable five-minute period when the police followed Navarette (D) undermines the reliability of the claim.

ANALYSIS

The majority labeled this decision a "close case" and the 5-4 split among the justices corroborates this description. In any stop based on an anonymous tip, the issues will be (1) whether the tip itself is reliable and (2) whether the tip alleges some type of criminal activity. After finding the tip reliable, the majority put significant weight into the type of incident alleged—that Navarette (D) tried to run the caller off the road. Defense counsel will try to distinguish that type of serious allegation in future cases where the alleged single incident is more along the lines of swerving on the highway or changing lanes without signaling.

Continued on next page.

Quicknotes

EXCITED UTTERANCE An exception to the hearsay rule for statements made or caused by the happening of a startling occurrence and that is related to that occurrence.

REASONABLE SUSPICION That which would cause an ordinary prudent person under the circumstances to suspect that a crime has been committed based on specific and articulable facts.

Heien v. North Carolina

Individual (D) v. State (P)

574 U.S. 54 (2014)

NATURE OF CASE: Appeal from the North Carolina Supreme Court's decision against the defendant.

FACT SUMMARY: A police officer pulled over Heien's (D) vehicle after noticing that it had only one functioning rear brake light. During the ensuing search, the officer found cocaine in Heien's (D) vehicle.

RULE OF LAW

A mistake of law will not render an investigatory stop illegal so long as the mistake is reasonable.

FACTS: A police officer pulled over Heien's (D) vehicle after noticing that it had only one functioning rear brake light. After being pulled over, Heien (D) consented to a search of the vehicle. The officer found cocaine in the vehicle. Heien (D) moved to suppress the cocaine on the grounds the stop was impermissible. The North Carolina Court of Appeals concluded that the state's regulatory language regarding rear brake lights mandated that each vehicle needed only one functioning brake light. That court reversed the conviction, finding that the stop was not valid. The North Carolina Supreme Court disagreed and held that the regulatory code required two functioning brake lights. It reinstated the conviction against Heien (D). Heien appealed to the United States Supreme Court.

ISSUE: Will a mistake of law render an investigatory stop illegal so long as the mistake is reasonable?

HOLDING AND DECISION: (Roberts, C.J.) No. A mistake of law will not render an investigatory stop illegal so long as the mistake is reasonable. This Court has previously held that searches and seizures based on a mistake of fact are not per se unreasonable. The same concept applies to mistakes of law. The limit on these mistakes in both areas is that they must be reasonable. Heien (D) contends that snap factual judgments in the field are understandable. Heien (D) argues the law is clear and officers' mistaken beliefs about the law should not grant officers greater authority. However, officers also have to make quick judgments in the field regarding the applicability of certain laws. For example, a law may prohibit cars from a public park, but officers may have to decide if that law or ordinance applies to other types of transportation like a Segway. Here, the Court finds the mistake regarding the requirement for one or two brakes lights was reasonable. Affirmed.

DISSENT: (Sotomayor, J.) While it is clear officers have leeway to assess the facts on the ground as they effectuate a stop, the same leeway should not be afforded to officers' interpretation of the applicable laws or regulations. That is the province of the courts. Allowing officers to apply their own understanding of such laws or regulations and then upholding their actions by finding their alleged mistakes reasonable greatly expands their authority. In addition, permitting reasonable mistakes of law to support investigatory stops has the effect of deterring officers from educating themselves about the current state of the law in their jurisdiction.

ANALYSIS

The fact that the North Carolina Court of Appeals and the North Carolina Supreme Court differed in their interpretations of the applicable regulations regarding brake lights supported the United States Supreme Court's decision in this case. The decision clearly expands the scope of permissible investigatory stops beyond the simple mistake of fact scenarios. It remains to be seen if future decisions will limit or further expand this authority.

Quicknotes

INVESTIGATORY STOP A brief, non-intrusive stop, requiring the police officer to have a reasonable suspicion that a crime has been committed based on specific and articulable facts.

MISTAKE OF FACT An unintentional mistake in knowing or recalling a fact without the will to deceive.

MISTAKE OF LAW An error involving a misunderstanding or incorrect application of law.

Chimel v. California

Convicted burglar (D) v. State (P)

395 U.S. 752 (1969)

NATURE OF CASE: Appeal from a burglary conviction.

FACT SUMMARY: California (P) contended it could search Chimel's (D) entire premises pursuant to his lawful arrest there.

RULE OF LAW

A search incident to a lawful arrest is limited to the suspect's person and the area within which he or she could reach for a weapon or evidence.

FACTS: Chimel (D) was arrested in the living room of his home on a burglary charge. The police, without a warrant, searched the entire premises and finally found the evidence of the burglary in the master bedroom. They justified the search as pursuant to the lawful arrest. Chimel (D) moved to suppress on the basis the search was constitutionally limited to his area of control. The motion was denied and the California Supreme Court upheld the conviction. The United States Supreme Court granted certiorari.

ISSUE: Is a search conducted incident to a lawful arrest limited to the suspect's person and the area within which he or she could reach for a weapon or destroy evidence?

HOLDING AND DECISION: (Stewart, J.) Yes. A search incident to a lawful arrest is limited to the person and the area within which he or she could reach for a weapon or destroy evidence. The search is to allow the officer to protect him- or herself and preserve evidence. It does not extend to extremities of the premises where the suspect could never obtain a weapon or destroy evidence. Thus the search of the bedroom was not lawful without a warrant or consent and the evidence should have been suppressed. Reversed.

DISSENT: (White, J.) When there is probable cause to search and there are exigent circumstances making it "impracticable" to obtain a search warrant, a warrantless search is reasonable under the Fourth Amendment. Such an exigent circumstance is supplied by the fact of an arrest. Almost always, there is a strong possibility that if officers leave the scene of the arrest to obtain a warrant, confederates of the arrestee will remove that evidence for which the officers had probable cause to search. It is, therefore, unreasonable, assuming that there is probable cause to search the premises where a person is lawfully arrested, to require the police to obtain a search warrant.

ANALYSIS

Some commentators, including Justice White, have criticized the holding in this case on the basis it does not meet with the requirements of reality. The officers in this case should have obtained a search warrant under this holding, yet to have done so would have allowed the defendant or accomplices to remove or destroy the evidence.

Quicknotes

FOURTH AMENDMENT Provides that persons be secure as to their person and private belongings against unreasonable searches and seizures.

SEARCH An inspection conducted in order to obtain evidence to be utilized for the prosecution of a crime.

WARRANT An order issued by a court directing an officer to undertake a certain act (e.g., arrest or search).

United States v. Robinson

Federal government (P) v. Convicted drug dealer (D)

414 U.S. 218 (1973)

NATURE OF CASE: Appeal from conviction of possessing heroin.

FACT SUMMARY: Robinson (D) contended the police had no probable cause to conduct a full body search and, therefore, the evidence obtained should have been suppressed.

RULE OF LAW

The fact of a lawful arrest establishes the authority to conduct a full-scale, reasonable search under the Fourth Amendment.

FACTS: Robinson (D) was stopped by police while driving his car and ordered out. The officer conducted a pat-down search and discovered something in the breast pocket that he did not identify by touch. The officer reached in and removed a cigarette package. Not knowing what was inside the package, the officer searched inside and removed heroin. Robinson (D) moved to suppress the evidence on the basis there was no probable cause to search because the cigarette package clearly contained no weapon. The Government (P) opposed the motion on the basis there was probable cause to arrest and a full-scale search was justified once the custodial arrest was made. Robinson (D) was convicted of possession of heroin, but the Court of Appeals for the District of Columbia Circuit reversed. The United States Supreme Court granted certiorari.

ISSUE: Does the fact of a lawful arrest establish the authority to conduct a full-scale, reasonable search under the Fourth Amendment?

HOLDING AND DECISION: (Rehnquist, J.) Yes. The fact of a lawful arrest establishes the authority to conduct a full-scale, reasonable search under the Fourth Amendment. This search is not limited to a pat-down search where the extent is controlled by the officer's ability to ensure his or her own safety. In this case, it was undisputed that at the time Robinson (D) was searched he had been placed under a full custodial arrest. Therefore, he was subject to a full search for both evidence and weapons. As a result, the evidence was lawfully obtained. Reversed.

CONCURRENCE: (Powell, J.) Once placed under a lawful custodial arrest, a suspect has no reasonable expectation of privacy and therefore any search is reasonable.

DISSENT: (Marshall, J.) No formula exists for what constitutes a reasonable search. The per se rule enunciated by the Court here violates this principle. In the context of this case, search of the cigarette pack was unreasonable.

ANALYSIS

A search occurs in the constitutional sense when a person's reasonable expectation of privacy is invaded. The validity of such search may be based upon the issuance of a warrant upon a showing of probable cause, and exception to the warrant requirement such as a search made pursuant to a lawful arrest, or where such searches are "reasonable." In this case, the majority holds that a full search is valid as pursuant to a lawful custodial arrest, and it is always reasonable. Thus, it qualifies as both an exception to the warrant requirement and as a situation where no warrant is necessary.

Quicknotes

FOURTH AMENDMENT Provides that persons be secure as to their person and private belongings against unreasonable searches and seizures.

PROBABLE CAUSE A reasonable basis for believing that a crime has been committed.

SEARCH An inspection conducted in order to obtain evidence to be utilized for the prosecution of a crime.

Arizona v. Gant

State (P) v. Individual (D)

556 U.S. 332 (2009)

NATURE OF CASE: Appeal from state high court decision in favor of defendant.

FACT SUMMARY: Local police arrested Gant (D) for an outstanding warrant for driving without a license. After the police placed Gant (D) in a police vehicle, a search of Gant's (D) vehicle revealed cocaine and a handgun.

RULE OF LAW

Police may search the passenger compartment of a vehicle incident to an occupant's arrest only if the occupant is within reaching distance of the vehicle or if it is reasonable to believe the vehicle contains evidence in support of the reasons for the arrest.

FACTS: After receiving an anonymous tip regarding alleged drug activity, Tucson police officers approached a house and spoke to Gant (D). After leaving the house, the police conducted a records check on Gant (D), revealing an outstanding warrant for driving with a suspended license. The police returned to the house and Gant (D) eventually drove into the house's driveway. The police immediately arrested Gant (D) on the outstanding warrant. The arrest took place ten to fifteen feet away from Gant's (D) vehicle. The police placed Gant (D) in a patrol car. A subsequent search of Gant's (D) vehicle, conducted while Gant (D) was arrested and in the back of the patrol car, revealed a handgun and cocaine. Gant (D) moved to suppress the evidence on the grounds the search was not a lawful search incident to his arrest. The trial court denied his motion, but the Arizona Supreme Court found the search was unreasonable because Gant (D) would not be able to reach the passenger compartment of the vehicle. Therefore, the exception to the warrant requirement for searches incident to arrests was not applicable. The State (P) appealed.

ISSUE: May police search the passenger compartment of a vehicle incident to an occupant's arrest only if the occupant is within reaching distance of the vehicle or if it is reasonable to believe the vehicle contains evidence in support of the reasons for the arrest?

HOLDING AND DECISION: (Stevens, J.) Yes. Police may search the passenger compartment of a vehicle incident to an occupant's arrest only if the occupant is within reaching distance of the vehicle or if it is reasonable to believe the vehicle contains evidence in support of the reasons for the arrest. In *New York v. Belton*, 453 U.S. 454 (1981), this Court held that searches incident to arrests may include the interior of a vehicle because of the assumption that the interior includes an area that an arrestee may reach, to either destroy evidence or retrieve a weapon. Since *Belton* was decided, lower courts have construed the decision to allow all searches of a motor vehicle incident to an arrest, regardless of whether an arrestee may actually have access to the interior to the vehicle. The Court holds today that *Belton* should not be interpreted so broadly. Rather, a search of a vehicle may only be conducted where the arrestee has actual access to the vehicle or if there is reason to believe the vehicle contains evidence related to the offense of the arrest. Here, Gant (D) was already handcuffed and in the patrol car at the time of the search. There was no way he could access the vehicle. Second, the police arrested Gant (D) for driving with a suspended license. The vehicle would not contain any additional evidence related to that offense. Accordingly, the search was unreasonable. Affirmed.

CONCURRENCE: (Scalia, J.) *Belton* should be overruled in its entirety. Instead, vehicle searches following arrests should be reasonable only when the object of the search is evidence of the crime related to the arrest. Because there could be no evidence related to Gant's (D) arrest in the vehicle, the search of his vehicle was unlawful. Also, this case applies only to those searches conducted after an arrest. The Court's abandonment of *Belton's* bright line rule may actually invite officers to leave a scene unsecured and delay placing occupants under arrest in order to conduct a search.

DISSENT: (Breyer, J.) Principles of stare decisis apply to this case. Because the facts are substantially similar, the Court should follow the *Belton* rule and find the search reasonable. Circumstances are not present in this case that would allow the Court to overrule the *Belton* case.

DISSENT: (Alito, J.) The *Belton* holding was unequivocal. That case held that whenever an officer makes an arrest of a person from a vehicle, a subsequent search of the passenger compartment constitutes a lawful search incident to the arrest. The Court did not limit its holding with reference to when a search was made. This Court should adhere to *Belton* because of law enforcement's reliance on the rule for the past 28 years. Circumstances have not changed since *Belton* that dictate a change in the law, nor has the *Belton* rule become unworkable. For these reasons, this court is bound by stare decisis. The

Continued on next page.

Court should have found the search of Gant's (D) vehicle reasonable and consistent with the *Belton* rule.

ANALYSIS

This decision limited *Belton's* holding regarding the ability to search vehicles incident to arrests and modified police practice of always searching vehicle compartments after arrests, regardless of the location of the arrestee. The issue dividing the Court is the ability of an arrested person to ever reach a vehicle compartment. Justice Scalia essentially offers a compromise position, which is to do away with the issue of whether an arrestee can reach a vehicle compartment and focus solely on the evidence. He recommends that after an arrest, a search would be allowed only for evidence related to the arrest.

Quicknotes

PROBABLE CAUSE A reasonable basis for believing that a crime has been committed.

SEARCH INCIDENT TO A LAWFUL ARREST Exception to the requirement of a valid warrant for a search or seizure so long as the officer is lawfully in the location where the evidence is obtained, and it is apparent that the thing seized is evidence.

STARE DECISIS Doctrine whereby courts follow legal precedent unless there is good cause for departure.

Riley v. California

Arrestee (D) v. State (P)

573 U.S. 373 (2014)

NATURE OF CASE: Certiorari review of combined California and First Circuit cases.

FACT SUMMARY: Police conducted warrantless searches of cell phones of arrestees.

RULE OF LAW

A warrant generally is required prior to a law enforcement search of a cell phone seized incident to an arrest.

FACTS: In the first case, police stopped David Riley (D) on a traffic violation, searched the car, and arrested him for possession of concealed and loaded firearms. The officer seized Riley's (D) cell phone incident to the arrest and accessed information on the phone. The information showed what appeared to be Riley's (D) affiliation with the Bloods gang. Law enforcement later searched the digital data more thoroughly and found a photograph that led to additional charges against Riley (D). Riley (D) moved to suppress the cell phone evidence as a search in violation of the Fourth Amendment, but the trial court denied the motion. Riley (D) was convicted, the California Court of Appeal affirmed, and the California Supreme Court denied review. The U.S. Supreme Court granted certiorari.

In the second case, a police officer observed Brima Wurie (Wurie) (D) making a drug sale from his car. The officers arrested Wurie (D) and seized two cell phones incident to the arrest. At the station, one phone continually received calls from "My House," the officers reviewed the phone data and found information leading them to Wurie's (D) residence, where they secured his apartment, obtained a search warrant, and found drugs and firearms. Wurie (D) was charged. Wurie (D) moved to suppress the cell phone search. The District Court denied his motion; Wurie (D) was convicted. A divided First Circuit reversed the denial of Wurie's (D) motion and vacated his convictions that arose as a result of the cell phone search. This Court granted certiorari. The Court combined the cases.

ISSUE: Is a warrant generally required prior to a law enforcement search of a cell phone seized incident to an arrest?

HOLDING AND DECISION: (Roberts, C.J.) Yes. A warrant generally is required prior to a law enforcement search of a cell phone seized incident to an arrest. The Fourth Amendment generally requires a warrant for law enforcement searches to be reasonable. There are specific exceptions to the warrant requirement, and a search incident to arrest is such an exception. This Court has a trilogy related to such searches. *Chimel v. California*, 395 U.S. 752 (1969), laid the groundwork for analyzing the reasonableness of warrantless searches incident to arrest. *Chimel* held it is reasonable for the arresting officer to search the person and the area within his or her immediate control for the officer's safety and to prevent concealment or destruction of evidence. An extensive search of an arrestee's home is not reasonable. In *United States v. Robinson*, 414 U.S. 218 (1973), this Court held it was not necessary for officers to conduct a case-by-case adjudication to determine the probability in a particular arrest situation whether that person would have weapons or destructible evidence. An officer's opening of a cigarette package seized from an arrestee was reasonable even though it was unlikely the package contained a weapon or evidence related to the arrestee's traffic crime. In *Arizona v. Gant*, 556 U.S. 332 (2009), this Court authorized searches of vehicles when the arrestee is unsecured and within reaching distance of the passenger compartment or when it is reasonable to believe evidence relevant to the crime of arrest might be in the vehicle. The Founders could not have conceived of the technology encased in a modern cell phone, so the Court is left without founding guidance. The Court must balance the privacy interests of the individual with the degree to which the digital data is needed for the promotion of legitimate governmental interests. Here, harm to officers and destruction of evidence are not present risks when searching digital data. *Robinson* cannot be extended to cell phone searches. In considering *Chimel* concerns, the cell phone data cannot be used as a weapon against the officer, and destruction of evidence on a cell phone, while possible, is neither prevalent nor unpreventable. The Government (P) argued about remote wiping or encryption, but there are ways to get around these possibilities. An arrestee does have diminished privacy interests, but a search of a cell phone is a massive intrusion into a person's private life. A cell phone regularly contains highly private documents, such as financial materials, photographs, and records of entire conversations among individuals. Further, the information on the cell phone may not only be on the actual cell phone but might be pulled from cloud computing, which is an additional search. The Government (P) requests an extension of *Gant*, but that case protects against vehicle searches for evidence of past crimes, and cell phones could hold incriminating evidence regardless of the time

Continued on next page.

of the crime. The Government's (P) other suggestions are equally unworkable, including its pre-digital counterpart proposal. It is unlikely someone would have been carrying a phone book, photo album, and video tape on his or her person, but that is exactly what is contained in a cell phone. It also would invite difficult line-drawing expeditions as law enforcement determined whether letters were pre-digital emails or voicemails were pre-digital telephone slips. This decision does have an impact on law enforcement's ability to combat crime. A cell phone is not immune from search, but a warrant is required unless other exceptions apply. Reversed (*Riley*); affirmed (*Wurie*).

CONCURRENCE: (Alito, J.) The search incident to arrest predates the Fourth Amendment by at least a century. Nothing indicates it should be based exclusively on officer safety or destruction of evidence. Nevertheless, that rule should not be mechanically applied to cell phones. The Court balances in favor of privacy interests, although that approach leads to anomalies. One person carrying a physical phone log can have that log searched, but the same phone log on a cell phone cannot be searched without a warrant. There is no workable alternative, however. Congress or state legislatures could draw reasonable distinctions among categories of information as Congress did with electronic surveillance.

ANALYSIS

The United States Supreme Court noted nearly 90 percent of Americans carry a cell phone, and, of those phones a large percentage are "smart" phones containing a massive amount of personal data. A warrantless search of a cell phone is the modern equivalent of an extensive search of a person's home and office and could be considered similar to wiretap as many people carry around records of their text messages and voicemails. Law enforcement now must distinguish between physical items (e.g., the cell phone itself as a possible weapon) and the data on those items (e.g., photographs, call logs) for warrant purposes.

Quicknotes

FOURTH AMENDMENT Provides that persons be secure as to their person and private belongings against unreasonable searches and seizures.

SEARCH INCIDENT TO A LAWFUL ARREST Exception to the requirement of a valid warrant for a search or seizure so long as the officer is lawfully in the location where the evidence is obtained and it is apparent that the thing seized is evidence.

Birchfield v. North Dakota

Three individuals (D) v. States (P)

579 U.S. 438 (2016)

NATURE OF CASE: Three consolidated appeals from state supreme courts' decisions against the defendants.

FACT SUMMARY: Three separate individuals were stopped for suspicion of drunk driving. Birchfield (D) refused to allow officers to draw his blood. After his arrest, Bernard (D) refused to take a breathalyzer test. Beylund (D) initially agreed to a blood test but then argued his consent was coerced by the police.

RULE OF LAW

Consistent with the search-incident-to-arrest doctrine, the Fourth Amendment allows law enforcement to administer a breath test without a warrant after an arrest has been made for drunk driving.

FACTS: Three separate individuals were stopped in different incidents for suspicion of drunk driving. In North Dakota, Birchfield (D) refused to allow officers to draw his blood. North Dakota has made it a crime, as opposed to a civil penalty, to refuse a breath test or blood test after a lawful arrest for drunk driving. After his arrest in Minnesota, Bernard (D) refused to take a breathalyzer test. He was charged with failing to take the breath test and sentenced to three years imprisonment. In North Dakota, Beylund (D) initially agreed to a blood test but then argued his consent was coerced by the police. He alleged the officer informed him that his refusal to submit to the blood test would be a crime. Each of the defendants was convicted on various grounds. Their appeals to the United States Supreme Court were consolidated.

ISSUE: Consistent with the search-incident-to-arrest doctrine, does the Fourth Amendment allow law enforcement to administer a breath test without a warrant after an arrest has been made for drunk driving?

HOLDING AND DECISION: (Alito, J.) Yes. Consistent with the search-incident-to-arrest doctrine, the Fourth Amendment allows law enforcement to administer a breath test without a warrant after an arrest has been made for drunk driving. We have previously held that the exigent circumstances doctrine does not always allow for the warrantless taking of a blood sample. That exception applies only on a case-by-case analysis. The search-incident-to-arrest doctrine has long held that officers conducting a lawful arrest may also complete a warrantless search of the arrestee's person. The issue in these cases is whether that exception to the warrant requirement applies to breath tests and blood tests following a lawful arrest of a person for drunk driving. To determine whether a search may be exempt from the warrant requirement, the Court must analyze (1) the degree to which the search invades one's privacy and (2) whether the search promotes a legitimate governmental interest. A breath test does not implicate privacy concerns. The physical intrusion is minimal. One must only blow into the device for a few seconds. Blood tests are different. Here, one must allow the piercing of one's skin and the extraction of part of one's body. Those samples can also be preserved where additional medical information can be obtained. Turning to part two of the analysis, state and federal governments clearly have a strong interest in the safety of their residents. Simply removing drunk drivers from the road is not enough. Preserving evidence and prosecuting them serves as a deterrent to the defendants and others to not drink and drive. Mandating that law enforcement obtain a warrant to administer breath tests would unnecessarily burden the court system and jeopardize the loss of evidence, that is, the dissipation of the alcohol within the blood stream. Because breath tests are significantly less intrusive than blood tests and in most cases amply serve law enforcement interests, we conclude that a breath test, but not a blood test, may be administered as a search incident to a lawful arrest for drunk driving. As in all cases involving reasonable searches incident to arrest, a warrant is not needed in this situation.

CONCURRENCE AND DISSENT: (Sotomayor, J.) The majority is correct that the Fourth Amendment requires the issuance of a warrant before law enforcement may administer a blood test. Warrants should also be issued before law enforcement conducts a breath test. Once a drunk driver is arrested and is off the road, the danger is removed. Officers then have sufficient time to obtain the necessary warrant to conduct the breath test. In addition, there would likely be no extra burden on courts to grant these types of warrants. Finally, granting law enforcement a categorical rule to administer breath tests without a warrant provides too much authority. The incidents in question are fact intensive and do not lend themselves well to the application of a categorical rule such as this.

CONCURRENCE AND DISSENT: (Thomas, J.) A search incident to a lawful arrest has always required no further justification. The majority splits hairs unnecessarily in this case. Either the search-incident-to-arrest doctrine allows for bodily searches (both breath and

Continued on next page.

blood tests) to prevent the destruction of evidence or it does not.

ANALYSIS

While the United States Supreme Court focused on the legal issue of whether warrantless breath tests or blood tests were legal, the underlying holding in this decision is that states may criminalize the refusal to submit to warrantless breath tests. Most states still only use a civil penalty such as the suspension of a driver's license or a fine. This decision may compel other states to follow the examples of North Dakota and Minnesota.

Quicknotes

EXIGENT CIRCUMSTANCES Circumstances requiring an extraordinary or immediate response; an exception to the prohibition on a warrantless arrest or search when police officers believe probable cause to exist and there is no time for obtaining a warrant.

FOURTH AMENDMENT Provides that persons be secure as to their person and private belongings against unreasonable searches and seizures.

SEARCH INCIDENT TO A LAWFUL ARREST Exception to the requirement of a valid warrant for a search or seizure so long as the officer is lawfully in the location where the evidence is obtained and it is apparent that the thing seized is evidence.

Atwater v. City of Lago Vista

Driver (P) v. City (D)

532 U.S. 318 (2001)

NATURE OF CASE: Civil rights claim stemming from arrest for misdemeanor traffic violation.

FACT SUMMARY: Atwater (P) claimed that her arrest for a misdemeanor seatbelt violation violated her Fourth Amendment rights against warrantless searches and seizures.

RULE OF LAW

The Fourth Amendment does not forbid a warrantless arrest for a minor criminal offense, such as a misdemeanor seatbelt violation punishable only by a fine.

FACTS: Atwater (P) was driving in a pickup truck with her three-year-old son and five-year-old daughter in the front seat. None of them was wearing a seatbelt. Texas law made it a misdemeanor for a driver, in a car equipped with a seatbelt, not to wear a seatbelt or not to secure any small child riding in the front seat with one. Atwater (P) ultimately pled no contest to the seatbelt charge and paid the fine. She then filed a 42 U.S.C. § 1983 action against the police officer, city of Lago Vista, and the chief of police (D), alleging her Fourth Amendment rights were violated. The district court granted summary judgment for the City (D), concluding the claim was meritless. A panel of the Court of Appeals for the Fifth Circuit reversed, but the court en banc vacated the previous decision and affirmed the summary judgment.

ISSUE: Does the Fourth Amendment forbid a warrantless arrest for a minor criminal offense, such as a misdemeanor seatbelt violation punishable only by a fine?

HOLDING AND DECISION: (Souter, J.) No. The Fourth Amendment does not forbid a warrantless arrest for a minor criminal offense, such as a misdemeanor seatbelt violation punishable only by a fine. We confirm what prior cases have suggested, that probable cause applies to all arrests. There is no need to apply a balancing test of interests involved in the particular situation. If an official has probable cause to believe that an individual has committed even a very minor criminal offense in his or her presence, the officer may arrest the offender without violating the Fourth Amendment. Affirmed.

DISSENT: (O'Connor, J.) The Court's position is inconsistent with the Fourth Amendment's guarantees. A custodial arrest, such as the one here, is a seizure. When it is affected without a warrant, the Fourth Amendment requires such search to be reasonable. The record here shows that Atwater's (P) arrest was unreasonable. The police officer (D) was not justified by law or reason in his decision to arrest Atwater (P) rather than to give her a citation, and severely infringed Atwater's (P) liberty and privacy interests.

ANALYSIS

Atwater (P) argued that common-law principles prohibited police officers from making warrantless misdemeanor arrests except in cases of "breach of the peace," a narrow category including only non-felony offenses "involving or tending toward violence." The United States Supreme Court rejects this argument, stating that neither the legislative history of the Fourth Amendment nor subsequent decisions supported this position.

Quicknotes

COMMON LAW A body of law developed through the judicial decisions of the courts as opposed to the legislative process.

FOURTH AMENDMENT Provides that persons be secure as to their person and private belongings against unreasonable searches and seizures.

MISDEMEANOR Any offense that does not constitute a felony; generally less severe than a felony and results in a lesser punishment.

PROBABLE CAUSE A reasonable basis for believing that a crime has been committed.

SEARCH An inspection conducted in order to obtain evidence to be utilized for the prosecution of a crime.

SEIZURE The taking of property by unlawful activity or in satisfaction of a judgment entered by the court.

WARRANT An order issued by a court directing an officer to undertake a certain act (e.g., arrest or search).

Whren v. United States

Convicted drug dealer (D) v. Federal government (P)

517 U.S. 806 (1996)

NATURE OF CASE: Appeal from criminal conviction for possession of drugs upon the denial of the motion to suppress evidence.

FACT SUMMARY: Plainclothes policemen patrolling a "high drug area" observed and then stopped a suspicious sports utility vehicle (SUV) ostensibly to warn the driver about traffic violations. Whren (D), a passenger in the SUV, was found holding plastic bags of crack cocaine.

RULE OF LAW

The temporary detention of a motorist on probable cause that he or she has violated the traffic laws does not violate the Fourth Amendment's prohibition against unreasonable seizures, even if a reasonable officer would not have stopped the motorist absent some additional law enforcement objective.

FACTS: Plainclothes policemen of the District of Columbia were patrolling a "high-drug area" in an unmarked car. During the policemen's patrol, their suspicions were aroused when they observed a sports utility vehicle (SUV) with temporary license plates and youthful passengers. As the officers drove past the SUV, the officers noticed that the driver was looking down into the lap of the passenger immediately to the driver's right. One officer also observed that the SUV waited at a stop sign at an intersection for an unusually long time—approximately 20 seconds. As the unmarked police car executed a U-turn, the SUV then made a sudden right turn, without signaling, and sped off at an "unreasonable" speed. The officers stopped the SUV, ostensibly to warn the driver about traffic violations. Upon approaching the SUV, however, the officer observed two plastic bags of what appeared to be crack cocaine in passenger Whren's (D) hands. Whren (D) and the other passengers (D) were arrested and charged with violating various federal drug laws. Prior to trial, they moved for suppression of the evidence, arguing that the stop had not been justified by either a reasonable suspicion or probable cause to believe that they were engaged in illegal drug-dealing activity, and that the officers' ground for approaching the vehicle was pretextual. The district court denied the motion to suppress. Whren (D) and the others (D) were convicted. The court of appeals affirmed, and certiorari was granted by the United States Supreme Court.

ISSUE: Does the temporary detention of a motorist on probable cause that he or she has violated the traffic laws violate the Fourth Amendment's prohibition against unreasonable seizures even if a reasonable officer would not have stopped the motorist absent some additional law enforcement objective?

HOLDING AND DECISION: (Scalia, J.) No. The temporary detention of a motorist on probable cause that he or she has violated the traffic laws does not violate the Fourth Amendment's prohibition against unreasonable seizures, even if a reasonable officer would not have stopped the motorist absent some additional law enforcement objective. As a general matter, the decision to stop an automobile is reasonable where the police have probable cause to believe that a traffic violation has occurred. In this case, the officers had probable cause to believe that various provisions of the District of Columbia traffic code had been violated. Ulterior motives, even if held by police officers during a traffic stop, do not invalidate police conduct if the officers had justifiable probable cause that a violation of law has occurred. Motive is only relevant to inventory and administrative inspections because such searches are exempt from a probable cause requirement; thus, the Supreme Court has invalidated inventory or administrative searches that were not made for the ostensible regulatory purpose. As Whren (D) correctly argues, the Constitution prohibits selective enforcement of the law based on considerations such as race. But the constitutional basis for objecting to intentionally discriminatory application of laws is the Equal Protection Clause, not the Fourth Amendment. Lastly, contrary to what Whren (D) suggests, balancing inherent in Fourth Amendment inquiry does not require the courts to weigh governmental and individual interests implicated in a traffic stop. Affirmed.

ANALYSIS

In this case, Whren (D) attempted to argue for an objective standard under a "reasonable officer" test. That test would be whether a police officer, acting reasonably, would have made the stop for the reason given. However, the Court was undeterred by Whren's (D) use of empirical terms. Instead, the United States Supreme Court emphasized its unwillingness to go through such a burdensome exercise as to second-guess an officer's intentions.

Continued on next page.

Quicknotes

EQUAL PROTECTION CLAUSE A constitutional provision that each person be guaranteed the same protection of the laws enjoyed by other persons in like circumstances.

FOURTH AMENDMENT Provides that persons be secure as to their person and private belongings against unreasonable searches and seizures.

PROBABLE CAUSE A reasonable basis for believing that a crime has been committed.

Horton v. California

Convicted felon (D) v. State (P)

496 U.S. 128 (1990)

NATURE OF CASE: Appeal from criminal conviction upon denial of motion to suppress evidence.

FACT SUMMARY: Sergeant LaRault searched the home of Horton (D) with a search warrant for proceeds of a crime, found weapons in plain view, and seized them.

RULE OF LAW

Where the police have a warrant or other justification for a search, and evidence of an immediately apparent incriminating nature is in plain view in a place where the officers have a lawful right of access, the police may seize the evidence whether or not they came upon it inadvertently.

FACTS: Sergeant LaRault swore out an affidavit describing the proceeds of a crime and the weapons used. A search warrant was issued for the proceeds only. When LaRault searched Horton's (D) home he did not find the proceeds, but he discovered the weapons in plain view and seized them. At trial, Horton (D) argued that the weapons could not be introduced as evidence because LaRault's admission that he found other evidence while searching for the proceeds he was interested in meant that the discovery of the weapons was not inadvertent and, therefore, under *Coolidge v. New Hampshire*, 403 U.S. 443 (1971), not covered by the "plain view" doctrine. The trial judge disagreed and admitted the evidence. Horton (D) was convicted, and he appealed to the United States Supreme Court.

ISSUE: Where the police have a warrant or other justification for a search, and evidence of an immediately apparent incriminating nature is in plain view in a place where the officers have a lawful right of access, may the police seize the evidence whether or not they came upon it inadvertently?

HOLDING AND DECISION: (Stevens, J.) Yes. Where the police have a warrant or other justification for a search, and evidence of an immediately apparent incriminating nature is in plain view in a place where the officers have a lawful right of access, the police may seize the evidence whether or not they came upon it inadvertently. Evenhanded law enforcement is best achieved by application of objective standards, rather than standards depending on the subjective state of mind of the officer. There is no danger of officers using specific warrants or exigent circumstances to conduct general searches because the scope of the search is proscribed by the warrant's description of the place to be searched or the exigencies that justify the intrusion. This decision overrules the part of *Coolidge* that requires that an officer inadvertently come upon an object to seize it under the "plain view" doctrine. Affirmed.

DISSENT: (Brennan, J.) The Fourth Amendment not only protects privacy interests by requiring that a warrant describe the place to be searched, but also protects possessory interests by requiring that a warrant particularly describe the things to be seized. Eliminating the inadvertency requirement excuses officers from obtaining a warrant particularly describing evidence, giving them discretion to invade possessory interests in property.

ANALYSIS

The remaining requirements for "plain view" seizure have also come under United States Supreme Court review. In *Coolidge*, automobiles were in plain view, but they were parked on private property to which the police did not have legal access, so their seizure was unconstitutional. In *Arizona v. Hicks*, 480 U.S. 321 (1987), an officer lawfully searching an apartment for evidence of a shooting noticed expensive stereo components that seemed out of place in the badly furnished apartment. He moved the components to read the serial numbers, one serial number matched a stolen property list, and he seized the item. The seizure was ruled unconstitutional because the fact that the item was stolen was not immediately apparent and the moving of the components amounted to a separate search without probable cause.

Quicknotes

FOURTH AMENDMENT Provides that persons be secure as to their person and private belongings against unreasonable searches and seizures.

PLAIN VIEW DOCTRINE Exception to the requirement of a valid warrant for a search or seizure so long as the officer is lawfully in the location where the evidence is obtained and it is apparent that the thing seized is evidence.

Chambers v. Maroney

Convicted robber (D) v. Government (P)

399 U.S. 42 (1970)

NATURE OF CASE: Appeal from a robbery conviction.

FACT SUMMARY: Chambers (D) contended that the search of an automobile taken to the station house after his arrest was invalid.

RULE OF LAW

Where there is probable cause to believe that a vehicle is carrying contraband or fruits of the crime, a warrantless search of the vehicle is permissible, even where the vehicle itself is seized and held without a warrant for whatever period is necessary to obtain a warrant for the search.

FACTS: Chambers (D) was indicted for robbing two gas stations. Partially because of a witness's statement that one of the robbers was wearing a green sweater, and that the robbers were driving a station wagon, Chambers (D) was arrested, and the station wagon was taken to the police station and searched. There was no warrant. Search of the station wagon revealed evidence linking Chambers (D) with the crimes. The materials taken from the station wagon were admitted into evidence. Chambers (D) was convicted and sentenced to prison. Chambers (D) did not take a direct appeal from these convictions but applied for a writ of habeas corpus. After state and federal appeals courts denied granting the writ, the United States Supreme Court granted certiorari.

ISSUE: Where there is probable cause to believe that a vehicle is carrying contraband or fruits of the crime, is a warrantless search of the vehicle permissible, even where the vehicle itself is seized and held without a warrant for whatever period is necessary to obtain a warrant for search?

HOLDING AND DECISION: (White, J.) Yes. Where there is probable cause to believe that a vehicle is carrying contraband or fruits of the crime, a warrantless search of the vehicle is permissible, even where the vehicle itself is seized and held without a warrant for whatever period is necessary to obtain a warrant for the search. Automobiles may be searched without a warrant in circumstances where the intrusion would not be permissible for a house. The opportunity to search a car is fleeting since it is movable. Here, the station wagon could have been searched on the spot, since there was probable cause to search and it was a fleeting target for a search. Affirmed.

CONCURRENCE AND DISSENT: (Harlan, J.) Seizure of the car for the period necessary to enable the officers to obtain a warrant is the lesser intrusion, and therefore the more desirable action. The Court's approval of a warrantless search in this instance is not consistent with the Fourth Amendment's mandate of obedience to judicial procedure. This is so where the lesser intrusion is available.

ANALYSIS

This case is in accord with the proposition that the Fourth Amendment is less strict with cars than it is with homes. The ability of the car to be moved, the lesser aspect of privacy, and the plain view of the auto on the highway contribute to this proposition.

Quicknotes

FOURTH AMENDMENT Provides that persons be secure as to their person and private belongings against unreasonable searches and seizures.

PROBABLE CAUSE A reasonable basis for believing that a crime has been committed.

SEARCH An inspection conducted in order to obtain evidence to be utilized for the prosecution of a crime.

SEIZURE The taking of property by unlawful activity or in satisfaction of a judgment entered by the court.

WARRANT An order issued by a court directing an officer to undertake a certain act (e.g., arrest or search).

WRIT OF HABEAS CORPUS A proceeding in which a defendant brings a writ to compel a judicial determination of whether he or she is lawfully being held in custody.

California v. Acevedo

State (P) v. Accused (D)

500 U.S. 565 (1991)

NATURE OF CASE: Appeal from the grant of a motion to suppress.

FACT SUMMARY: Without first obtaining a warrant, police officers searched a closed container that Acevedo (D) placed in his trunk.

RULE OF LAW

Police officers may search closed containers within an automobile without a warrant, pursuant to a valid search of the vehicle.

FACTS: Drug enforcement agents intercepted a package of marijuana being sent to Daza and notified Daza when it arrived at Federal Express. Officers followed Daza when he picked up the package and drove it to his apartment. Acevedo (D) arrived at Daza's apartment and left shortly thereafter carrying a paper bag of the same size as the marijuana package. Acevedo (D) placed the bag in the trunk of his car and started to drive away. The officers stopped him and opened the trunk and the bag and found the marijuana. Acevedo (D) claimed that the search of the bag was illegal. The appeals court agreed, and the State (P) appealed.

ISSUE: May police officers search closed containers within an automobile without a warrant, pursuant to a valid search of the vehicle?

HOLDING AND DECISION: (Blackmun, J.) Yes. Police officers may search closed containers within an automobile without a warrant, pursuant to a valid search of the vehicle. Two previous cases decided by this Court have raised some confusion in this area. In *United States v. Chadwick*, 433 U.S. 1 (1977), the Court held that a closed container placed in a car could not be searched without a warrant when there was probable cause only as to the container. On the other hand, in *United States v. Ross*, 456 U.S. 798 (1982), we found that a warrantless search of an automobile could include a search of containers inside when there was probable cause to search the car. The contradiction between these cases could result in officers conducting more intrusive searches as they seek to generate probable cause to search an entire car rather than just a container within the car. Furthermore, the rule in *Chadwick* has not protected privacy and has confused courts and police officers. It is better to adopt a single clear-cut rule to govern auto searches. Thus, the warrant requirement for closed containers set forth in *Chadwick* is overruled. Reversed.

CONCURRENCE: (Scalia, J.) While the dissent makes the correct point that the new rule will produce anomalous results, the Fourth Amendment does not require a prior warrant for searches; it requires only that the search not be unreasonable. This is the concept that should govern this area of the law.

DISSENT: (White, J.) The judgment below should be confirmed for the reason stated by Justice Stevens.

DISSENT: (Stevens, J.) When the police have probable cause to search a particular container, they can seize that container and have no need to search an entire vehicle. The majority opinion creates a situation in which a search of a container is prohibited while the owner is carrying it in the open but allowed once the owner has placed the container in a locked trunk.

ANALYSIS

This decision does not eliminate challenges based on an excessive search under the auto exception. A defendant may still claim that a search of other areas of a car was invalid if the officers had probable cause with regard to the container only. Lower courts have not been consistent in interpreting the new rule.

Quicknotes

FOURTH AMENDMENT Provides that persons be secure as to their person and private belongings against unreasonable searches and seizures.

SEARCH An inspection conducted in order to obtain evidence to be utilized for the prosecution of a crime.

WARRANT An order issued by a court directing an officer to undertake a certain act (e.g., arrest or search).

Brigham City v. Stuart

Government (P) v. Convicted felons (D)

547 U.S. 398 (2006)

NATURE OF CASE: Fourth Amendment appeal for entrance into a home without a warrant.

FACT SUMMARY: Police saw a fight through a window in a home and entered the home without a warrant to break up the fight.

RULE OF LAW

Police may enter a home without a warrant when they have an objectively reasonable basis for believing that an occupant is seriously injured or imminently threatened with such injury.

FACTS: Officer Jeff Johnson (P) along with three other officers, responded to a complaint of a loud party at 3 a.m. on July 23, 2001. From the driveway, Johnson (P) observed two underage males drinking alcohol and entered the backyard to get a better view inside the house. He peered through the back windows and a screen door and saw four adults restraining a teenager against a refrigerator. The teenager broke free and punched one of the adults in the face, and Johnson (P) and another officer decided to enter the house without a search warrant. The officers arrested all four adults, including Charles Stuart (D), Shayne Taylor (D), and Sandra Taylor (D), on charges of contributing to the delinquency of a minor, disorderly conduct, and intoxication. The Supreme Court of Utah decided that the officers acted illegally, and the United States Supreme Court granted certiorari.

ISSUE: May police enter a home without a warrant when they have an objectively reasonable basis for believing that an occupant is seriously injured or imminently threatened with such injury?

HOLDING AND DECISION: (Roberts, C.J.) Yes. Police may enter a home without a warrant when they have an objectively reasonable basis for believing that an occupant is seriously injured or imminently threatened with such injury. The role of a peace officer includes preventing violence and restoring order, not simply rendering first aid to casualties. The court concluded that under the circumstances, the officers had an objectively reasonable basis for believing both that the injured adult might need help and that the violence in the kitchen was just beginning. Nothing in the Fourth Amendment required them to wait until the fight continued and rendered someone unconscious or semi-conscious or worse before entering. Reversed and remanded.

ANALYSIS

This case illustrates that the public-safety exception applies in cases where the officers are not pursuing public safety, but instead are pursuing law enforcement.

Quicknotes

FOURTH AMENDMENT Provides that persons be secure as to their person and private belongings against unreasonable searches and seizures.

WARRANT An order issued by a court directing an officer to undertake a certain act (e.g., arrest or search).

Kentucky v. King

State (P) v. Individual (D)

563 U.S. 452 (2011)

NATURE OF CASE: Appeal from state high-court decision in favor of defendant.

FACT SUMMARY: After observing a suspect purchase cocaine, police officers followed him to a breezeway in an apartment complex. The officers did not know which apartment the suspect entered. Smelling marijuana from one apartment and hearing things moving around in the apartment, the officers entered that apartment and discovered King (D) with drugs, cash, and other drug paraphernalia.

RULE OF LAW

The exigent circumstances rule may be used to uphold a warrantless search only if police officers do not gain entry into a residence by an actual or threatened violation of the Fourth Amendment.

FACTS: Police officers were following a suspect involved in a controlled purchase of cocaine. The suspect entered the breezeway of an apartment complex. The officers, following the suspect into the breezeway, did not know into which apartment he disappeared, the one on the left or the right. The officers smelled the odor of marijuana emanating from the apartment on the left. The officers knocked on the door of that apartment and announced their presence. They then heard things being moved around quickly in the apartment. This led the officers to believe that evidence was about to be destroyed. The officers then entered the apartment and found King (D), who was not the original suspect, with drugs, cash, and other drug paraphernalia. Before trial, King (D) moved to suppress the evidence on the grounds the officers' search was an illegal warrantless search and no exceptions existed to uphold the search. The trial court denied the motion and a jury convicted King (D) on various drug charges. The Kentucky Supreme Court then overturned the decision, holding that the police could not rely upon the exigent circumstances exception when the police themselves created the emergency. The State (P) appealed to the United States Supreme Court.

ISSUE: May the exigent circumstances rule be used to uphold a warrantless search only if police officers do not gain entry into a residence by an actual or threatened violation of the Fourth Amendment?

HOLDING AND DECISION: (Alito, J.) Yes. The exigent circumstances rule may be used to uphold a warrantless search only if police officers do not gain entry into a residence by an actual or threatened violation of the Fourth Amendment. First, the exigent circumstances rule allows officers to conduct a search without a warrant if exigent circumstances exist that preclude officers from first obtaining a warrant. Such circumstances include the imminent destruction of evidence or imminent harm to one inside a residence. However, lower federal courts have developed the "police created exigency" doctrine, which holds that police may not conduct a search without a warrant if the police themselves create or manufacture the exigent circumstances. This Court now holds that the exigent circumstances exception may still be used as long as the police do not gain entry by an actual or threatened violation of the Fourth Amendment. A review of the officers' actions in exigent circumstance cases must be objective, and the Kentucky Supreme Court's use of a subjective test is inappropriate under the Fourth Amendment. Rather than ruminate whether the officers subjectively created the emergency by loudly knocking on the door of the apartment, the facts must be viewed objectively in light of all circumstances. Another test posited by the lower courts, whether it was reasonably foreseeable that the officers' actions would create the exigent circumstances, is also unworkable. There is always some possibility a suspect in the drug trade may have drugs in the residence. Use of the reasonable foreseeability test would include an analysis of the level of predictability that must be reached before the exigent circumstances rule would apply. Lastly, some courts have faulted police when circumstances supporting probable cause exist but the police fail to stop their activities and obtain a warrant. This approach interferes with law enforcement strategies. The police are under no obligation to halt their activities and obtain a search warrant once the minimum standard for probable cause has been reached. Reversed.

DISSENT: (Ginsburg, J.) The officers had probable cause to obtain a search warrant based upon the suspect's entrance into the breezeway and the smell of marijuana from the apartment. Nothing made it impracticable for the police to obtain the appropriate search warrant at that time prior to their entry into the apartment.

ANALYSIS

This decision reaffirms the original exigent circumstances rule and severely limits the "police created exigency" exception to that rule. In essence, as long as police do not gain entry by means of an actual or threatened violation of the Fourth Amendment, the

Continued on next page.

warrantless search may be upheld. Note here, the United States Supreme Court did not engage in a specific analysis as to whether exigent circumstances were present. It assumed this for the purposes of its review but remanded the case to the Kentucky Supreme Court for a determination of whether exigent circumstances were actually present.

Quicknotes

EXIGENT CIRCUMSTANCES Circumstances requiring an extraordinary or immediate response; an exception to the prohibition on a warrantless arrest or search when police officers believe probable cause to exist and there is no time for obtaining a warrant.

FOURTH AMENDMENT Provides that persons be secure as to their person and private belongings against unreasonable searches and seizures.

Illinois v. McArthur

State (P) v. Drug possessor (D)

531 U.S. 326 (2001)

NATURE OF CASE: Misdemeanor drug charge.

FACT SUMMARY: Charles McArthur (D) moved to suppress evidence seized from his home on the basis that it was the "fruit" of an unlawful search.

RULE OF LAW

In determining whether a search is unreasonable and in violation of the Fourth Amendment, the court must balance the privacy-related and law enforcement-related concerns to determine whether the intrusion was reasonable.

FACTS: Tera McArthur asked two police officers to accompany her to the trailer where she and her husband, Charles (D), lived so that they could keep the peace while she retrieved some of her belongings. Assistant Chief Love and Officer Skidis went with Tera to the trailer. Tera then informed Chief Love that Charles (D) had some drugs in the trailer. Chief Love knocked on the trailer door, told Charles (D) what Tera had said, and asked for permission to search the trailer. Charles (D) did not grant permission. Chief Love remained at the location while Officer Skidis went to obtain a search warrant. Chief Love told Charles (D), who was on the porch at this point, that he could not reenter the trailer unless a police officer accompanied him. Charles (D) subsequently reentered the trailer two or three times. Each time Chief Love stood just inside the door to observe what Charles (D) did. Officer Skidis obtained the warrant and returned to the trailer with other officers. The officers searched the trailer, finding under the sofa a marijuana pipe, a box for marijuana, and a small amount of marijuana. Charles (D) was arrested and charged. Charles (D) moved to suppress the evidence (pipe, box, and marijuana) on the basis that it was the "fruit" of an unlawful seizure. The trial court granted the motion and the appellate court affirmed.

ISSUE: In determining whether a search is unreasonable and in violation of the Fourth Amendment, must the court balance the privacy-related and law enforcement-related concerns to determine whether the intrusion was reasonable?

HOLDING AND DECISION: (Breyer, J.) Yes. In determining whether a search is unreasonable and in violation of the Fourth Amendment, the court must balance the privacy-related and law enforcement-related concerns to determine whether the intrusion was reasonable. Here the restriction at issue was reasonable in light of the fact that the police had probable cause to believe Charles's (D) trailer home contained evidence of a crime and contraband and that the police had time to speak to his wife and assess her reliability. The police also had good reason to believe that unless restrained, Charles (D) would destroy the evidence. The police made reasonable efforts to reconcile their law enforcement needs with the demands of personal privacy and imposed the restraint for only a limited time period of two hours. The restraint was compatible with the Fourth Amendment's requirements. Reversed.

ANALYSIS

In determining whether the Fourth Amendment is violated, the court must invoke a "reasonableness" inquiry. In general, seizures of personal property are presumptively unreasonable unless conducted pursuant to a warrant issued by a neutral magistrate after finding probable cause.

Quicknotes

CONTRABAND Items that are illegal to have in one's possession or to trade or produce.

FOURTH AMENDMENT Provides that persons be secure as to their person and private belongings against unreasonable searches and seizures.

PROBABLE CAUSE A reasonable basis for believing that a crime has been committed.

UNREASONABLE SEARCH The Fourth Amendment protects against unreasonable searches and seizures; in order to invoke the Fourth Amendment prohibition, the individual must have a reasonable expectation of privacy in respect to the location searched or thing seized.

WARRANT An order issued by a court directing an officer to undertake a certain act (e.g., arrest or search).

New York v. Burger

State (P) v. Junkyard owner (D)

482 U.S. 691 (1987)

NATURE OF CASE: Review of grant of a motion to suppress evidence in a criminal prosecution for possession of stolen property.

FACT SUMMARY: Burger (D) contended that police officers' inspection of his automobile junkyard without a warrant but pursuant to a state statute violated the Fourth Amendment.

RULE OF LAW

Administrative inspections of closely regulated businesses fall within an exception to the warrant requirement of the Fourth Amendment.

FACTS: Burger (D), the owner of an automobile junkyard, sought to suppress evidence that he possessed stolen property that was obtained by officers who searched his business pursuant to New York Vehicle and Traffic Law §415-a5. The statute required junkyard operators to make records and inventory available for inspection by police officers. Burger (D) contended that the statute violated the Fourth Amendment since it did not require a warrant for a search designed to gather criminal evidence. The trial court denied Burger's (D) motion, but the New York Court of Appeals reversed, holding that the statute was unconstitutional. The United States Supreme Court granted certiorari.

ISSUE: Do administrative inspections of closely regulated businesses fall within an exception to the warrant requirement of the Fourth Amendment?

HOLDING AND DECISION: (Blackmun, J.) Yes. Administrative inspections of closely regulated businesses fall within an exception to the warrant requirement of the Fourth Amendment. The expectation of privacy in commercial premises is less than the expectation for homes. The Court has recognized that certain industries have a history of government oversight such that no reasonable expectation of privacy exists. In these closely regulated businesses, administrative schemes allow for warrantless inspections provided that: there is a substantial government interest; the warrantless inspection is necessary to further the regulatory scheme; and the regularity of the program provides an adequate substitution for the safeguards supplied by a warrant. Searches made pursuant to §415-a5 clearly fall within this exception to the warrant requirement because the junkyard business has been heavily regulated since the inception of the industry. Additionally, the State (P) has a substantial interest in regulating the industry because of the problem of auto theft associated with junkyards. The theft problem is addressed effectively by the administrative scheme of §415-a5. Finally, the program limits the time, place, and scope of inspections, providing an adequate substitution for warrant safeguards. Therefore, §415-a5 is constitutional; the New York Court of Appeals is reversed.

DISSENT: (Brennan, J.) Vehicle dismantling businesses are not closely regulated, and even if they were, §415-a5 does not provide enough guidance or limits on searches to be an adequate substitute for a warrant. Instead, the State (P) has used an administrative scheme as a pretext to search without probable cause for evidence of criminal violations.

ANALYSIS

The United States Supreme Court rejected arguments that there was significance in the fact that police officers, rather than administrative agents, had conducted the inspections. The Court reasoned that as long as the regulatory scheme was properly administrative, a state could assign any type of official to enforce the program. However, lower courts applying more detailed statutes have held the presence of a law enforcement agent sufficient to render an administrative search unconstitutional. See *United States v. Johnson*, 994 F.2d 740 (10th Cir. 1993).

Quicknotes

FOURTH AMENDMENT Provides that persons be secure as to their person and private belongings against unreasonable searches and seizures.

WARRANT An order issued by a court directing an officer to undertake a certain act (e.g., arrest or search).

Maryland v. King

State (P) v. Arrestee (D)

569 U.S. 455 (2013)

NATURE OF CASE: Certiorari review of Fourth Amendment search in appeal of criminal rape conviction.

FACT SUMMARY: Alonzo King (King) (D) was arrested and charged in Maryland (P) with first- and second-degree assault. As part of the booking process, his DNA sample was taken by applying a cotton swab or filer paper to the inside of his cheeks—a common procedure known as a "buccal swab." A later analysis determined King's (D) DNA matched one taken from rape victim years earlier. King (D) was tried and convicted for the rape.

RULE OF LAW

It is reasonable under the Fourth Amendment for officers to take and analyze a buccal swab of an arrestee's DNA when the arrest is for a serious offense and is supported by probable cause and the arrestee is brought to the police station for legitimate police booking procedures.

FACTS: In 2003, a masked man broke into a woman's home in Salisbury, Maryland, and raped her. The perpetrator's DNA was collected from the victim, but the perpetrator was not identified or located. In 2009, King (D) was arrested and charged for first- and second-degree assault for menacing a group of people with a shotgun. Police processed King (D) for detention, and, as part of the booking process, took a DNA sample from him by applying a cotton swab or filter paper to the inside of his cheeks—a common procedure known as a "buccal swab." The DNA matched that from the 2003 rape sample. King (D) was tried and convicted for the rape. On appeal the Maryland Court of Appeals set aside the rape conviction on the grounds that obtaining and using the cheek swab during the 2009 booking was an unreasonable search of the person. [The United States Supreme Court granted certiorari.]

ISSUE: Is it reasonable under the Fourth Amendment for officers to take and analyze a buccal swab of an arrestee's DNA when the arrest is for a serious offense and is supported by probable cause and the arrestee is brought to the police station for legitimate police booking procedures?

HOLDING AND DECISION: (Kennedy, J.) Yes. It is reasonable under the Fourth Amendment for officers to take and analyze a buccal swab of an arrestee's DNA when the arrest is for a serious offense and is supported by probable cause and the arrestee is brought to the police station for legitimate police booking procedures. The Maryland DNA Collection Act (the Act) authorizes law enforcement officials to collect DNA samples from those arrested for crimes of violence, attempts to commit crimes of violence, burglary, or attempted burglary. The DNA sample then may not be entered into any database without the arrestee's consent until the arrestee is arraigned. The sample is destroyed if no probable cause is found to support the charges, no conviction is obtained, the conviction is reversed or vacated, or the convicted is later pardoned. Further, the DNA sample may be used only for identification and no other purpose. Here, the DNA sample was entered into and identified by the Combined DNA Index System (CODIS), which collects DNA profiles and connects DNA laboratories at the local, state, and national level. The buccal swab, while minimally invasive, is a search nevertheless. Warrentless searches may be permissible when the search involves no discretion by those administering the search. This is the case here, so no warrant was required. The search must still be reasonable in its scope and manner of execution. The legitimate government interest accomplished with the DNA swab is the need for law enforcement officers safely and accurately to process and identify those in their custody. A suspect's criminal history is a critical part of his or her identity and it is common for arrestees to conceal their true identity. Police already compare booking photographs and sketches and make computerized comparison of fingerprints. The use of DNA for identification is no different. Identifying those who have committed prior crimes is important also to ascertain who might be likely to flee if permitted conditional leave from custody. A person with a past criminal action might be more likely to flee to avoid more serious charges. Finally, use of DNA may free an innocent person wrongfully imprisoned for the same offense. DNA identification is superior to fingerprinting and the time to accomplish DNA identification is shrinking. There is little reason to question the government's legitimate interest in knowing for certainty the identity of the person it has arrested. In comparison, the intrusion of a cheek swab is minimal. The privacy concerns of an arrestee also are diminished. Merely being in custody does not make any search of an arrestee a reasonable one, but this is a reasonable search. The Act provides sufficient protections against further invasion of the arrestee's privacy. Reversed.

DISSENT: (Scalia, J.) The very heart of the Fourth Amendment is the prohibition against unreasonable

Continued on next page.

and baseless search of a person for evidence of a crime. When the Court has permitted a suspicionless search, it has required a justifying motive apart from the investigation of a crime. No such justifying motive exists here. The Court elaborates on its identification purpose, but knowing the facts of the DNA search at issue here instantly disabuses one that identification has anything to do with using King's (D) DNA sample. The Act prohibited Maryland P) from using the DNA sample until King's (D) arraignment, which was three days after arrest. Surely Maryland (P) knew who it had in custody during those three days and whom it was arraigning. The search had nothing to do with establishing his identity. The Combined DNA Index System (CODIS) works by comparing Convict and Arrestee Collection DNA samples with those in the Unsolved Crimes Collection; that does not reveal King's (D) identity. The Act permits identification testing of a DNA sample to identify human remains or missing individuals. No mention is made about identifying arrestees. Taking a person's photograph is not a search. Cases do not readily answer whether fingerprinting is a search, but officers' post-arrest use of fingerprints is for identification while post-arrest use of DNA is to solve crimes. The Court repeatedly says DNA testing and database entry affects only those arrested for serious offenses. No principle possibly could justify this limitation, and DNA collection for any reason, right or wrong, is the predictable consequence.

ANALYSIS

When the United States Supreme Court granted certiorari in *Maryland v. King*, 49 states filed amicus briefs in support of Maryland. The Court noted 26 states and the federal government take DNA samples upon arrest, and the amicus briefs generally argued the legitimate government interests outweighed the rights and interests of the arrestees. All 50 states and the federal government take DNA samples from convicted offenders. The Combined DNA Index System (CODIS) now maintains a database of millions of offender and arrestee profiles.

Quicknotes

FOURTH AMENDMENT Provides that persons be secure as to their person and private belongings against unreasonable searches and seizures.

PROBABLE CAUSE A reasonable basis for believing that a crime has been committed.

City of Indianapolis v. Edmond

City (D) v. Motorists (P)

531 U.S. 32 (2000)

NATURE OF CASE: Class action challenging constitutionality of vehicle checkpoints.

FACT SUMMARY: Motorists (P) challenged the constitutional validity of city-imposed vehicle checkpoints as violative of the Fourth Amendment's prohibition against unlawful searches and seizures.

RULE OF LAW

Where a vehicle checkpoint program is designed primarily to uncover evidence of criminal wrongdoing, such program constitutes an unlawful search and seizure in violation of the Fourth Amendment.

FACTS: The City of Indianapolis (D) began to operate vehicle checkpoints in an effort to intercept unlawful drugs. Checkpoint locations were selected weeks in advance, based on certain considerations such as area crime statistics and traffic flow. Edmond (P) and Palmer (P) were each stopped at such a narcotics checkpoint. They filed a lawsuit on behalf of themselves and the class of all motorists who had been stopped or were subject to being stopped in the future at the checkpoints. They claimed the roadblocks violated the Fourth Amendment and the search and seizure provision of the state constitution and moved for a preliminary injunction. The district court denied, holding the Fourth Amendment was not violated. The court of appeals reversed and the United States Supreme Court granted certiorari.

ISSUE: Where a vehicle checkpoint program is designed primarily to uncover evidence of criminal wrongdoing, does such program constitute an unlawful search and seizure in violation of the Fourth Amendment?

HOLDING AND DECISION: (O'Connor, J.) Yes. Where a vehicle checkpoint program is designed primarily to uncover evidence of criminal wrongdoing, such program constitutes an unlawful search and seizure in violation of the Fourth Amendment. Our checkpoint cases have recognized only limited exceptions to the general rule that a seizure must be accompanied by some measure of individualized suspicion. When law enforcement authorities pursue primarily general crime control purposes at checkpoints such as these, such stops may only be justified by some measure of individualized suspicion. Because the primary purpose of the program was indistinguishable from its general interest in crime control, the checkpoints violate the Fourth Amendment. Affirmed.

DISSENT: (Rehnquist, C.J.) The program in issue here complies with our previous decisions regarding roadblock seizures of automobiles, and the addition of a dog sniff does not change the intrusiveness of the stop. It is constitutionally irrelevant that the law enforcement also hoped to intercept narcotics.

DISSENT: (Thomas, J.) Prior decisions compel upholding the program at issue here; however, I do not believe those cases were correctly decided. A program of indiscriminate stops of individuals not suspected of wrongdoing is not consistent with the intent of the Fourth Amendment.

ANALYSIS

The Fourth Amendment requires that searches be "reasonable" in order to be held valid. A search is presumptively unreasonable if there is a lack of probable cause. A special category of searches is excluded from the reasonable requirement where it is required to serve "special needs, beyond the normal need for law enforcement." The United States Supreme Court has upheld such special needs as border control and sobriety checkpoints, while rejecting discretionary, suspicionless spot checks of driver's license and registration. The constitutionality of such programs is based on a balancing test between the interests at stake and the program's effectiveness.

Quicknotes

FOURTH AMENDMENT Provides that persons be secure as to their person and private belongings against unreasonable searches and seizures.

PROBABLE CAUSE A reasonable basis for believing that a crime has been committed.

SEIZURE The removal of property from one's possession due to unlawful activity or in satisfaction of a judgment entered by the court.

United States v. Flores-Montano

Federal government (P) v. Convicted drug smuggler (D)

541 U.S. 149 (2004)

NATURE OF CASE: Appeal of conviction for drug smuggling.

FACT SUMMARY: Manuel Flores-Montano (D) was arrested after border patrol in California discovered 81 pounds of marijuana in his gas tank. He claimed the search was unreasonable.

RULE OF LAW

Under the Fourth Amendment, customs officers at the international border need not have reasonable suspicion to remove, disassemble, and search a vehicle's fuel tank for contraband.

FACTS: Manuel Flores-Montano (D) was arrested after a border search that uncovered 37 kilograms (around 81 pounds) of marijuana hidden in the gas tank of his vehicle. He was indicted in a California federal court on one count of unlawfully importing marijuana and one count of possession with intent to distribute it. Flores-Montano (D) moved to suppress the marijuana evidence, arguing that the border search that uncovered the drugs was a "non-routine" border search requiring reasonable suspicion. The district court held that the search of the gas tank was "non-routine" and therefore reasonable suspicion was required to justify the search. The Ninth Circuit Court of Appeals affirmed.

ISSUE: Under the Fourth Amendment, must customs officers at the international border have reasonable suspicion to remove, disassemble, and search a vehicle's fuel tank for contraband?

HOLDING AND DECISION: (Rehnquist, C.J.) No. Under the Fourth Amendment, customs officers at the international border need not have reasonable suspicion to remove, disassemble, and search a vehicle's fuel tank for contraband. The government's interest in preventing the entry of unwanted persons and materials is highest at the border, and the United States has the right to protect itself by examining persons and property crossing into this country. A high number of drug seizures has occurred at California ports of entry, many through gas tank searches. The expectation of privacy is less at the border than it is in the interior of the United States, and is not greater in the gas tank than it is in the passenger compartment, and the disassembly and reassembly of his gas tank did not damage his vehicle. Reversed.

CONCURRENCE: (Breyer, J.) Customs also keeps track of the border searches that are conducted, which minimizes concerns that gas tank searches might be taken abusively.

ANALYSIS

Court documents associated with this case indicate that the Government's (P) argument did not rely on a reasonable-suspicion theory, even though the defendant avoided eye contact and had shaky hands when questioned at the border, which would have provided the Government (P) with reasonable grounds to suspect, and therefore to search the car. The Government (P) appears to have intended to call into question the rule that searches without reasonable suspicion at the border were unconstitutional.

Quicknotes

FOURTH AMENDMENT Provides that persons be secure as to their person and private belongings against unreasonable searches and seizures.

REASONABLE BELIEF A reasonable basis for believing that a crime is being or has been committed.

Mapp v. Ohio

Convicted felon (D) v. State (P)

367 U.S. 643 (1961)

NATURE OF CASE: Appeal from denial of motion to suppress evidence.

FACT SUMMARY: Ohio (P) contended evidence obtained against Mapp (D) in violation of the Fourth Amendment was admissible.

RULE OF LAW

The exclusionary rule under the Fourth Amendment applies in state court prosecutions.

FACTS: Mapp (D) was convicted of possessing lewd books based on evidence seized illegally without a search warrant. Mapp (D) appealed her conviction on the basis that the evidence should have been suppressed under the exclusionary rule. The court of appeals affirmed, and the United States Supreme Court granted certiorari.

ISSUE: Does the exclusionary rule under the Fourth Amendment apply in state court prosecutions?

HOLDING AND DECISION: (Clark, J.) Yes. The exclusionary rule under the Fourth Amendment applies in state court prosecutions. The rationale behind applying the rule federally applies equally to the states. Evidence obtained in derogation of constitutionally protected rights cannot be admitted to support a prosecution. This is essential to deter oppressive police conduct. The exclusionary rule is a critical component of the enforceability of the Fourth and Fourteenth Amendments. As a result, the conviction must be overturned.

DISSENT: (Harlan, J.) Uniformity of sanction is not a logical reason to extend the exclusionary rule to the states.

ANALYSIS

This case illustrates the United States Supreme Court extending its earlier decision in *Wolf v. Colorado*, 338 U.S. 25 (1949). In that case, the Court held that the Fourth Amendment guarantees applied against the states, yet it also held that the exclusionary rule did not apply. With this case, the Fourth Amendment has equal application on both federal and state levels.

Quicknotes

EXCLUSIONARY RULE A rule precluding the introduction at trial of evidence unlawfully obtained in violation of the federal constitutional safeguards against unreasonable searches and seizures.

FOURTEENTH AMENDMENT Declares that no state shall make or enforce any law that shall abridge the privileges and immunities of citizens of the United States; no state shall deny to any person within its jurisdiction the equal protection of the laws.

FOURTH AMENDMENT Provides that persons be secure as to their person and private belongings against unreasonable searches and seizures.

United States v. Leon

Federal government (P) v. Alleged drug trafficker (D)

468 U.S. 897 (1984)

NATURE OF CASE: Appeal from grant of motion to suppress in drug prosecution.

FACT SUMMARY: Police officers found narcotics in Leon's (D) house pursuant to a search warrant obtained in good faith but later held to be invalid.

RULE OF LAW

The Fourth Amendment exclusionary rule does not bar the introduction of evidence for use in the prosecution's case-in-chief that was seized by law enforcement officers and reasonably relied on a warrant issued by a detached and neutral magistrate but that is ultimately found to be unsupported by probable cause.

FACTS: Police obtained from a neutral magistrate a facially valid search warrant to search Leon's (D) residence. In the affidavit supporting the warrant, police cited information from a confidential informant of unproven reliability and the results of an extensive police investigation, which included surveillance of Leon (D). Upon execution of the warrant, illegal narcotics were found in Leon's (D) residence. The district court held that the affidavit failed to establish probable cause under *Aguilar v. State of Texas*, 378 U.S. 108 (1964), and *Spinelli v. United States*, 393 U.S. 410 (1969), and suppressed part of the evidence. A divided panel of the court of appeals affirmed. The Government (P) appealed, contending the officers relied on the warrants in good faith.

ISSUE: Does the Fourth Amendment exclusionary rule bar the introduction of evidence for use in the prosecution's case-in-chief that was seized by law enforcement officers and reasonably relied on a warrant issued by a detached and neutral magistrate but that is ultimately found to be unsupported by probable cause?

HOLDING AND DECISION: (White, J.) No. The Fourth Amendment exclusionary rule does not bar the introduction of evidence for use in the prosecution's case-in-chief that was seized by law enforcement officers and reasonably relied on a warrant issued by a detached and neutral magistrate but that is ultimately found to be unsupported by probable cause. The exclusionary rule articulates a judicially created remedy designed to deter police misconduct, not cure the invasion of the defendant's Fourth Amendment rights. Therefore, the social costs of applying the remedy must be weighed against its benefits. Excluding inherently trustworthy tangible evidence obtained in reliance on a search warrant issued by a neutral magistrate that ultimately is found to be defective substantially interferes with the truth-finding function of the courts, causing guilty defendants to go free or receive reduced sentences. This is a substantial social cost. By contrast, the deterrent value of excluding such evidence is slight because, by hypothesis, police officers are acting in the objectively reasonable belief that their conduct does not violate the Fourth Amendment. Neither will exclusion deter magisterial errors because judges and magistrates are judicially neutral officers with no stake in the outcome of a particular criminal prosecution. It therefore serves no purpose to punish police for the errors of magistrates. The warrant application here related the results of an extensive investigation in sufficient detail to divide opinion within the court of appeals panel reviewing the issue whether sufficient probable cause existed to justify issuance of the warrant. The officers' reliance on the facially valid warrant was therefore objectively reasonable. Reversed.

CONCURRENCE: (Blackmun, J.) This empirical judgment about the effect of exclusionary rule is provisional by necessity, and the Court should be ready to reconsider it in light of its effect on law enforcement activity.

DISSENT: (Brennan, J.) Police searches and seizures are generally executed for the purpose of introducing their fruits as evidence in a criminal trial. Therefore, the exclusionary rule is necessary to give meaning to the Fourth Amendment and states a fundamental constitutional right. Application of cost-benefit analysis to a constitutional guarantee is inappropriate because the Fourth Amendment directly contemplates that some reliable and incriminating evidence will be lost to the government. It is the Fourth Amendment itself, and not the exclusionary rule, that imposes this cost.

DISSENT: (Stevens, J.) This decision incomprehensibly states that a search was constitutionally unreasonable but that the seized evidence is admissible because the same search was reasonable. The Court in so holding ignores its practice of deciding cases on the narrowest grounds possible and does grave damage to the deterrent function of the Fourth Amendment exclusionary rule.

ANALYSIS

It is conceivable that sometime in the future the United States Supreme Court will consider whether

Continued on next page.

the good-faith exception will be applied to warrantless searches. Justice White, the author of the present case, has indicated that he might apply the exception in the case of warrantless searches. See *INS v. Lopez-Mendoza*, 468 U.S. 1032 (1984). If it is ultimately held that the exception will apply, law enforcement officers may decide to forgo applications for warrants.

Quicknotes

EXCLUSIONARY RULE A rule precluding the introduction at trial of evidence unlawfully obtained in violation of the federal constitutional safeguards against unreasonable searches and seizures.

FOURTH AMENDMENT Provides that persons be secure as to their person and private belongings against unreasonable searches and seizures.

Herring v. United States

Individual (D) v. Federal government (P)

555 U.S. 135 (2009)

NATURE OF CASE: Appeal from Eleventh Circuit Court of Appeals in favor of the Government (P).

FACT SUMMARY: After receiving information from a neighboring county that Herring (D) had an outstanding warrant against him, police officers in Coffee County arrested Herring (D). A search of Herring's (D) vehicle revealed a gun and illegal drugs. The police then learned the warrant had previously been recalled.

RULE OF LAW

When police mistakes leading to an unlawful search are the result of isolated negligence attenuated from the search, rather than systemic error or reckless disregard of constitutional requirements, the exclusionary rule does not apply.

FACTS: Police in Coffee County investigated whether Herring (D) had any outstanding warrants against him. A search of a neighboring county's database initially revealed that Herring (D) had a warrant against him for failure to appear for a felony charge. Acting on the information, the police officers arrested Herring (D). A search of his vehicle incident to his arrest turned up a gun and illegal drugs. Shortly after the search, police dispatch informed the arresting officers that the warrant had actually been recalled five months earlier and was no longer valid. Federal charges were subsequently brought against Herring (D), and Herring (D) moved to suppress the evidence from the search on the grounds the arrest and search were in violation of his Fourth Amendment rights. The trial court and the Eleventh Circuit Court of Appeals found that because the mistake was caused by the mere negligence of the police record-keeping system, the exclusionary rule did not apply. Herring (D) appealed.

ISSUE: When police mistakes leading to an unlawful search are the result of isolated negligence attenuated from the search, rather than systemic error or reckless disregard of constitutional requirements, does the exclusionary rule apply?

HOLDING AND DECISION: (Roberts, C.J.) No. When police mistakes leading to an unlawful search are the result of isolated negligence attenuated from the search, rather than systemic error or reckless disregard of constitutional requirements, the exclusionary rule does not apply. The mere fact that a search is unreasonable does not mean the exclusionary rule automatically applies. The Court has previously held the rule does not apply when police reasonably relied upon an invalid warrant issued by a court. The only issue here is whether negligence by the police, as opposed to others, will lead to the suppression of evidence. The Court holds that it should not. The exclusionary rule was created to deter police misconduct. The conduct must have a deliberate or indifferent nature to invoke the exclusionary rule. Those circumstances are not present here. An error arising from nonrecurring negligence, as opposed to systemic negligence, does not implicate the concerns the exclusionary rule was designed to protect. Affirmed.

DISSENT: (Ginsburg, J.) The Court's decision may lead to the arrest of innocent persons based upon information that is negligently maintained. Police departments across the country will have little incentive to ensure the accuracy of their warrant databases. The exclusionary rule is the only remedy Herring (D) and others in his situation have. A subsequent lawsuit against the police for wrongful arrest will be barred by qualified immunity. Just as in tort law, the risk of exclusion of evidence would encourage police departments at the state and federal level to monitor the warrant databases and ensure their accuracy.

DISSENT: (Breyer, J.) In addition to Justice Ginsburg's arguments, another reason to apply the exclusionary rule is that the police were responsible for the error. Prior cases have allowed evidence when the police rely in good faith on the incorrect information provided by third parties. This Court has never held that evidence may be allowed when the police are themselves responsible for the incorrect information.

ANALYSIS

Debate has ensued over the scope of this 5–4 decision. Some commentators believe the scope is limited to police errors in regard to record keeping only. However, others believe police departments may rely on the decision to argue that any of their good-faith mistakes will prohibit the application of the exclusionary rule. It does appear though that the holding concerns only those isolated and negligent mistakes that are "attenuated from the search." The precise contours of this "attenuation" factor have yet to be defined.

Quicknotes

EXCLUSIONARY RULE A rule precluding the introduction at trial of evidence unlawfully obtained in violation of the

Continued on next page.

federal constitutional safeguards against unreasonable searches and seizures.

FOURTH AMENDMENT Provides that persons be secure as to their person and private belongings against unreasonable searches and seizures.

WARRANT An order issued by a court directing an officer to undertake a certain act (e.g., arrest or search).

Rakas v. Illinois

Auto passenger (D) v. State (P)

439 U.S. 128 (1978)

NATURE OF CASE: Appeal of criminal convictions.

FACT SUMMARY: Various defendants sought to suppress evidence in which they had no proprietary interest seized from a vehicle in which they were passengers.

RULE OF LAW

A person may not move to suppress evidence in which he or she has no proprietary interest nor expectation of privacy.

FACTS: Police stopped a vehicle that matched the description of a getaway car. A search of the vehicle revealed a shotgun and shotgun shells. The shotgun and shells belonged to the owner of the vehicle, who was also the driver. Charged with various crimes [not specified in the casebook excerpt], the passengers (D) moved to suppress the gun and shells. This was denied, and the passengers (D) were convicted, along with the driver. The Illinois appellate courts affirmed. The United States Supreme Court accepted the passengers' (D) writ for certiorari.

ISSUE: May a person move to suppress evidence in which he or she has no proprietary interest or expectation of privacy?

HOLDING AND DECISION: (Rehnquist, J.) No. A person may not move to suppress evidence in which he or she has no proprietary interest or expectation of privacy. The rights secured by the Fourth Amendment are personal; a person cannot move to suppress evidence seized in violation of another's rights. For a person to have a personal interest in the evidence sufficient to confer a right to seek suppression, one of two things must occur. One, the movant may have some sort of ownership or possessory interest in the evidence; such a seizure would violate a personal interest. In the alternative, the party seeking suppression must demonstrate that the items were seized from some sort of area in which he or she had a legitimate expectation of privacy. Absent these circumstances, a person cannot make a Fourth Amendment claim. Here, the passengers (D) had no proprietary interest in the seized articles. Further, they had no expectation of privacy in the interior of another person's vehicle. Consequently, they suffered no Fourth Amendment violation. Affirmed.

CONCURRENCE: (Powell, J.) Cases such as this demand a case-by-case analysis.

DISSENT: (White, J.) The majority holds that the Fourth Amendment protects property, not people. The ruling undercuts the force of the exclusionary rule in its deterrence of bad-faith Fourth Amendment violations. The police are now invited to engage in patently unreasonable searches every time an automobile contains more than one person.

ANALYSIS

Prior to *Rakas,* the United States Supreme Court considered the type of analysis made here to be one of standing. The Court believed this to be an inappropriate focus on procedure. In the opinion, the Court takes pains to point out that it was dealing with substantive Fourth Amendment law, not procedure.

Quicknotes

EXCLUSIONARY RULE A rule precluding the introduction at trial of evidence unlawfully obtained in violation of the federal constitutional safeguards against unreasonable searches and seizures.

EXPECTATION OF PRIVACY Requirement that in order to invoke the Fourth Amendment's protection against unreasonable searches and seizures, the individual must have a reasonable expectation of privacy in respect to the location searched or thing seized.

FOURTH AMENDMENT Provides that persons be secure as to their person and private belongings against unreasonable searches and seizures.

Brown v. Illinois

Convicted felon (D) v. State (P)

422 U.S. 590 (1975)

NATURE OF CASE: Appeal of conviction for murder.

FACT SUMMARY: Brown (D) was illegally arrested and taken to the police station where he was twice given *Miranda* warnings and twice confessed.

RULE OF LAW

Where an illegal arrest leads to a search or confession that produces evidence, the evidence is inadmissible as "fruit of the poisonous tree," unless the causal connection between the illegal arrest and the discovery of the evidence is so attenuated as to dissipate the taint. (However, the mere recitation of *Miranda* warnings prior to confession does not dissipate the taint.)

FACTS: As Brown (D) arrived at his apartment two police officers pointed guns at him, informed him he was under arrest, searched him in his apartment, and took him to the police station. About 90 minutes after arriving at the station, Brown (D) was given *Miranda* warnings and confessed to a murder. Seven hours later, Brown (D) was again given *Miranda* warnings, and again he confessed. At trial, Brown (D) moved to suppress the confessions as fruit of an illegal arrest, but the motion was denied and he was convicted. On appeal, the Illinois Supreme Court found the arrest had been made without probable cause but held that the *Miranda* warnings broke the causal chain, making the confessions admissible. Brown (D) appealed to the United States Supreme Court.

ISSUE: Where an illegal arrest leads to a search or confession that produces evidence, is the evidence inadmissible as "fruit of the poisonous tree," unless the causal connection between the illegal arrest and the discovery of the evidence is so attenuated as to dissipate the taint?

HOLDING AND DECISION: (Blackmun, J.) Yes. Where an illegal arrest leads to a search or confession that produces evidence, the evidence is inadmissible as "fruit of the poisonous tree," unless the causal connection between the illegal arrest and the discovery of the evidence is so attenuated as to dissipate the taint. The mere recitation of *Miranda* warnings prior to confession does not per se dissipate the taint. *Miranda* warnings deal with Fifth Amendment concerns, while the exclusionary rule is designed to effectuate the Fourth, which protects against all unlawful searches and seizures, whether or not they produce incriminating material or testimony. *Miranda* warnings are only one factor in the determination of whether a confession was obtained by exploitation of an illegal arrest or whether the taint was dissipated. Other factors include how much time passed between arrest and confession; the presence of intervening circumstances, especially an act of free will by the defendant; and, particularly, the purpose and flagrancy of the police misconduct. In this case, the first confession occurred less than two hours after the arrest and there was no significant intervening event. The police misconduct had a quality of purposefulness, with the officers knowing they lacked probable cause and effectuating the arrest in a way calculated to cause surprise, fright, and confusion. Reversed.

CONCURRENCE IN PART: (Powell, J.) Conviction was correctly reversed, but the case should have been remanded for reconsideration using the factors stated in the majority opinion. This factual analysis should be left to state courts. Moreover, to further the exclusionary rule's purpose of deterring the worst police behavior, the degree of attenuation required to dissipate the taint should increase where police misconduct is more egregious and decrease where the Fourth Amendment violation is more "technical."

ANALYSIS

The opinions in *Brown* contain lengthy discussions of *Wong Sun v. United States*, 371 U.S. 471 (1963), the leading case on causation and attenuation. In *Wong Sun*, federal agents broke into defendant Toy's home, arrested him without probable cause, and elicited a statement concerning Toy's involvement in a drug sale. Toy's statement led to Yee, who possessed the drugs and who implicated a third party known as "Sea Dog." Toy said that "Sea Dog" was defendant Wong Sun and led police to Wong Sun's residence. Wong Sun was arrested, arraigned, and released on his own recognizance. Several days later, Wong Sun voluntarily returned to the police station and gave a confession. Toy's statements and the drugs taken from Yee were suppressed as fruits of the illegal arrest of Toy since there was no independent intervening act of free will to break the causal chain and purge the taint of the illegal arrest. Wong Sun's arrest was also tainted, but his confession was admissible in light of his lawful arraignment and release on his own recognizance and his voluntary return several days later to confess. The connection between Wong Sun's arrest and confession had become so attenuated as to dissipate the taint.

Continued on next page.

Quicknotes

CAUSATION The aggregate effect of preceding events that bring about a tortious result; the causal connection between the actions of a tortfeasor and the injury that follows.

EXCLUSIONARY RULE A rule precluding the introduction at trial of evidence unlawfully obtained in violation of the federal constitutional safeguards against unreasonable searches and seizures.

FIFTH AMENDMENT Provides that no person shall be compelled to serve as a witness against him- or herself, be subject to trial for the same offense twice, or be deprived of life, liberty, or property without due process of law.

FOURTH AMENDMENT Provides that persons be secure as to their person and private belongings against unreasonable searches and seizures.

FRUIT OF POISONOUS TREE Doctrine that evidence obtained as a result of illegal procedures is tainted and is usually inadmissible at trial.

***MIRANDA* WARNINGS** Specified warnings that must be communicated to a person prior to a custodial interrogation; in the absence of the communication of such warnings, any communications made during the interrogation are inadmissible at trial.

Utah v. Strieff

State (P) v. Individual (D)

579 U.S. 232 (2016)

NATURE OF CASE: Appeal from Utah Supreme Court's decision in favor of the defendant.

FACT SUMMARY: Police suspected Strieff (D) of drug possession and stopped him in a parking lot. After learning his name, the officer discovered Strieff (D) had an outstanding arrest warrant. In a subsequent search incident to the arrest, the police found methamphetamine on Strieff's (D) person.

RULE OF LAW

Evidence remains admissible when the link between unconstitutional police action and the evidence obtained has been broken by an intervening circumstance, such that the protections of the Fourth Amendment that have been violated would not be furthered by the subsequent suppression of the evidence.

FACTS: Police in Utah suspected a certain house was the center of illegal drug activity. While conducting surveillance, officers observed Strieff (D) leave the house and walk to a nearby convenience store. A police officer, suspecting Strieff (D) of drug possession, stopped him in the parking lot and demanded his name. The officer then requested warrant information from his dispatchers. The dispatchers informed the officer that Strieff (D) had an outstanding arrest warrant for a traffic violation. In a subsequent search incident to the arrest, the police found methamphetamine on Strieff's (D) person. At trial Strieff (D) moved to suppress the evidence on the grounds the stop was without reasonable suspicion. The State (P) conceded the stop was illegal but argued the evidence should remain admissible. The trial court agreed. On appeal, the Utah Supreme Court reversed in favor of Strieff (D). The State (P) appealed to the United States Supreme Court.

ISSUE: Does evidence remain admissible when the link between unconstitutional police action and the evidence obtained has been broken by an intervening circumstance, such that the protections of the Fourth Amendment that have been violated would not be furthered by the subsequent suppression of the evidence?

HOLDING AND DECISION: (Thomas, J.) Yes. Evidence remains admissible when the link between unconstitutional police action and the evidence obtained has been broken by an intervening circumstance, such that the protections of the Fourth Amendment that have been violated would not be furthered by the subsequent suppression of the evidence. Three factors exist to determine if the discovery of a valid arrest warrant is an intervening cause to break the link between the unlawful stop of Strieff (D) and the discovery of drugs on his person. First, we examine the temporal proximity between the unconstitutional conduct and the discovery of the evidence. This factor favors suppressing the evidence. Here, the officer discovered the methamphetamine within minutes of learning of the outstanding arrest warrant. The second factor is the existence of the intervening circumstances. This factor favors the State (P). Here, the warrant was valid, and the officer had an obligation to arrest Strieff (D) once he became aware of it. The officer's actions were thus independently compelled. Once he made the arrest, the subsequent search incident to the arrest was lawful. The third factor is the purpose and flagrancy of the officer's conduct. This factor also favors the State (P). The exclusionary rule exists to deter officer's purposeful or flagrant conduct when carrying out a stop or search. In this matter, the officer was, at most, negligent. The officer made two good-faith errors. He failed to note when Strieff (D) entered the home and failed to inquire if Strieff (D) would speak with him voluntarily, as opposed to demanding his name. These errors do not rise to a flagrant violation of Strieff's (D) rights. Accordingly, we find the discovery of the valid warrant was an intervening cause between the illegal stop and the discovery of the drugs of Strieff's (D) person. Reversed.

DISSENT: (Sotomayor, J.) The majority decision here means that the discovery of a warrant for an unpaid parking ticket relieves a police officer from any prior violations of Fourth Amendment rights during an encounter. Police officers can now ask residents for their identification and perform a search for outstanding warrants, even without any reasonable suspicion. Clearly, the officer had a strong anticipation that Strieff (D) would have an outstanding warrant. The state of Utah has 180,000 outstanding warrants currently. The officer knew the discovery of the warrant would trump any illegalities of the initial stop. Because the officer found the drugs by exploiting the illegal stop, the evidence should be suppressed.

DISSENT: (Kagan, J.) The officer's investigatory stop was calculated. He knew there was a good chance that there would be a warrant on Strieff (D). The stop was so unjustified that the State (P) did not even defend it at trial. This decision will embolden police officers to make unlawful stops now that they are aware the discovery of a valid arrest warrant will forgive the unlawful stop or seizure.

Continued on next page.

ANALYSIS

Among the three factors to determine if the warrant was an intervening circumstance, the final factor regarding the officer's purposeful or flagrant conduct appears to give reviewing courts wide discretion. The majority and the dissents differed greatly in their interpretation of this factor. The majority felt the officer's errors were simply negligent while the dissenting justices clearly found them to be unconstitutional. It remains to be seen if future cases will further define this type of police conduct.

Quicknotes

ARREST WARRANT An order issued by a court directing an officer to arrest a particular individual.

EXCLUSIONARY RULE A rule precluding the introduction at trial of evidence unlawfully obtained in violation of the federal constitutional safeguards against unreasonable searches and seizures.

FOURTH AMENDMENT Provides that persons be secure as to their person and private belongings against unreasonable searches and seizures.

INVESTIGATORY STOP A brief, non-intrusive stop, requiring the police officer to have a reasonable suspicion that a crime has been committed based on specific and articulable facts.

Murray v. United States

Convicted drug possessor (D) v. Federal government (P)

487 U.S. 533 (1988)

NATURE OF CASE: Appeal from conviction for marijuana possession.

FACT SUMMARY: Agents saw marijuana when they illegally entered a warehouse, then obtained a search warrant without using any information discovered during the illegal entry, reentered the warehouse, and seized the marijuana that was used to convict Murray (D).

RULE OF LAW

Under the "independent source" doctrine, evidence initially uncovered, but not seized, during an illegal search will not be suppressed if the police later obtain a search warrant that does not rely on any facts discovered during the illegal search, and then seize the evidence during a second search pursuant to the warrant.

FACTS: Federal agents saw Murray (D) and others driving vehicles in and out of a warehouse that the agents believed contained drugs. Two drivers were lawfully arrested and their vehicles were found to contain marijuana. The agents entered the warehouse illegally and saw bales of marijuana, but without seizing the drugs they left the warehouse and applied for a search warrant. The warrant was issued despite the application making no mention of any information discovered during the illegal entry of the warehouse. The agents reentered the warehouse with the warrant and seized marijuana and other evidence. At trial, Murray (D) moved to suppress the evidence as fruit of the illegal search, the motion was denied, and he was convicted. The Court of Appeals for the First Circuit affirmed, and Murray (D) appealed to the United States Supreme Court.

ISSUE: Under the "independent source" doctrine, will evidence initially uncovered, but not seized, during an illegal search be suppressed if the police later obtain a search warrant that does not rely on any facts discovered during the illegal search, and then seize the evidence during a second search pursuant to the warrant?

HOLDING AND DECISION: (Scalia, J.) No. Under the "independent source" doctrine, evidence initially uncovered, but not seized, during an illegal search will not be suppressed if the police later obtain a search warrant that does not rely on any facts discovered during the illegal search, and then seize the evidence during a second search pursuant to the warrant. Society's interest in deterring unlawful police behavior and society's interest in having juries review all probative evidence of a crime are properly balanced by putting the police in the same position they would have been in but for their illegal conduct. If, as here, police discover evidence illegally, but later acquire it through a lawful, independent source, suppressing the evidence would put the police in a worse position than they would have been absent the illegal conduct. This rule does not encourage officers to first search unlawfully and then get a warrant because if they already have probable cause, they risk suppression of the evidence should they be unable to satisfy the independent source doctrine. If they do not already have probable cause, no information obtained during the illegal search can be used to establish probable cause, and, moreover, if a court does not believe that the officers would have sought a search warrant absent the illegal search, then the evidence will be suppressed. Judgment vacated and remanded for determination of whether the warrant-authorized search was an independent source of the challenged evidence.

DISSENT: (Marshall, J.) Under this ruling officers have an incentive to search illegally first, then seek a warrant. If the illegal search turns up no evidence, the officers have saved the substantial time and inconvenience of obtaining a search warrant. If the illegal search does turn up evidence, it is a simple matter to exclude from the warrant application any information gained from the illegal entry. The defendant then will be reduced to the nearly unwinnable argument that the officers are lying when they testify that they would have sought the warrant absent the illegal search.

ANALYSIS

Closely related to the "independent source" doctrine, and another limit on "fruit of the poisonous tree" analysis, is the "inevitable discovery" doctrine announced in *Nix v. Williams*, 467 U.S. 431 (1984), which is discussed at length in *Murray*. In *Nix*, police learned the whereabouts of the victim's body by questioning the defendant in violation of his Sixth Amendment right to counsel. A search for the body had been under way but was called off when the defendant revealed the body's location. The United States Supreme Court, using much the same reasoning it used in *Murray*, held that evidence concerning the body was admissible because it inevitably would have been discovered by the searchers without the unlawful interrogation.

Continued on next page.

Quicknotes

FRUIT OF POISONOUS TREE Doctrine that evidence obtained as a result of illegal procedures is tainted and is usually inadmissible at trial.

INDEPENDENT SOURCE Pertaining to evidence derived from another source, independent of the evidence obtained with a defective warrant.

INEVITABLE DISCOVERY If it can be shown that discovery of evidence by lawful means was inevitable, the unlawfully obtained evidence can be used in a criminal case as an exception to the exclusionary rule.

SIXTH AMENDMENT Provides the right to a speedy and public trial by impartial jury, the right to be informed of the accusation, the right to confront witnesses, and the right to have the assistance of counsel in all criminal prosecutions

CHAPTER 3

Self-Incrimination and Confessions

Quick Reference Rules of Law

Lefkowitz v. Turley

Contractor (P) v. State (D)

414 U.S. 70 (1973)

NATURE OF CASE: Appeal from decision requiring witnesses to testify concerning state contracts.

FACT SUMMARY: Lefkowitz (P) challenged a New York state law requiring state contractors to waive Fifth Amendment immunity in investigations concerning state contracts.

RULE OF LAW

A state cannot compel testimony in violation of the Fifth Amendment without offering immunity from prosecution.

FACTS: Lefkowitz (P), a New York state contractor, challenged a New York law that required contractors to waive Fifth Amendment rights or have their contracts canceled. The State (D) contended it had an overriding interest in policing its contractors.

ISSUE: Can a state compel testimony in violation of the Fifth Amendment without offering immunity from prosecution?

HOLDING AND DECISION: (White, J.) No. A state cannot compel testimony in violation of the Fifth Amendment without offering immunity from prosecution. A waiver secured under threat of severe economic sanction cannot be termed voluntary. Thus, in this case, a citizen is compelled to give testimony, against his will, that likely will be used to prosecute him. This is precisely what the Fifth Amendment prohibits. Thus, the requirement is unconstitutional.

ANALYSIS

The Fifth Amendment prohibits the involuntary eliciting of incriminating evidence. However, it does not prohibit the use of such testimony when the declarant is given immunity. Thus, it can be compelled but not used against the declarant. There are two types of immunity, use and transactional, with use being the most wide-ranging.

Quicknotes

FIFTH AMENDMENT Provides that no person shall be compelled to serve as a witness against him- or herself, be subject to trial for the same offense twice, or be deprived of life, liberty, or property without due process of law.

PRIVILEGE AGAINST SELF-INCRIMINATION A privilege guaranteed by the Fifth Amendment to the federal Constitution in a criminal proceeding for communications made by an accused and protecting an accused or witness from having to give testimony that may incriminate him- or herself.

TRANSACTIONAL IMMUNITY Also called the privilege against self-incrimination; a person's constitutional right to refuse to render testimony that may incriminate him or her if called as a witness.

Fisher v. United States

Taxpayer (D) v. Federal government (P)

425 U.S. 391 (1976)

NATURE OF CASE: Action to enforce an Internal Revenue Service summons.

FACT SUMMARY: The Internal Revenue Service sought to compel Fisher's (D) attorney to turn over accountants' worksheets, tax returns, and accountant-client correspondence Fisher (D) had obtained from his accountant and turned over to his attorney when it looked as if an income tax case against Fisher (D) might arise.

RULE OF LAW

The Fifth Amendment does not protect against compelled production of a taxpayer's papers if such production would not involve testimonial self-incrimination.

FACTS: The Internal Revenue Service (IRS) was investigating Fisher (D) for possible civil or criminal liability under the federal income tax laws. Thus, Fisher (D) went to his accountant and recovered the accountant's worksheets, retained copies of the tax returns, and retained the accountant's copies of correspondence between the accounting firm and Fisher (D). He turned them over to his attorney, but the IRS issued a summons directing the attorney to produce those documents. The attorney refused, and the Government (P) began enforcement actions. Fisher's (D) attorney argued that the Fifth Amendment's protection against self-incrimination precluded forced production of these documents.

ISSUE: Does the Fifth Amendment protect against compelled production of a taxpayer's papers if such production would not involve testimonial self-incrimination?

HOLDING AND DECISION: (White, J.) No. The Fifth Amendment does not protect against compelled production of a taxpayer's papers if such production would not involve testimonial self-incrimination. The Fifth Amendment protects against compelled production of a taxpayer's papers only if such production would involve testimonial self-incrimination, which it would not under the circumstances of this particular case. It protects against "compelled self-incrimination," not the disclosure of private information. The attorney-client privilege applies only to documents in the hands of an attorney that would have been privileged in the hands of the client by reason of the Fifth Amendment, and the documents sought would not have been privileged in Fisher's (D) hands under the Fifth Amendment. Thus, they must be produced.

ANALYSIS

The United States Supreme Court in this case recognizes that even if Fisher (D) himself had been served with the subpoena, it would not violate his rights under the Fifth Amendment. Therefore, if the principal could be compelled, his agents clearly could be compelled to produce the documents.

Quicknotes

FIFTH AMENDMENT Provides that no person shall be compelled to serve as a witness against him- or herself, be subject to trial for the same offense twice, or be deprived of life, liberty, or property without due process of law.

Schmerber v. California

Drunken driver (D) v. State (P)

384 U.S. 757 (1966)

NATURE OF CASE: Appeal from conviction for drunk driving.

FACT SUMMARY: Schmerber (D) contended the drawing of his blood without consent to show its alcohol content was a violation of the right against self-incrimination.

RULE OF LAW

Only evidence of a testimonial or communicative nature is subject to the self-incrimination clause of the Fifth Amendment.

FACTS: Schmerber (D) was arrested at a hospital where he was being treated for injuries arising out of an automobile accident. The police ordered the hospital to take a blood sample and, based on the results, Schmerber (D) was convicted of driving under the influence of alcohol. Schmerber (D) appealed, contending the use of the sample violated his Fifth Amendment right against self-incrimination. The United States Supreme Court granted certiorari.

ISSUE: Is only evidence of a testimonial or communicative nature subject to the self-incrimination clause of the Fifth Amendment?

HOLDING AND DECISION: (Brennan, J.) Yes. Only evidence of a testimonial or communicative nature is subject to the self-incrimination clause of the Fifth Amendment. The Fifth Amendment privilege against self-incrimination protects an accused only from being compelled to testify against him- or herself or otherwise provide evidence of a testimonial or communicative nature. The withdrawal of blood is non-communicative in nature and thus is not subject to the privilege. As a result, the conviction must stand.

DISSENT: (Black, J.) The forcible taking of blood over the objection of the accused clearly violates his right against self-incrimination.

ANALYSIS

The basic distinction between communicative evidence and other evidence appears in subsequent Fifth Amendment cases. In *United States v. Wade*, 388 U.S. 218 (1967), the United States Supreme Court held that a suspect could be forced to participate in a lineup without offending the Fifth Amendment.

Quicknotes

FIFTH AMENDMENT Provides that no person shall be compelled to serve as a witness against him- or herself, be subject to trial for the same offense twice, or be deprived of life, liberty, or property without due process of law.

PRIVILEGE AGAINST SELF-INCRIMINATION A privilege guaranteed by the Fifth Amendment to the federal Constitution in a criminal proceeding for communications made by an accused and protecting an accused or witness from having to give testimony that may incriminate him- or herself.

Fisher v. United States

Taxpayer (D) v. Federal government (D)

425 U.S. 391 (1976)

NATURE OF CASE: Appeal from conviction for tax evasion.

FACT SUMMARY: Fisher (D) contended the Government (P) could not compel his accountants to produce his tax records as such would violate his right against self-incrimination.

RULE OF LAW

The Fifth Amendment privilege against self-incrimination does not prohibit the production of records held by a third party.

FACTS: Fisher (D) was under investigation for violation of civil and criminal tax laws. Records pertaining to the preparation of his returns were held by his accountants, who were served with subpoenas ordering them to produce the records. Fisher (D) objected on the grounds that such production would violate his right against self-incrimination. The United States Supreme Court granted certiorari.

ISSUE: Does the Fifth Amendment privilege against self-incrimination prohibit the production of records held by a third party?

HOLDING AND DECISION: (White, J.) No. The Fifth Amendment privilege against self-incrimination does not prohibit the production of records held by a third party. The Amendment applies only to testimonial evidence, that is, only to compelling the accused to testify against himself. The papers involved in this case were the accountant's work papers. They were not Fisher's (D) and contained no testimonial declarations made by him. Thus, they were not privileged.

ANALYSIS

Some commentators argue that the United States Supreme Court left many unanswered questions in this case such as, if the papers had been owned by or prepared by Fisher (D), would they be protected? Why are work papers different from actual returns? Would they be protected if they were prepared at Fisher's (D) direction?

Quicknotes

FIFTH AMENDMENT Provides that no person shall be compelled to serve as a witness against him- or herself, be subject to trial for the same offense twice, or be deprived of life, liberty, or property without due process of law.

PRIVILEGE AGAINST SELF-INCRIMINATION A privilege guaranteed by the Fifth Amendment to the federal Constitution in a criminal proceeding for communications made by an accused and protecting an accused or witness from having to give testimony that may incriminate him- or herself.

Hiibel v. Sixth Judicial District Court of Nevada, Humboldt County

Criminal (D) v. State (P)

542 U.S. 177 (2004)

NATURE OF CASE: Appeal of state court judgment conviction for refusing to cooperate with criminal investigation.

FACT SUMMARY: Dudley Hiibel (D) refused to give a police officer his name on grounds it might incriminate him.

RULE OF LAW

Statutes requiring suspects to identify themselves during police investigations do not violate either the Fourth or the Fifth Amendment.

FACTS: [Police stopped Dudley Hiibel (D) on a reasonable suspicion that he was involved in a domestic assault. Hiibel (D) refused to reveal his identity to the police. Hiibel (D) did not challenge the stop, but he did challenge the statute criminalizing his refusal to provide identification during the stop.] Hiibel (D) was convicted and appealed.

ISSUE: Do statutes requiring suspects to identify themselves during police investigations violate either the Fourth or the Fifth Amendment?

HOLDING AND DECISION: (Kennedy, J.) No. Statutes requiring suspects to identify themselves during police investigations do not violate either the Fourth or the Fifth Amendment. Hiibel's (D) refusal to disclose his name was not based on a fear that his name would be used to incriminate him or that it would link him to a crime. He only thought his name was none of the officer's business. The Fifth Amendment does not override the Nevada legislature's judgment that his name is the business of an officer properly investigating a possible crime, absent a reasonable belief that the disclosure would tend to incriminate him. In addition, giving one's name is insignificant in the scheme of things and is therefore incriminating only in unusual circumstances. Affirmed.

DISSENT: (Stevens, J.) Hiibel (D) was the target of a criminal investigation. While the majority holds that we should not assume that the disclosure of a person's name would be used to incriminate him or her or provide a link to his or her prosecution, there is no other reason the officer would ask for it. A name can provide the key to a criminal prosecution, and to force a person to give it violates his or her Fifth Amendment rights.

ANALYSIS

The rule for determining the validity of the privilege against self-incrimination is whether the information requested of a witness might possibly tend to incriminate the witness in the future, an easy test to meet. Even if one accepts that providing an officer with one's name probably will not lead to a criminal case against the person, it certainly could, and one would therefore think this case would have had a different result.

Quicknotes

FIFTH AMENDMENT Provides that no person shall be compelled to serve as a witness against him- or herself, be subject to trial for the same offense twice, or be deprived of life, liberty, or property without due process of law.

FOURTH AMENDMENT Provides that persons be secure as to their person and private belongings against unreasonable searches and seizures.

PRIVILEGE AGAINST SELF-INCRIMINATION A privilege guaranteed by the Fifth Amendment to the federal Constitution in a criminal proceeding for communications made by an accused and protecting an accused or witness from having to give testimony that may incriminate him- or herself.

Miranda v. Arizona

Accused (D) v. State (P)

384 U.S. 436 (1966)

NATURE OF CASE: Appeal from convictions for murder.

FACT SUMMARY: In this consolidation of several cases, Miranda (D) and others appealed from their convictions, claiming that their confessions were elicited through violation of their constitutional rights.

RULE OF LAW

The prosecution may not use statements stemming from custodial interrogation of the defendant, unless the prosecution demonstrates the use of procedural safeguards effective to secure the privilege against self-incrimination.

FACTS: In the *Miranda* case, the police arrested Miranda (D) and took him to a special room where they secured a confession. In *Vignera v. New York*, Vignera (D) made oral admissions to the police after interrogation. In *Westover v. United States*, Westover (D) was handed over to the Federal Bureau of Investigation (FBI) by local authorities after they had detained and interrogated him for a lengthy period. The FBI obtained signed statements from Westover (D). Lastly, in *California v. Stewart*, the local police held Stewart (D) for five days in the station interrogating him until they secured his inculpatory statement. In none of these cases was the defendant given a full and effective warning of his rights at the outset of the interrogation process. In all of the cases, the questioning elicited oral admissions, and in three of them, signed statements as well, which were admitted at the defendants' trials. Miranda (D) and the others appealed from their convictions on the ground that their admissions were secured through means that violated their constitutional rights.

ISSUE: May the prosecution use statements stemming from custodial interrogation of the defendant?

HOLDING AND DECISION: (Warren, C.J.) No. The prosecution may not use statements stemming from custodial interrogation of the defendant, unless the prosecution demonstrates the use of procedural safeguards effective to secure the privileges against self-incrimination. Prior to any questioning, the person must be warned that he or she has a right to remain silent, that any statement he or she does make may be used as evidence against him or her, and that he or she has a right to the presence of an attorney. The defendant may waive effectuation of these rights, provided the waiver is made voluntarily, knowingly, and intelligently. Likewise, if the individual is alone and indicates in any manner that he or she does not wish to be interrogated, the police may not question him or her. In each of the cases at bar, Miranda (D) and the others were subjected to menacing custodial interrogation without the benefits of any procedural safeguards in derogation of their Fifth Amendment rights against self-incrimination. Reversed.

CONCURRENCE AND DISSENT: (Clark, J.) [Dissent in the cases of *Vignera*, *Westover*, and *Miranda*, and Concurrence in the case of *Stewart*.] The Court should have been more restrained in these cases. There is a decided lack of information and empirical data on the practical operation of requirements comparable to those announced today.

DISSENT: (Harlan, J.) The decision of the Court today in abandoning its historical case-by-case approach represents poor constitutional law. The Court's new rules are designed to "ultimately discourage any confession at all." Such an approach cannot be sustained by constitutional or policy considerations. Constitutionally, there is no basis for extending the Fifth Amendment to the police station. Historically, the ban against self-incrimination has applied only in criminal proceedings, not in "extra-legal" situations, such as interrogations. Furthermore, even if it can be applied to custodial interrogations, it has never been held to forbid all pressures on an accused, as the Court today attempts to do. Similarly, there is no constitutional basis for applying the right to counsel to custodial interrogations. The danger of injustice by allowing an untrained person to defend him- or herself in a technical court situation is the basis for this right, and that rationale is not applicable to custodial situations. In conclusion, neither the constitutional interpretations nor the consequences of today's ruling are justifiable.

DISSENT: (White, J.) Other methods would be more successful in determining which confessions have been coerced. Observers to confessions, time limits, or other remedies more tailored to fit each case should be required instead of the rule announced today. Even if it were true that all confessions obtained by police questioning are obtained as the result of compulsion, the rule is still irrational. By the same reasoning, a waiver obtained by the police before questioning should never be accepted, based on the same alleged compulsion.

Continued on next page.

ANALYSIS

In *Michigan v. Mosley*, 423 U.S. 96 (1975), detectives gave the defendant the *Miranda* warnings and then questioned him about the robbery charges for which he had been arrested. When he said he did not want to be questioned any further, the questioning stopped. A few hours later, after repeating the warnings, other detectives questioned the defendant about a homicide for which he had not been arrested. His answers incriminated him, and he was prosecuted for murder. The United States Supreme Court held that the resumption of questioning, each session being independent of the other and accompanied by warnings, did not violate *Miranda;* that is to say, *Miranda* did not create a per se proscription of indefinite duration.

Quicknotes

CUSTODIAL INTERROGATION The questioning of a suspect by police while in custody.

FIFTH AMENDMENT Provides that no person shall be compelled to serve as a witness against him- or herself, be subject to trial for the same offense twice, or be deprived of life, liberty, or property without due process of law.

Dickerson v. United States

Bank robber (D) v. Federal government (P)

530 U.S. 428 (2000)

NATURE OF CASE: Appeal from denial of motion to suppress statement based on *Miranda* violation.

FACT SUMMARY: Dickerson (D) sought to suppress a statement he made while in a Federal Bureau of Investigation field office prior to being given his *Miranda* warnings.

RULE OF LAW

When a decision of the court involves interpretation and application of the Constitution, Congress may not legislatively supersede such decision.

FACTS: Dickerson (D) was indicted for bank robbery and conspiracy to commit bank robbery. Before trial he moved to suppress a statement he made at a Federal Bureau of Investigation field office on the grounds that he had not received *Miranda* warnings before being interrogated. The district court granted the motion, and the Government (P) took an interlocutory appeal to the court of appeals, which reversed, stating that § 3501 was satisfied since the statement was made voluntarily. Dickerson (D) appealed.

ISSUE: Where a decision of the court involves interpretation and application of the Constitution, may Congress legislatively supersede such decision?

HOLDING AND DECISION: (Rehnquist, C.J.) No. When a decision of the court involves interpretation and application of the Constitution, Congress may not legislatively supersede such decision. *Miranda*, 384 U.S. 436 (1966), and its progeny govern the admissibility of statements made during custodial interrogation in both state and federal courts. Section 3501 provides that the admissibility of a custodial suspect's statements should depend on whether they are voluntarily made. Prior to *Miranda*, the admissibility of a suspect's confession was evaluated under a voluntariness test. The requirement of voluntariness was based on the Fifth Amendment right against self-incrimination and the Due Process Clause of the Fourteenth Amendment. The Court's decisions in *Miranda* and *Malloy v. Hogan*, 378 U.S. 1 (1964), changed the focus of the due process inquiry. In *Malloy*, the Court held that the Fifth Amendment's Self-Incrimination Clause is incorporated into the Due Process Clause of the Fourteenth Amendment and this applies to the states. In *Miranda*, the Court recognized that the coercion inherent in custodial interrogation makes it difficult to determine whether a statement is voluntary or involuntary and heightens the risk of self-incrimination. Section 3501 was enacted two years after the decision in *Miranda* and was intended by Congress to overrule the Court's decision in that case. The issue is whether Congress has the constitutional authority to do so. While Congress retains the ultimate authority to modify or set aside any judicially created rules of evidence and procedure that are not required by the Constitution, it may not legislatively supersede the Court's decisions that interpret and apply the Constitution. *Miranda* is a constitutional decision. The Court specifically stated that it was intended "to explore some facets of the problems of . . . applying the privilege against self-incrimination to in-custody interrogation and to give concrete constitutional guidelines for law enforcement agencies and courts to follow." The decision is otherwise replete with references to constitutional rules and standards. *Miranda* announced a constitutional rule that Congress may not supersede legislatively. Reversed.

DISSENT: (Scalia, J.) To justify the majority's result, the Court is adopting a significant new, if not entirely comprehensible, principle of constitutional law. The majority has held that statutes of Congress can be disregarded, not only when what they prescribe violates the Constitution, but also when what they prescribe contradicts a decision of the Supreme Court.

ANALYSIS

The United States Supreme Court also relies on the principle of stare decisis as weighing heavily against overruling *Miranda*, since *Miranda* warnings have become "embedded in routine police practice to the point where the warnings have become part of our national culture." Justice Scalia rejects such rationale on the basis that the court rules are both "mutable and modifiable" and that they "must make sense."

Quicknotes

FOURTEENTH AMENDMENT DUE PROCESS CLAUSE Provides that protections mandated by the U.S. Constitution and observed by the federal government are equally applicable, and therefore must be observed by the States.

FIFTH AMENDMENT Provides that no person shall be compelled to serve as a witness against him- or herself, be

Continued on next page.

subject to trial for the same offense twice, or be deprived of life, liberty, or property without due process of law.

***MIRANDA* RULE** A required warning given before any questioning by law enforcement authorities can take place. Individuals in custody receive warnings regarding their privilege against self-incrimination, right to remain silent, and right to be represented by an attorney.

***MIRANDA* WARNINGS** Specified warnings that must be communicated to a person prior to a custodial interrogation; in the absence of the communication of such warnings, any communications made during the interrogation are inadmissible at trial.

STARE DECISIS Doctrine whereby courts follow legal precedent unless there is good cause for departure.

Missouri v. Seibert

State (P) v. Murder suspect (D)

542 U.S. 600 (2004)

NATURE OF CASE: Appeal from reversal of a murder conviction.

FACT SUMMARY: Patrice Seibert (D) argued that since her murder confession was obtained by the police technique of interrogating in successive, unwarned and warned phases, known as "question first," the requirements of *Miranda*, 384 U.S. 436 (1966), were violated.

RULE OF LAW

The police technique of interrogating in successive, unwarned and warned phases violates the requirements of *Miranda*.

FACTS: In questioning Patrice Seibert (D), a murder suspect, the police interrogator employed a widely used interrogation technique known as "question first," in which the interrogator questions the suspect first, then gives the *Miranda* warnings, and then repeats the questioning until the interrogator obtains the confession or incriminating statement that the suspect has already previously provided. After employing this technique of interrogating in successive, unwarned and warned phases, Seibert (D) confessed to murder prior to her warnings and then again after being given the warnings. The trial court suppressed Seibert's (D) pre-warning confession but admitted her post-warning confession. She was convicted of murder. The Missouri Supreme Court reversed, holding that here where the interrogation was "nearly continuous," the second statement was clearly "the product of the invalid first statement" and should have been suppressed. Missouri (P) appealed.

ISSUE: Does the police technique of interrogating in successive, unwarned and warned phases violate the requirements of *Miranda*?

HOLDING AND DECISION: (Souter, J.) Yes. The police technique of interrogating in successive, unwarned and warned phases violates the requirements of *Miranda*. *Miranda* addressed interrogation practices likely to disable an individual from making a free and rational choice about speaking and held that a suspect must be "adequately and effectively" advised of the choice the Constitution guarantees. The object of the "question first" technique here utilized against Seibert (D) was to render *Miranda* warnings ineffective by waiting for a particularly opportune time to give them, after the suspect had already confessed. Just as no talismanic incantation is required to satisfy *Miranda*'s strictures, it would be absurd to think that mere recitation of the litany suffices to satisfy *Miranda* in every conceivable circumstance. The issue when interrogators question first and warn later is thus whether the warnings reasonably convey to a suspect his or her *Miranda* rights. Unless the warnings could place a suspect who has just been interrogated in a position to make an informed choice as to whether to speak, there is no practical justification for accepting the formal warnings as compliance with *Miranda*, or for treating the second stage of interrogation as distinct from the first, unwarned and inadmissible segment. By any objective measure, applied to circumstances exemplified here, it is likely that if the interrogators employ the technique of withholding warnings until after interrogation succeeds in eliciting a confession, the warnings will be ineffective in preparing the suspect for successive interrogation, close in time and similar in content. Accordingly, the question first tactic effectively threatens to thwart *Miranda*'s purpose of reducing the risk that a coerced confession would be admitted. Affirmed.

CONCURRENCE: (Breyer, J.) Courts should exclude the "fruits" of the initial unwarned questioning unless the failure to warn was in good faith.

CONCURRENCE: (Kennedy, J.) Not every violation of *Miranda* requires suppression of the evidence obtained. The scope of the *Miranda* suppression remedy depends on a consideration of whether admission of the evidence under the circumstances would frustrate *Miranda*'s "central concerns and objectives."

DISSENT: (O'Connor, J.) Because here the isolated fact of the interrogating officer's intent could not have had any bearing on Seibert's (D) capacity to comprehend and knowingly relinquish her right to remain silent, it could not by itself affect the voluntariness of her confession.

ANALYSIS

As the United States Supreme Court makes clear in *Seibert*, the reason for the increased popularity of the question first method of interrogation is to obtain a confession the suspect would not make if the suspect understood his or her rights at the outset. The underlying police assumption, which is accurate, is that with one confession in hand before the warnings, the interrogator can usually count on getting a duplicate. It is unrealistic, explained the Court, to treat two bouts of integrated and proximately conducted questioning as independent interrogations subject to independent

Continued on next page.

evaluation simply because *Miranda* warnings formally punctuate them in the middle.

Quicknotes

CUSTODIAL INTERROGATION The questioning of a suspect by police while in custody.

***MIRANDA* RULE** A required warning given before any questioning by law enforcement authorities can take place. Individuals in custody receive warnings regarding their privilege against self-incrimination, right to remain silent, and right to be represented by an attorney.

***MIRANDA* WARNINGS** Specified warnings that must be communicated to a person prior to a custodial interrogation; in the absence of the communication of such warnings, any communications made during the interrogation are inadmissible at trial.

Rhode Island v. Innis

State (P) v. Convicted murderer (D)

446 U.S. 291 (1980)

NATURE OF CASE: Appeal from a murder conviction.

FACT SUMMARY: On the way to the police station in a police car after his arrest, Innis (D) overheard remarks between the officers expressing concern that handicapped children in the area might find the hidden shotgun, whereupon Innis (D) told them to turn around so he could show them where he had hidden it.

RULE OF LAW

Any words or actions on the part of the police that they should know are reasonably likely to elicit an incriminating response from the suspect constitute "interrogation" under *Miranda* and bring the *Miranda* safeguards into play.

FACTS: After being arrested for murder, Innis (D) received the *Miranda* warnings and said he wanted to speak with an attorney. While being taken to the station in a police car, he overheard a conversation between the officers. "God forbid," one officer said, ["that one of the students at the school for the handicapped find a gun and hurt himself"]. At that point, Innis (D) told the officers to turn the car around so that he could show them where he had hidden the gun used in the murder. The gun that was thus found was used in evidence when Innis (D) was later convicted of murder. The Rhode Island Supreme Court reversed the conviction, holding that the officers had engaged in "interrogation" in violation of *Miranda*, 384 U.S. 436 (1966).

ISSUE: Do any words or actions on the part of the police that they should know are reasonably likely to elicit an incriminating response from the suspect constitute "interrogation" under *Miranda* and bring the *Miranda* safeguards into play?

HOLDING AND DECISION: (Stewart, J.) Yes. Any words or actions on the part of the police that the police should know are reasonably likely to elicit an incriminating response from the suspect constitute "interrogation" under *Miranda* and bring the *Miranda* safeguards into play. That is, the term "interrogation" as used in *Miranda* covers express questioning or its functional equivalent. In this particular case the facts are that the officers engaged in an entire conversation that consisted of no more than a few offhand remarks. The Court cannot say, on that basis, that the officers should have known that it was reasonably likely that Innis (D) would suddenly be moved to make a self-incriminating response to this overheard conversation. Therefore, whatever "subtle compulsion" Innis (D) experienced cannot be equated with "interrogation" bringing *Miranda* into play. Reversed.

DISSENT: (Marshall, J.) The Court's definition of "interrogation" for *Miranda* purposes, is equivalent, for practical purpose, to my own formulation—*Miranda* safeguards apply whenever police conduct is intended or likely to produce a response from a suspect in custody. I am, however, utterly at a loss to understand how the objective standard adopted by the Court, when applied to this case, can rationally lead to the conclusion that there was no interrogation. One can scarcely imagine a stronger appeal to the conscience of a suspect than the assertion that if the weapon is not found an innocent, handicapped child will be hurt or killed.

DISSENT: (Stevens, J.) Any statement that would normally be understood by the average listener as calling for a response is the functional equivalent of a direct question, whether or not it is punctuated by a question mark. The Court takes a narrower view in defining "interrogation" for *Miranda* purposes in a holding that represents a plain departure from the principles set forth in *Miranda*. It prohibits only those relatively few statements or actions that a police officer should know are likely to elicit an incriminating response, when statements appear to call for a response from the suspect, as well as those that are designed to do so, should be considered interrogation. What the Court does in this decision is to narrow the scope of protection afforded a suspect.

ANALYSIS

In *Harryman v. Estelle*, 616 F.2d 879 (5th Cir. 1980), Harryman was arrested as a burglary suspect. A search of his person revealed a condom containing white powder tucked under the waistband of his trousers. The officer, who later claimed he spoke out of shock and surprise, asked, "What is this?" Harryman answered: "Oh, you know what it is. It is heroin." Noting that the rigidity of the *Miranda* rules and the way they are to be applied is recognized as the decision's greatest strength, the court of appeals found *Miranda* had been violated by this interchange between officer and suspect. In its opinion, the Court stated, "It is enough to decide that

Continued on next page.

what the officer said could reasonably have had the force of a question on the accused."

Quicknotes

***MIRANDA* RULE** A required warning given before any questioning by law enforcement authorities can take place. Individuals in custody receive warnings regarding their privilege against self-incrimination, right to remain silent, and right to be represented by an attorney.

***MIRANDA* WARNINGS** Specified warnings that must be communicated to a person prior to a custodial interrogation; in the absence of the communication of such warnings, any communications made during the interrogation are inadmissible at trial.

Berghuis v. Thompkins

State (D) v. Convicted criminal (P)

560 U.S. 370 (2010)

NATURE OF CASE: Appeal from reversal of denial of habeas corpus request.

FACT SUMMARY: After Thompkins (P) was advised of his *Miranda* rights, Thompkins (P) did not expressly say he wanted to remain silent, did not want to talk with the police, or want an attorney. Eventually, toward the end of a three-hour interrogation during which Thompkins (P) was largely silent, he answered "yes" when asked if he prayed to God to forgive him for the shooting of victim who had died. Thompkins (P) was found guilty of murder and sentenced to life without parole. In his habeas corpus petition, Thompkins (P) argued that he had invoked his Fifth Amendment right to remain silent, that he had not waived that right, and that his inculpatory statements were involuntary.

RULE OF LAW

(1) A criminal suspect's silence during an interrogation does not invoke his or her right to remain silent.

(2) A criminal suspect waives his or her right to remain silent when he or she knowingly and voluntarily makes a statement to the police.

(3) The police are not required to obtain a waiver of a criminal suspect's *Miranda* rights before interrogating the suspect.

FACTS: After advising respondent Thompkins (P) of his rights, in full compliance with *Miranda v. Arizona*, 384 U.S. 436 (1966), detective Helgert and another officer interrogated him about a shooting in which one victim died. At no point did Thompkins (P) say that he wanted to remain silent, that he did not want to speak with the police, or that he wanted an attorney. He refused, however, to sign a written acknowledgment that he had been advised of or understood his *Miranda* rights. He was largely silent during the three-hour interrogation, but near the end, he answered "yes" when asked if he prayed to God to forgive him for the shooting. He moved to suppress his statements, claiming that he had invoked his Fifth Amendment right to remain silent, that he had not waived that right, and that his inculpatory statements were involuntary. The trial court denied the motion, the state's intermediate court affirmed, and the state's highest court denied review. The jury found Thompkins (P) guilty, and he was sentenced to life in prison without parole. The district court denied his subsequent habeas request, reasoning that Thompkins (P) did not invoke his right to remain silent and was not coerced into making statements during the interrogation, and that it was not unreasonable for the state's intermediate appellate court to determine that he had waived his right to remain silent. The court of appeals reversed, holding that the state court was unreasonable in finding an implied waiver of Thompkins's (P) right to remain silent. The Unites States Supreme Court granted certiorari.

ISSUE:

(1) Does a criminal suspect's silence during an interrogation invoke his or her right to remain silent?

(2) Does a criminal suspect waive his or her right to remain silent when he or she knowingly and voluntarily makes a statement to the police?

(3) Are the police required to obtain a waiver of a criminal suspect's *Miranda* rights before interrogating the suspect?

HOLDING AND DECISION: (Kennedy, J.)

(1) No. A criminal suspect's silence during an interrogation does not invoke his or her right to remain silent. A suspect's *Miranda* right to counsel must be invoked "unambiguously." If the accused makes an "ambiguous or equivocal" statement or no statement, the police are not required to end the interrogation, or ask questions to clarify the accused's intent. There is no principled reason to adopt different standards for determining when an accused has invoked the *Miranda* right to remain silent and the *Miranda* right to counsel. Both protect the privilege against compulsory self-incrimination by requiring an interrogation to cease when either right is invoked. The unambiguous invocation requirement results in an objective inquiry that "avoid[s] difficulties of proof and ... provide[s] guidance to officers" on how to proceed in the face of ambiguity. Had Thompkins (P) said that he wanted to remain silent or that he did not want to talk, he would have invoked his right to end the questioning. He did neither, and therefore did not invoke his right to remain silent.

(2) Yes. A criminal suspect waives his or her right to remain silent when he or she knowingly and voluntarily makes a statement to the police. A waiver must be "the product of a free and deliberate choice rather than intimidation, coercion, or deception" and "made with a full awareness of both the nature of the right being abandoned and the consequences of the decision to abandon it." Such a waiver may

Continued on next page.

be "implied" through a "defendant's silence, coupled with an understanding of his or her rights and a course of conduct indicating waiver." If the State (D) establishes that a *Miranda* warning was given and that it was understood by the accused, an accused's uncoerced statement establishes an implied waiver. The record here shows that Thompkins (P) waived his right to remain silent. First, the lack of any contention that he did not understand his rights indicates that he knew what he gave up when he spoke. Second, his answer to the question about God is a "course of conduct indicating waiver" of that right. Had he wanted to remain silent, he could have said nothing in response or unambiguously invoked his *Miranda* rights, ending the interrogation. That he made a statement nearly three hours after receiving a *Miranda* warning does not overcome the fact that he engaged in a course of conduct indicating waiver. Third, there is no evidence that his statement was coerced. He does not claim that police threatened or injured him or that he was fearful. The interrogation took place in a standard-sized room in the middle of the day, and there is no authority for the proposition that a three-hour interrogation is inherently coercive. The fact that the question referred to religious beliefs also does not render Thompkins's (P) statement involuntary.

(3) No. The police are not required to obtain a waiver of a criminal suspect's *Miranda* rights before interrogating the suspect. Thompkins (P) argues that, even if his answer to Helgert could constitute a waiver of his right to remain silent, the police were not allowed to question him until they first obtained a waiver. However, a rule requiring a waiver at the outset would be inconsistent with precedent holding that courts can infer a waiver "from the actions and words of the person interrogated." Any waiver, express or implied, may be contradicted by an invocation at any time, terminating further interrogation. When the suspect knows that *Miranda* rights can be invoked at any time, he or she can reassess his or her immediate and long-term interests as the interrogation progresses. After giving a *Miranda* warning, police may interrogate a suspect who has neither invoked nor waived *Miranda* rights. Thus, the police were not required to obtain a waiver of Thompkins's (P) *Miranda* rights before interrogating him. Reversed.

DISSENT: (Sotomayor, J.) Under the majority's decisions, criminal suspects must now unambiguously invoke their right to remain silent—which, counterintuitively, requires them to speak. At the same time, suspects will be legally presumed to have waived their rights even if they have given no clear expression of their intent to do so. Those results are not supported by *Miranda* or subsequent precedent and are inconsistent with the fair-trial principles on which those precedents are grounded. The question whether a suspect has validly waived his or her right is "entirely distinct" as a matter of law from whether he or she invoked that right. The questions are related, however, in terms of the practical effect on the exercise of a suspect's rights. A suspect may at any time revoke his or her prior waiver of rights, or guard against the possibility of a future finding that he or she implicitly waived those rights, by invoking the rights and thereby requiring the police to cease questioning. Thus, analytically, the first question should be whether Thompkins (P) waived his right to remain silent. Precedent places a heavy burden on the prosecution to show waiver, and the presumption is that the suspect did not waive his or her rights. Waiver may not be presumed merely because a confession was eventually obtained. Here, the circumstances of the interrogation show that Thompkins (P) never waived his right to remain silent. He never expressly waived that right, and his refusal to sign even an acknowledgment that he understood his *Miranda* rights evinces, if anything, intent not to waive those rights. So does his silence during the interrogation for nearly three hours. Essentially, his course of conduct did not manifest waiver. Thus, it is objectively unreasonable to conclude the prosecution met its "heavy burden" of proof on a record "consisting of three one-word answers, following 2 hours and 45 minutes of silence punctuated by a few largely nonverbal responses to unidentified questions." By so concluding, however, the majority turns long-standing *Miranda* precedent on its head and significantly dilutes its protections and lowers the prosecution's hitherto high burden of proof. Because *Miranda* and its precedents perceive custodial interrogation to be inherently coercive, requiring proof of a course of conduct beyond the inculpatory statements themselves is critical to ensuring that those statements are voluntary admissions and not the dubious product of an overborne will. Because Thompkins (P) should prevail on his waiver argument, the issue of whether he invoked his right to remain silent should not have been reached, as it was by the majority. Nonetheless, even as to Thompkins's (P) argument that in any event his conduct invoked his right to remain silent, the majority is wrong in holding that a suspect must expressly invoke that right by speaking. Such a novel clear-statement rule for invocation invites police to question a suspect at length—notwithstanding his or her persistent refusal to answer questions—in the hope of eventually obtaining a single inculpatory response that will suffice to prove waiver of rights. Contrary to the majority's reasoning, there has been a precedential distinction between protections involving the right to counsel and the right to remain silent. The appropriate rule is that when a suspect's conduct is sufficiently unambiguous as to invocation, the police must scrupulously honor that conduct. While this

Continued on next page.

does not provide a bright-line rule, as does the majority's clear-statement rule, the police nonetheless have been following the prior fact-specific rule for over three decades and no evidence has been presented that the status quo has proved unworkable. The clear-statement rule is also a poor fit for the right to silence, since advising a suspect that he or she has a "right to remain silent" is unlikely to convey that he or she must speak (and must do so in some particular fashion) to ensure the right will be protected. By contrast, telling a suspect "he [or she] has the right to the presence of an attorney, and that if he [or she] cannot afford an attorney one will be appointed for him [or her] prior to any questioning if he [or she] so desires," implies the need for speech to exercise that right. Moreover, if a suspect's statements or conduct is ambiguous, it is not an undue burden to have the police ask questions clarifying the suspect's intent, such as, "Do you want to talk to us?" Such an approach is a more faithful application of precedents than the majority's clear-statement approach.

ANALYSIS

Prior to this decision, courts had to grapple with doctrinal questions of what it took to make a legally valid invocation of, or waiver of, *Miranda* rights. If a suspect's conduct fell between these extremes, there was also the issue of what was acceptable police conduct. The *Thompkins* decision has seemingly done away with those issues. Now, where the police have given the suspect the proper *Miranda* warnings and the suspect understands those warnings and has not been coerced, until the moment when the suspect clearly invokes one of his or her *Miranda* rights, the police may continue to seek a waiver of those rights, and, even absent a clear waiver, as soon as the suspect says anything to the police he or she will be held to have impliedly waived his or her rights.

Quicknotes

FIFTH AMENDMENT Provides that no person shall be compelled to serve as a witness against him- or herself, be subject to trial for the same offense twice, or be deprived of life, liberty, or property without due process of law.

HABEAS CORPUS A proceeding in which a defendant brings a writ to compel a judicial determination of whether he or she is lawfully being held in custody.

INCULPATORY A statement or other evidence tending to show a person's guilt in committing a criminal act.

***MIRANDA* RULE** A required warning given before any questioning by law enforcement authorities can take place. Individuals in custody receive warnings regarding their privilege against self-incrimination, right to remain silent, and right to be represented by an attorney.

***MIRANDA* WARNINGS** Specified warnings that must be communicated to a person prior to a custodial interrogation; in the absence of the communication of such warnings, any communications made during the interrogation are inadmissible at trial.

Massiah v. United States

Convicted drug dealer (D) v. Federal government (P)

377 U.S. 201 (1964)

NATURE OF CASE: Appeal from conviction for violating narcotic laws.

FACT SUMMARY: Massiah (D) was convicted after he gave incriminating statements to a person he did not know was a Government (P) agent.

RULE OF LAW

Authorities cannot use incriminating statements gained from an accused through stealth after indictment and in the absence of counsel.

FACTS: Massiah (D) was arrested on drug charges after being indicted. He was released on bail and made incriminating statements to a former accomplice who was secretly working for the police. He was convicted on the basis of the statements, and he appealed, contending he had been forced to self-incriminate. The court of appeals affirmed, and the United States Supreme Court granted certiorari.

ISSUE: Can authorities use incriminating statements gained from an accused through stealth and after indictment and in the absence of counsel?

HOLDING AND DECISION: (Stewart, J.) No. Authorities cannot use incriminating statements gained from an accused through stealth after indictment and in the absence of counsel. Massiah (D) was denied his Sixth Amendment right by the admission of evidence at trial of his own incriminating words, which federal agents had deliberately elicited from him after he had been indicted and in the absence of his counsel. He believed he was speaking to an accomplice. He was not warned that he was speaking to a police agent. Therefore, he was compelled to self-incriminate and the statements must be held inadmissible. Reversed.

DISSENT: (White, J.) Massiah (D) was never denied counsel. He could have conferred with counsel at any time. The admissions were made voluntarily and thus were admissible.

ANALYSIS

A problem arose in the wake of *Massiah*. The United States Supreme Court never clearly explained when a defendant was "formally charged," so that the right to counsel and self-incrimination protections are triggered. Clearly, after an indictment, the rights are triggered, but short of that, no clear pronouncement was made.

Quicknotes

PRIVILEGE AGAINST SELF-INCRIMINATION A privilege guaranteed by the Fifth Amendment to the federal Constitution in a criminal proceeding for communications made by an accused and protecting an accused or witness from having to give testimony that may incriminate him- or herself.

RIGHT TO COUNSEL Right conferred by the Sixth Amendment that the accused shall be provided effective legal assistance in a criminal proceeding.

SIXTH AMENDMENT Provides the right to a speedy and public trial by impartial jury, the right to be informed of the accusation, the right to confront witnesses, and the right to have the assistance of counsel in all criminal prosecutions.

Brewer v. Williams

Government (P) v. Convicted murderer (D)

430 U.S. 387 (1977)

NATURE OF CASE: Appeal from grant of petition for habeas corpus.

FACT SUMMARY: Williams (D) contended his conviction was invalid as it was based on evidence obtained through the denial of his right to counsel.

RULE OF LAW

Once the right to counsel is invoked and the suspect refuses to answer questions, any evidence gained through subsequent interrogation is inadmissible.

FACTS: Williams (D), who was arrested for the murder of a young girl, immediately invoked his right to counsel and his right to remain silent in counsel's absence. He was transported, without counsel, between cities and was asked by the transporting officer to reveal the location of the body so that it could receive a "Christian burial." Williams (D) led the officer to the body and was subsequently convicted. He brought a petition for habeas corpus, contending the evidence, i.e., the body, was obtained in violation of his right to counsel. The district court granted the petition, and the court of appeals affirmed. The United States Supreme Court granted certiorari.

ISSUE: Once the right to counsel is invoked and the suspect refuses to answer questions, is any evidence gained through subsequent interrogation admissible?

HOLDING AND DECISION: (Stewart, J.) No. Once the right to counsel has been invoked and the suspect refuses to answer, any evidence obtained through continued custodial interrogation is inadmissible. The questioning in the car was clearly aimed at obtaining evidence in contravention of Williams's (D) asserted right to remain silent and to have his counsel present during questioning. The right clearly was not waived and thus was violated. As a result, the evidence was inadmissible. Affirmed.

CONCURRENCE: (Marshall, J.) Detective Leaming isolated Williams (D) from his lawyers and intentionally "persuaded" him to give incriminating evidence. It is the intentional police misconduct the Court rightly condemns.

CONCURRENCE: (Powell, J.) The interpretation of the facts finding custodial interrogation occurred after the right to the assistance of counsel attached leads inevitably to the result in this case.

CONCURRENCE: (Stevens, J.) The invocation of the right to counsel came at a critical stage of the proceedings. The state cannot be permitted to dishonor its promise to an accused's attorney to postpone interrogation.

DISSENT: (Burger, C.J.) This decision carries the exclusionary rule to an absurd extent, punishing the public for the mistakes and misdeeds of law enforcement officers instead of punishing the officer directly.

DISSENT: (White, J.) Williams (D) clearly waived his right to counsel by speaking to the police. Thus, the evidence was admissible.

DISSENT: (Blackmun, J.) This was not an example of purposeful police conduct. The trip was necessary to transport Williams (D) to Des Moines. Merely making a Christian plea on behalf of the family seems to me not unreasonable and is simply not the type of coercion for which a reversal should be granted.

ANALYSIS

Williams (D) was retried and again found guilty. On certiorari, the United States Supreme Court held that the body would have been found eventually by law enforcement officers, and thus under the rule of inevitable discovery, the evidence was admissible.

Quicknotes

EXCLUSIONARY RULE A rule precluding the introduction at trial of evidence unlawfully obtained in violation of the federal constitutional safeguards against unreasonable searches and seizures.

HABEAS CORPUS A proceeding in which a defendant brings a writ to compel a judicial determination of whether he or she is lawfully being held in custody.

INEVITABLE DISCOVERY If it can be shown that discovery of evidence by lawful means was inevitable, the unlawfully obtained evidence can be used in a criminal case as an exception to the exclusionary rule.

RIGHT TO COUNSEL Right conferred by the Sixth Amendment that the accused shall be provided effective legal assistance in a criminal proceeding.

Montejo v. Louisiana

Individual (D) v. State (P)

556 U.S. 778 (2009)

NATURE OF CASE: Appeal from state high-court decision affirming defendant's conviction.

FACT SUMMARY: After Montejo (D) admitted to a murder, a state judge ordered the appointment of an attorney. Following the appointment, Montejo (D) penned a letter to the victim's wife admitting that he murdered the victim. The prosecution used the letter at trial to convict Montejo (D) of the murder.

RULE OF LAW

The court-ordered appointment of legal counsel, by itself, does not preclude additional police-initiated interrogation outside the presence of counsel.

FACTS: In February 2002, police found the body of a man in a home. During their investigation, local police questioned Montejo (D) who, after waiving his *Miranda* rights, eventually admitted to the murder. The State (P) brought Montejo (D) to court and charged him with first-degree murder. During that initial hearing, the court appointed an attorney for Montejo (D). Later the same day, two police detectives visited Montejo's (D) jail cell and requested that he accompany them in a search for the murder weapon. The detectives read Montejo (D) his *Miranda* rights for a second time and he agreed to go with the officers. During the excursion, Montejo (D) wrote a letter to the victim's wife admitting to the murder. After returning to the police station, Montejo (D) then met with his court-appointed attorney for the first time. At trial, the prosecution admitted the letter and a jury convicted Montejo (D). The Louisiana Supreme Court affirmed the conviction. Montejo (D) appealed.

ISSUE: Does the court-ordered appointment of legal counsel, by itself, preclude additional police-initiated interrogation outside the presence of counsel?

HOLDING AND DECISION: (Scalia, J.) No. The court-ordered appointment of legal counsel, by itself, does not preclude additional police-initiated interrogation outside the presence of counsel. In *Michigan v. Jackson*, 475 U.S. 625 (1986), this Court forbade police from initiating further interrogations of a criminal defendant once the defendant has requested counsel at an arraignment or similar preliminary hearing. That decision is overruled. Our prior case law, including *Miranda*, 384 U.S. 436 (1966), provides adequate protection to accused persons for both their Fifth and Sixth Amendment rights. The right to counsel may be waived so long as the relinquishment is voluntary, knowing, and intelligent. The right may be waived whether or not the defendant is already represented. When a defendant is read his *Miranda* rights and agrees to waive those rights, such a waiver includes waiver of the right to counsel. In addition, where a defendant affirmatively requests an attorney at arraignment, our cases have held police cannot make further attempts to question a defendant, unless the defendant initiates the contact. For any further police-initiated contact, any subsequent waiver of the right to counsel will be held invalid. This rule protects against police badgering. At issue here is whether the court-ordered appointment of an attorney, as opposed to a defendant's affirmative request for an attorney, is an event that will make any subsequent waiver of the right to counsel involuntary. It does not. The simple appointment of an attorney for an accused does not constitute an accused's affirmative election to be represented by counsel. Therefore, an accused who stands silent while a court appoints counsel may still validly waive his or her right for counsel to be present during any additional police-initiated questioning. In this matter, there remains a question of fact whether Montejo (D) asserted his right to counsel when the police officers approached him after his arraignment. If he made a valid request for counsel at that time, any subsequent waiver of such right would have been invalid under our prior case law. Thus, the case should be remanded for a determination of those facts. Vacated and remanded.

DISSENT: (Stevens, J.) The majority flagrantly misinterprets the *Michigan v. Jackson* case and the rationale underlying its decision. *Jackson* relied on the express Sixth Amendment right to counsel. That right is to protect unsophisticated criminal defendants at all critical junctions of the criminal proceeding. Once the court ordered the appointment of an attorney, the police should not have been allowed to initiate any further questioning of him. In this matter, any subsequent waiver of the right to counsel after such police-initiated questioning would be invalid.

ANALYSIS

This was a 5-4 decision, with Justice Kennedy joining with conservative Justices Alito, Scalia, Thomas, and Roberts. In essence, the Court overruled *Michigan v. Jackson*, 475 U.S. 625 (1986), because it felt it was superfluous. The majority felt the *Miranda* protections were more than adequate to protect an accused's right

Continued on next page.

to counsel. In a similar decision, *Berghuis v. Thompkins*, 560 U.S. 370 (2010), the same conservative majority held that defendants must state affirmatively during police questioning that they wish to invoke their right to remain silent.

Quicknotes

FIFTH AMENDMENT Provides that no person shall be compelled to serve as a witness against him- or herself, be subject to trial for the same offense twice, or be deprived of life, liberty, or property without due process of law.

RIGHT TO COUNSEL Right conferred by the Sixth Amendment that the accused shall be provided effective legal assistance in a criminal proceeding.

SIXTH AMENDMENT Provides the right to a speedy and public trial by impartial jury, the right to be informed of the accusation, the right to confront witnesses, and the right to have the assistance of counsel in all criminal prosecutions.

WAIVER The intentional or voluntary forfeiture of a recognized right.

CHAPTER 4

Identifying Suspects

Quick Reference Rules of Law

United States v. Wade

Federal government (P) v. Convicted bank robber (D)

388 U.S. 218 (1967)

NATURE OF CASE: Appeal from conviction for bank robbery.

FACT SUMMARY: Wade (D) contended he had a right to counsel at a post-indictment pretrial lineup.

RULE OF LAW

A post-indictment lineup is a critical stage in a criminal prosecution, and the accused is entitled to the assistance of counsel at this time.

FACTS: Wade (D) was convicted of bank robbery based on witness identifications that stemmed from a pretrial, post-indictment lineup. Wade (D) was not given an opportunity to have his counsel present at this lineup. His attorney unsuccessfully moved for an acquittal on the basis that Wade (D) had been denied his Sixth Amendment right to counsel. The Government (P) argued that pretrial lineups are not critical stages in the prosecution, and, therefore, no right to counsel existed. The United States Supreme Court granted certiorari.

ISSUE: Is a post-indictment lineup a critical stage in a criminal prosecution, and is the accused entitled to the assistance of counsel at this time?

HOLDING AND DECISION: (Brennan, J.) Yes. A post-indictment lineup is a critical stage in a criminal prosecution, and the accused is entitled to the assistance of counsel at this time. Because of the inherently unreliable nature of eyewitness testimony, lineups present an unusually ripe time for manipulation of witness perception. Because the result of such procedures bears directly on the question of guilt or innocence, the conduct of the lineup must be closely monitored. The presence of the suspect's counsel is essential for this purpose. In this case it is unclear whether the in-court identification was inextricably intertwined with the faulty pretrial lineup. If the in-court identification was independent, it may be admitted. Vacated.

CONCURRENCE AND DISSENT: (White, J.) The Court improperly announces a per se rule of constitutional law. Whether or not a pretrial lineup requires invocation of the right for counsel is a factual question and must be determined on a case-by-case basis.

ANALYSIS

In *Powell v. Alabama*, 287 U.S. 45 (1964), the United States Supreme Court announced the basic guideline governing when the Sixth Amendment right to counsel is triggered. It held that such right exists at each "critical stage" of a criminal prosecution. Thus, by definition, if the time period within which a suspect is denied counsel is not considered to be critical to the ultimate determination of guilt or innocence, then the right to counsel does not exist.

Quicknotes

PER SE By itself, without more; taken alone; not requiring additional evidence for proof, as a matter of law.

RIGHT TO COUNSEL Right conferred by the Sixth Amendment that the accused shall be provided effective legal assistance in a criminal proceeding.

SIXTH AMENDMENT Provides the right to a speedy and public trial by impartial jury, the right to be informed of the accusation, the right to confront witnesses, and the right to have the assistance of counsel in all criminal prosecutions.

Manson v. Brathwaite

Government (P) v. Convicted drug dealer (D)

432 U.S. 98 (1977)

NATURE OF CASE: Appeal from the reversal of a conviction for the sale of narcotics.

FACT SUMMARY: Glover, a police officer, after describing the man who had sold him heroin, was given a photograph of the suspect for identification purposes.

RULE OF LAW

If identification is independently reliable, it will not be excluded solely because police identification techniques were suggestive.

FACTS: Glover, an undercover policeman, purchased heroin from Brathwaite (D). During the purchase, which took several minutes, Glover was no more than two or three feet from him. Glover returned to headquarters and described the individual whom he had seen in great detail. From the description, another officer pulled a picture of Brathwaite (D) from their files. Glover saw the photograph two days later and promptly identified Brathwaite (D) as the seller. The photograph and identification were subsequently admitted at trial without objection. Brathwaite (D) was found guilty and was sentenced to prison. Fourteen months later, Brathwaite (D) challenged the photographic identification on the ground it was too suggestive, thereby rendering the identification itself per se excludable. The court of appeals reversed the conviction on this basis, holding that independent indicia of reliability could not overcome the suggestibility of the identification technique.

ISSUE: If identification is independently reliable, will it be excluded solely because police identification techniques were suggestive?

HOLDING AND DECISION: (Blackmun, J.) No. If identification is independently reliable, it will not be excluded solely because police identification techniques were suggestive. The circuits have split over whether or not a per se rule should apply to excluding identification based on suggestive identification procedures. Some favor per se exclusion. Others take each case separately in order to determine if the identification would be otherwise reliable, and, if so, allowing it in evidence. We think the latter theory is correct. To hold otherwise would exclude relevant information from the jury merely because of improper police procedure. The case-by-case approach will be a deterrent to the police and will prevent the guilty from being freed. The linchpin in this area is the independent reliability of the identification. Here we have a trained police officer who viewed Brathwaite (D) closely for several minutes from within two feet. Glover then described Brathwaite (D) in detail shortly thereafter. The pictorial identification was two days later. All of this indicates independent reliability based on a trained observer, a prompt identification, and a reasonable opportunity to view the suspect. Independently reliable identifications need not be excluded to satisfy due process requirements. Reversed.

CONCURRENCE: (Stevens, J.) While this case is extremely close, I am convinced of the independent reliability of the identification.

DISSENT: (Marshall, J.) In this case, the Court disregards distinctions in analysis developed in previous decisions and fashions a rule that is not supported by precedent. The use of a single picture on the presentation of a single suspect is inherently suggestive.

ANALYSIS

The per se rule is used to discourage police abuses. The majority appears to indicate that non-police witnesses will be less likely to survive an ad hoc, case-by-case approach because they are more prone to misidentification since they are not trained observers. The stress on them is also deemed greater, which may cause faulty identifications. No hard and fast rules can be developed in this area, but the United States Supreme Court apparently focuses on (1) the length of time in which the accused was viewed; (2) the nature of the witness; (3) the circumstances; (4) the length of time between the incident and the identification; and (5) the ability to give an initial description of the accused.

Quicknotes

PER SE By itself, without more; taken alone; not requiring additional evidence for proof, as a matter of law.

State v. Martinez

State (P) v. Convicted first-degree murderer (D)

N.M. Sup. Ct., 478 P.3d 880 (2020)

NATURE OF CASE: Appeal by convicted murderer from denial of motion to suppress eyewitness testimony.

FACT SUMMARY: Ricardo Martinez (Martinez) (D), who was convicted of murder in the first degree, moved to suppress eyewitness testimony against him, contending that the standard used for admitting the evidence, which followed the federal rule articulated in *Manson v. Brathwaite,* 432 U.S. 98 (1977), was no longer viable in light of advances in scientific knowledge of eyewitness memory, perception, and recall, and, therefore, violated his due process rights.

RULE OF LAW

(1) Where a prevailing test for the admissibility at trial of eyewitness identification evidence is demonstrably untethered to advances in scientific knowledge of eyewitness memory, perception, and recall made since the test was first articulated, due process requires that the test be abandoned and replaced with a test that comports with sound, current scientific knowledge.

(2) A per se rule of exclusion, whereby an identification of a defendant made by a witness as a result of a police identification procedure that is unnecessarily suggestive and conducive to irreparable misidentification, and any subsequent identification by the same witness, is suppressed, comports with sound, current scientific knowledge of eyewitness memory, perception, and recall, and, therefore, due process.

FACTS: Ricardo Martinez (Martinez) (D) was convicted of murder in the first degree. Martinez (D) sought reversal and a new trial on grounds that the trial court erred by denying his motion to suppress out-of-court and in-court eyewitness identification testimony. In admitting the evidence, the trial court had applied the prevailing federal test for eyewitness reliability, articulated in *Manson v. Brathwaite,* 432 U.S. 98 (1977), which asks whether police identification procedures were "unnecessarily suggestive" and, if so, then weighs specified factors in deciding the "linchpin" issue of whether the eyewitness identification was nonetheless sufficiently reliable to satisfy federal due process requirements. Martinez (D) contended that the analytical assumptions underlying the *Manson* test were no longer valid in the face of advances in scientific knowledge of eyewitness memory, perception, and recall, so that the trial court's admission of eyewitness evidence against him pursuant to *Manson* violated his state due process rights. The state's highest court granted review.

ISSUE:

(1) Where a prevailing test for the admissibility at trial of eyewitness identification evidence is demonstrably untethered to advances in scientific knowledge of eyewitness memory, perception, and recall made since the test was first articulated, does due process require that the test be abandoned and replaced with a test that comports with sound, current scientific knowledge?

(2) Does a per se rule of exclusion, whereby an identification of a defendant made by a witness as a result of a police identification procedure that is unnecessarily suggestive and conducive to irreparable misidentification, and any subsequent identification by the same witness, is suppressed, comport with sound, current scientific knowledge of eyewitness memory, perception, and recall, and, therefore, due process?

HOLDING AND DECISION: (Vigil, C.J.)

(1) Yes. Where a prevailing test for the admissibility at trial of eyewitness identification evidence is demonstrably untethered to advances in scientific knowledge of eyewitness memory, perception, and recall made since the test was first articulated, due process requires that the test be abandoned and replaced with a test that comports with sound, current scientific knowledge. The reliability and significance of post-*Manson* scientific studies addressing the psychological factors affecting eyewitness identifications are now widely acknowledged by the courts, as are the shortcomings of the *Manson* framework. A vast body of social science research conducted after *Manson* was decided has demonstrated that most of the five *Manson* "reliability" factors do not correlate at all with the reliability of an eyewitness's identification, and that as a consequence of the powerful effect eyewitness identification has on juries, especially when stated in a confident manner, mistaken identification evidence is the most significant cause of wrongful convictions in the United States. In this regard, the scientific literature demonstrates multiple reasons why eyewitness testimony can be erroneous despite the fact that a witness testifies in good faith and with a high degree of confidence. Scientific studies have

Continued on next page.

shown that an eyewitness's memory of a crime frequently does not contain the degree of detail sought by criminal investigators. Instead, when an eyewitness recalls a crime, the witness unconsciously reconstructs their memory of the crime, and unknowingly fills in the gaps in their factual memory of the crime based on such factors as the eyewitness's expectations, attitude, beliefs, and knowledge of similar events. These different sources of information are automatically blended together in the eyewitness's memory to produce an account of the crime that is apparently seamless and coherent but that may contain inaccuracies. Additionally, an eyewitness's biases influence not only what they recall about a crime, but also what they perceive and encode into memory about the crime. Eyewitness testimony may also be erroneous as a result of what is known as the "misinformation effect," whereby the eyewitness's memory of a crime—which is reconstructed by the eyewitness—can be altered by information that the eyewitness learns after the crime from other sources such as other eyewitnesses, the police, the prosecutor, and the media. Another reason for misidentification stems from "source monitoring errors." This category of cognitive error occurs when eyewitnesses become confused about where they learned information about a crime or where they saw an individual, and, in addition, there is "hindsight bias," which refers to the cognitive error that occurs when an individual knows how an event turns out and this knowledge influences the individual's memory of what the individual believes about what actually occurred. Thus, when an eyewitness learns that a suspect has been indicted and is going to be tried for a crime, this information can alter an eyewitness's memory of the crime and what the eyewitness remembers or was thinking when the crime occurred. Other factors that lead to misidentifications are "eyewitness overconfidence" and tendencies toward "relative judgment." As to eyewitness overconfidence, because people tend to overestimate the accuracy of their perceptions and memory, eyewitnesses are likely to be overconfident about the accuracy of their account of the crime and their identification of the suspect as the perpetrator of the crime. Also, because confidence in a memory is malleable, post-event information can increase an eyewitness's confidence in a false memory. As to relative judgments, in the context of a lineup or photo array, eyewitnesses are likely to make a relative judgment in identifying a perpetrator such that eyewitnesses will choose the person who most closely resembles their memory of the perpetrator of the crime. Relative judgments stem from two assumptions frequently made by eyewitnesses: (1) law enforcement would not conduct a lineup if they did not have a suspect, and (2) eyewitnesses feel pressure from law enforcement, relatives, friends, and themselves to make an identification. Apart from these factors, experts agree that certain additional factors, described as "variables," may inherently impair the ability of witnesses to accurately process what they observe. "System" variables relate to the identification procedure itself, whereas "estimator" variables relate to the circumstances of the crime and a witness's observation of it. System variables bear on the suggestiveness of an identification procedure used by law enforcement. "Estimator" variables are used to evaluate an identification's reliability, such as variables relating to the focus of a witness's attention during the commission of a crime, a factor that is often dependent on a witness's level of stress or distraction at the time. For example, if a weapon is visibly present during an encounter, that can negatively affect a witness's memory for faces and identification accuracy because witnesses tend to focus their attention on the weapon instead of on the face or appearance of the perpetrator, or on other details of the encounter. According to the legal literature, the *Manson* reliability test does not account for these factors, and, therefore, can readily result in misidentifications. There is broad consensus that three of the five *Manson* factors—view, attention, and certainty—are insufficiently independent from each other and from the suggestiveness of a given identification procedure to be accurate predictors of reliability and accuracy. These concerns have prompted commentators to call for the adoption of new, science-driven admissibility standards in place of the reliability-based formulation set out in *Manson*, and the courts and legislatures in some jurisdictions have responded by adopting measures that align to a greater or lesser degree with modern empirical realities. In fact, this state's legislature has enacted such remedial legislation (the Accurate Eyewitness Identification Act) that requires law enforcement to use specific eyewitness identification procedures designed to minimize the possibility of mistaken identifications. Because advances in scientific knowledge reveal serious flaws in the assumptions and premises underlying *Manson*, blind adherence to the outdated *Manson* reliability test would be a failing, especially given that by adhering to it the risks of misidentification are great and the stakes, including wrongful convictions, are high. Accordingly, given that the *Manson* standard is both scientifically and jurisprudentially unsound and flawed, it violates due process under this state's constitution, and must be abandoned and replaced with a rule that accounts

Continued on next page.

for modern scientific knowledge of eyewitness identification.

(2) Yes. A per se rule of exclusion, whereby an identification of a defendant made by a witness as a result of a police identification procedure that is unnecessarily suggestive and conducive to irreparable misidentification, and any subsequent identification by the same witness, is suppressed, comports with sound, current scientific knowledge of eyewitness memory, perception, and recall, and, therefore, due process. Such a bright-line exclusionary rule, triggered on the basis of suggestiveness alone, has replaced the *Manson* rule in its entirety in Massachusetts and New York in response to the *Manson* rule's inherent frailties. In addition to adopting such a rule, the Massachusetts Supreme Judicial Court has established a protocol for the police to follow in conducting a photographic identification procedure, based on the court's recognition that there is a near consensus in the relevant scientific community that the failure to follow such a protocol increases the risk of misidentification. Under the rule now adopted, the question of whether the identification is unnecessarily suggestive focuses not only on the identification procedure itself, but also on whether the police have a good reason to use a suggestive identification procedure in the first instance. Under this approach, the initial burden falls on the accused to establish prima facie that some aspect of the identification procedure employed by the police was suggestive in nature. If the accused does not meet that burden, suppression is not required. However, if the accused demonstrates that the identification procedure contained one or more suggestive elements, the burden shifts to the state to prove by clear and convincing evidence either that (1) the procedure employed was not so suggestive as to materially taint the identification made by the eyewitness, i.e., that any departure from proper procedure could not have increased the risk of misidentification, or (2) good reason existed for the police to employ the suggestive procedure in the first instance. If the state fails to carry its responsive burden, the identification evidence and any subsequent in-court identification must be suppressed.

ANALYSIS

Under the rule set forth in *Manson v. Brathwaite*, 432 U.S. 98 (1977), federal due process requires a court to determine whether the procedure used for eyewitness identification was so impermissibly suggestive as to give rise to a very substantial likelihood of irreparable misidentification and whether, under the totality of the circumstances, the identification was still reliable. Pursuant to this due process standard, even if the procedures used for the identification are determined to be impermissibly suggestive, the identification may still be admitted if its reliability sufficiently outweighs the corrupting effect of the suggestive procedures. Thus, *Manson* sets a high bar for exclusion of eyewitness identification evidence, requiring a court to find the evidence to be both produced through an unnecessarily suggestive procedure and unreliable. By contrast, the per se exclusion rule adopted by the New Mexico Supreme Court in *Martinez* affords a criminal defendant broader due process rights by requiring the defendant to demonstrate only that the identification procedure contained one or more suggestive elements, which then shifts to the state the burden of proof regarding the procedure's suggestiveness, or necessity therefor. If the state fails to carry its responsive burden, the identification evidence and any subsequent in-court identification must be suppressed.

Quicknotes

EXCLUSIONARY RULE A rule precluding the introduction at trial of evidence unlawfully obtained in violation of the federal constitutional safeguards against unreasonable searches and seizures.

PER SE By itself; without more; taken alone; not requiring additional evidence for proof; as a matter of law.

Perry v. New Hampshire

Individual (D) v. State (P)

132 S. Ct. 716 (2012)

NATURE OF CASE: Appeal from decision of the New Hampshire Supreme Court upholding defendant's criminal conviction.

FACT SUMMARY: Police received a call that an African American man was breaking into vehicles in a parking lot. When police spoke with witness Nubia Blandon, she identified Perry (D) as the man she had seen breaking into the vehicles.

RULE OF LAW

The Due Process Clause does not require a preliminary judicial inquiry into the reliability of eyewitness identification when the identification was not obtained by a suggestive identification procedure employed by law enforcement personnel.

FACTS: At 3:00 a.m. on August 15, 2008, Nashua, New Hampshire, police received a call about an African American man breaking into vehicles in a parking lot. When police arrived at the scene, one officer, Nicole Clay, approached Perry (D) who was holding two radio amplifiers in his hands. Perry (D) denied that he had stolen the amplifiers. Clay then spoke with Nubia Blandon about the incidents. Blandon stated that she had witnessed from her kitchen window an African American man roaming the parking lot and looking into vehicles. Clay then asked Blandon to describe the person. Blandon pointed through her kitchen window to Perry (D), who was standing with another officer in the parking lot. A month later, when police showed Blandon a photographic array that included a picture of Perry (D), she was unable to identify him. The State (P) charged Perry (D) with one count of theft. Perry (D) moved to suppress Blandon's out-of-court identification of him, because it essentially constituted a one-person lineup. The trial court denied the motion and both Blandon and Clay testified as to Blandon's out-of-court identification. A jury convicted Perry (D) and the New Hampshire Supreme Court affirmed the conviction. The United States Supreme Court granted Perry's (D) application for review.

ISSUE: Does the Due Process Clause require a preliminary judicial inquiry into the reliability of eyewitness identification when the identification was not obtained by a suggestive identification procedure employed by law enforcement personnel?

HOLDING AND DECISION: (Ginsburg, J.) No. The Due Process Clause does not require a preliminary judicial inquiry into the reliability of eyewitness identification when the identification was not obtained by a suggestive identification procedure employed by law enforcement personnel. This Court has developed a two-step analysis to determine whether the Due Process Clause requires suppression of out-of-court identifications tainted by police misconduct. The first step is to determine whether law enforcement employed an identification procedure that was suggestive in nature. If so, the reviewing court must next consider whether the improper identification procedure tainted the resulting identification in a manner that would render it unreliable and therefore inadmissible. Reliability of the eyewitness identification is the linchpin of the analysis. Where the indicators of the witness's ability to make an accurate identification outweigh the corrupting effect of the tainted law enforcement suggestion, the evidence should be allowed. Such indicators include the opportunity of the witness to view the defendant at the time of the crime, the accuracy of the description, and the level of certainty. Perry (D) argues the rule requiring pretrial judicial inquiries should not be limited to those situations involving police conduct. Rather, courts should review all eyewitness identifications any time identification is made under suggestive circumstances. Perry (P) is incorrect. A primary purpose of excluding identification under suggestive circumstances created by law enforcement is to deter police officers from using suggestive lineup and photo arrays. The deterrence rationale does not exist where, as in this case, police engaged in no improper conduct resulting in the identification. Moreover, requiring pretrial judicial review of all such eyewitness testimony would place a large burden on criminal trial courts. The jury, not the judge, traditionally determines the reliability of evidence. Other safeguards protect criminal defendants from unreliable out-of-court statements. Those safeguards include the defendant's ability to cross-examine the witness. Eyewitness jury instructions warn the jury to take care when evaluating specific evidence relating to eyewitness identifications. Lastly, the government has the high burden of proving the defendant's guilt beyond reasonable doubt. Accordingly, the introduction of Blandon's out-of-court identification of Perry (D) did not render his trial fundamentally unfair. Affirmed.

CONCURRENCE: (Thomas, J.) The majority correctly concludes that pretrial inquiries into out-of-court identifications are only required where police action is involved in the identification process. However, the majority is incorrect that the Due Process Clause includes

Continued on next page.

a substantive due process right to fundamental fairness. The Clause only deals with the right to process, and not substantive rights.

DISSENT: (Sotomayor, J.) The majority improperly concludes that the primary purpose of requiring pretrial judicial inquiries into out-of-court identifications is deterrence of improper law enforcement conduct. The primary purpose of the requirement is to ensure reliability of such statements before they are submitted to a jury. By requiring the presence of police action as part of the identification, the majority introduces a mens rea or intent inquiry into the rule. This Court's precedents, however, make no distinction between intentional and unintentional suggestive conduct regarding identification. Here, even though the identification was unplanned, it still involved the police. Lastly, scientific analysis of eyewitness identification revealed, in one study, that 76 percent of convictions overturned due to DNA evidence occurred based on faulty eyewitness identifications. Accordingly, the majority should not limit pretrial judicial inquires to those identifications that involve potential police misconduct.

ANALYSIS

Reliability of evidence is typically within the province of the jury. A criminal defendant can always file a motion to suppress an out-of-court identification (or any other out-of-court statements). Perry (D) was seeking a preliminary evidentiary hearing where the judge would hear from the witness regarding the out-of-court statement. However, the New Hampshire trial court found, as did the United States Supreme Court in this decision, that because police conduct was not suggestive, the reliability of the statement was for the jury to consider.

Quicknotes

DUE PROCESS The constitutional mandate requiring the courts to protect and enforce individuals' rights and liberties consistent with prevailing principles of fairness and justice and prohibiting the federal and state governments from such activities that deprive its citizens of life, liberty, or property interest.

MENS REA Criminal intent.

SUBSTANTIVE DUE PROCESS A constitutional safeguard limiting the power of the state, irrespective of how fair its procedures may be; substantive limits placed on the power of the state.

CHAPTER 5

The Right to Counsel

Quick Reference Rules of Law

	PAGE
1. *Powell v. Alabama.* In a capital case, where the defendant is unable to employ counsel and is incapable of adequately defending him- or herself, the Due Process Clause requires that effective counsel be appointed for him or her.	*104*
2. *Gideon v. Wainwright.* An indigent criminal defendant is entitled to court-appointed counsel.	*105*
3. *Argersinger v. Hamlin.* A person has a right to appointed counsel in any case in which he or she may be sentenced to jail.	*106*
4. *Mempa v. Rhay.* An accused is entitled to be represented by counsel at every stage of a criminal proceeding where substantial rights of a criminal accused may be affected.	*107*

Powell v. Alabama

Accused (D) v. State (P)

287 U.S. 45 (1932)

NATURE OF CASE: Appeal from convictions for rape.

FACT SUMMARY: Seven Black defendants were convicted of raping two White girls.

RULE OF LAW

In a capital case, where the defendant is unable to employ counsel and is incapable of adequately defending him- or herself, the Due Process Clause requires that effective counsel be appointed for him or her.

FACTS: Seven Black defendants were charged with the rape of two White girls. The seven defendants were all young, "ignorant, and illiterate." They came from other states and had no family or friends in the immediate area. Six days after an indictment and arraignment at which they were not represented by counsel, the seven defendants were tried. Until the morning of the trial, no lawyer had been named to represent them. All seven defendants were found guilty and sentenced to death. The Alabama Supreme Court affirmed the judgments, ruling that the seven defendants had been properly represented by counsel. The United States Supreme Court granted certiorari.

ISSUE: In a capital case, where the defendant is unable to employ counsel and is incapable of adequately defending him- or herself, does the Due Process Clause of the Fourteenth Amendment require that effective counsel be appointed for him or her?

HOLDING AND DECISION: (Sutherland, J.) Yes. In a capital case, where the defendant is unable to employ counsel and is incapable of adequately defending him- or herself, the Due Process Clause of the Fourteenth Amendment requires that effective counsel be appointed for him or her. The record of this case clearly illustrates that from the time of their arraignment until the trial, the defendants did not have the aid of counsel in any real sense. This is often the most critical stage of a criminal trial, during which consultation and investigation must be carried out. The right to a hearing has always included the right to counsel, for the right to be heard is often useless unless it includes the right to be heard by counsel; even the intelligent layperson is often unable to adequately defend him- or herself. Thus, the failure of the trial court to give the seven defendants reasonable time and opportunity to employ counsel was a denial of due process. In addition, assuming their inability to secure counsel even if they had been given the opportunity, the failure of the trial court to make an effective appointment of counsel was also a denial of due process. Reversed.

ANALYSIS

Powell v. Alabama is the first case to recognize the constitutional right of an indigent defendant to the assistance of court-appointed counsel. Although the *Powell* decision was limited to capital cases, its underlying due process rationale suggested the need for the appointment of counsel generally.

Quicknotes

DUE PROCESS CLAUSE Language in the Fifth and Fourteenth Amendments to the United States Constitution providing that no person shall be deprived of "life, liberty, or property, without due process of law."

FOURTEENTH AMENDMENT Declares that no state shall make or enforce any law that shall abridge the privileges and immunities of citizens of the United States; no state shall deny to any person within its jurisdiction the equal protection of the laws.

RIGHT TO COUNSEL Right conferred by the Sixth Amendment that the accused shall be provided effective legal assistance in a criminal proceeding.

Gideon v. Wainwright

Convicted robber (D) v. Government (P)

372 U.S. 335 (1963)

NATURE OF CASE: Appeal from denial of petition for habeas corpus.

FACT SUMMARY: Gideon (D), an indigent man, was convicted of a felony after having been denied court-appointed counsel.

RULE OF LAW
An indigent criminal defendant is entitled to court-appointed counsel.

FACTS: Gideon (D) was charged with breaking and entering. Prior to trial, he argued that he could not afford counsel and that he was entitled to a court-appointed attorney. The court denied the request, and Gideon (D) was convicted. His habeas corpus petition to the Florida Supreme Court was denied. The United States Supreme Court granted certiorari.

ISSUE: Is an indigent criminal defendant entitled to court appointed counsel?

HOLDING AND DECISION: (Black, J.) Yes. An indigent criminal defendant is entitled to court-appointed counsel. The Fourteenth Amendment guarantees that fundamental rights found in the United States Constitution will be applied to the states. There is no escaping the conclusion that right to counsel found in the Sixth Amendment is such a fundamental right. The state spends considerable money to hire prosecuting attorneys, and under our adversarial system, fairness demands that the indigent defendant be given at least the assistance of counsel. The legal system of this society is predicated on the assurance of fair trials, and a defendant without an attorney is unlikely to get a fair trial. Reversed and remanded.

ANALYSIS

Prior to this case, federal law had recognized the right to counsel in federal prosecutions. This was established in 1938, in *Johnson v. Zerbst*, 304 U.S. 458. The right, embodied in the Sixth Amendment, can be found in earlier English common law.

Quicknotes

FOURTEENTH AMENDMENT Declares that no state shall make or enforce any law that shall abridge the privileges and immunities of citizens of the United States; no state shall deny to any person within its jurisdiction the equal protection of the laws.

PETITION OF HABEAS CORPUS Petition to compel an independent review of whether a prisoner is being lawfully imprisoned.

RIGHT TO COUNSEL Right conferred by the Sixth Amendment that the accused shall be provided effective legal assistance in a criminal proceeding.

SIXTH AMENDMENT Provides the right to a speedy and public trial by impartial jury, the right to be informed of the accusation, the right to confront witnesses, and the right to have the assistance of counsel in all criminal prosecutions

Argersinger v. Hamlin

Petty offender (D) v. State (P)

407 U.S. 25 (1972)

NATURE OF CASE: Appeal from denial of writ of habeas corpus.

FACT SUMMARY: The Florida Supreme Court held that the right to counsel is not present in petty offense cases.

RULE OF LAW

A person has a right to appointed counsel in any case in which he or she may be sentenced to jail.

FACTS: Argersinger (D) was charged with carrying a concealed weapon. In Florida, this offense was a misdemeanor punishable by a sentence of up to six months in prison. He was not given appointed counsel and was sentenced to 90 days in jail. He petitioned for a writ of habeas corpus on the basis he had been denied his right to appointed counsel. The Florida Supreme Court denied the petition, holding no right to appointed counsel exists for petty offenses. The United States Supreme Court granted certiorari.

ISSUE: Does a person have a right to appointed counsel in any case in which he or she may be sentenced to jail?

HOLDING AND DECISION: (Douglas, J.) Yes. A person has a right to appointed counsel in any case in which he or she may be sentenced to jail. The inhibition on a person's liberty caused by imprisonment is so great that any time such is threatened, counsel must be appointed. As a result, before Argersinger (D) could have been placed in a position wherein he could have lost his liberty, he was entitled to appointed counsel. Reversed.

ANALYSIS

This case extends the right to appointed counsel to any case in which imprisonment may be imposed. The expansion of this Sixth Amendment right began with the landmark decision of *Gideon v. Wainwright*, 372 U.S. 335 (1963). In that case, Clarence Gideon (D) petitioned the United States Supreme Court in proper for a writ of certiorari hoping to have his conviction for burglary overturned. Under Florida law, only capital offenses triggered the right to appointed counsel. After the petition was granted, Gideon (D) was represented by future Supreme Court Justice Abraham Fortas. The Court ultimately overturned the conviction and held Gideon (D) had been denied his right to counsel.

Quicknotes

RIGHT TO COUNSEL Right conferred by the Sixth Amendment that the accused shall be provided effective legal assistance in a criminal proceeding.

SIXTH AMENDMENT Provides the right to a speedy and public trial by impartial jury, the right to be informed of the accusation, the right to confront witnesses, and the right to have the assistance of counsel in all criminal prosecutions.

WRIT OF HABEAS CORPUS A proceeding in which a defendant brings a writ to compel a judicial determination of whether he or she is lawfully being held in custody.

Mempa v. Rhay

Accused (D) v. State (P)

389 U.S. 128 (1967)

NATURE OF CASE: Appeal from revocation of probation and imposition of suspended sentence.

FACT SUMMARY: Mempa (D) participated in a burglary, as a result of which his probation for a prior crime was revoked and a deferred sentence was imposed.

RULE OF LAW

An accused is entitled to be represented by counsel at every stage of a criminal proceeding where substantial rights of a criminal accused may be affected.

FACTS: Mempa (D) was convicted of joyriding and was given a two-year probationary period with sentencing deferred unless and until Mempa (D) violated his probation. The State (P) later moved to have the probation revoked on the ground Mempa (D) had been involved in a burglary. Mempa (D) admitted involvement in the burglary. A probation officer testified to this effect, but without cross-examination. At no time during these court proceedings was Mempa (D) represented by counsel, nor was he asked if he desired counsel. The court imposed a deferred sentence of ten years in the penitentiary for joyriding.

ISSUE: Is an accused entitled to be represented by counsel at every stage of a criminal proceeding where substantial rights of a criminal accused may be affected?

HOLDING AND DECISION: (Marshall, J.) Yes. An accused is entitled to be represented by counsel at every stage of a criminal proceeding where substantial rights of a criminal accused may be affected. *Gideon v. Wainwright*, 372 U.S. 335 (1963), and preceding cases. Sentencing is clearly a critical stage of a criminal proceeding. The State (P) argues that the defendants were sentenced at the time they were originally placed on probation, and that the later imposition of sentence when probation is revoked is a mere formality and is thus not a critical stage. However, this argument is not supported by the facts of these cases. The later imposition of sentence is not a mere formality because the court makes recommendations, when it imposes the deferred sentence, to the prison administration on how much time is required to be served prior to parole. Such recommendations are given great weight by parole officials. Also, certain legal rights may be lost if they are not exercised at the time sentence is imposed. Counsel is certainly necessary to protect an accused from a summary proceeding. Therefore, a state may provide for a deferred sentencing procedure, but it must afford the accused the right to counsel. Reversed.

ANALYSIS

The United States Supreme Court uses, as the main basis for this decision, the holding in *Townsend v. Burke*, 334 U.S. 736 (1948), which stated that the absence of counsel during sentencing, coupled with the use of information concerning the accused's criminal record, denied the defendant due process. Counsel could have taken steps in that case to see that the sentencing was not based on misinformation and misreading of court records. The Sixth Amendment, as applied to the states by the Fourteenth Amendment, provides that in all criminal prosecutions the accused is entitled to have the assistance of counsel for his or her defense. *Gideon v. Wainwright*, 372 U.S. 335 (1963). However, *Mempa v. Rhay* may also indicate that the Court will substantially increase its inquiry into the correctional stage of the criminal process. There are a great many persons involved in such a stage and they comprise a minority who lack the resources and cohesion to gain a hearing on their grievances. Also, there is a distinct lack of specific statutes and administrative rules governing sentencing and correctional decision-making. The Court's inquiry into the correctional stage of criminal proceedings includes both the necessity of counsel and the necessity of procedural due process.

Quicknotes

FOURTEENTH AMENDMENT Declares that no state shall make or enforce any law that shall abridge the privileges and immunities of citizens of the United States; no state shall deny to any person within its jurisdiction the equal protection of the laws.

RIGHT TO COUNSEL Right conferred by the Sixth Amendment that the accused shall be provided effective legal assistance in a criminal proceeding.

SIXTH AMENDMENT Provides the right to a speedy and public trial by impartial jury, the right to be informed of the accusation, the right to confront witnesses, and the right to have the assistance of counsel in all criminal prosecutions.

CHAPTER 6

The Screening and Charging Process

Quick Reference Rules of Law

United States v. Armstrong

Federal government (P) v. Convicted drug dealer (D)

517 U.S. 456 (1996)

NATURE OF CASE: Appeal from granting of motion for discovery in selective-prosecution claims following indictment for drug offenses.

FACTS SUMMARY: Upon indictment for selling crack cocaine and using firearms in connection with drug trafficking, defendants (D) brought claims against the United States (P) for selective prosecution because of their race.

RULE OF LAW

For a defendant to be entitled to discovery on a claim that he or she was singled out for prosecution on the basis of race, the defendant must make a threshold showing that the government has declined to prosecute similarly situated suspects of other races.

FACTS: Armstrong (D), Hampton (D), and other defendants (D) were indicted in United States District Court on charges of conspiring to possess and to distribute cocaine (crack) and federal firearms offenses. Upon the indictment, defendants (D) filed a motion for discovery or for dismissal of the indictment, alleging that they were selected for federal prosecution because they were Black. They included in their affidavits a study that showed that in every one of the 24 similar cases handled by the local public defender's office, the defendants involved were Black. The district court granted the discovery motion, ordering the Government (P) to identify the race of the defendants in all cases from the last three years, as well as its criteria for prosecution. When the Government (P) refused to comply, the court dismissed the case. A divided three-judge panel of the Court of Appeals for the Ninth Circuit reversed, holding that defendants (P) must provide a basis for believing that others similarly situated have not been prosecuted to obtain discovery. The Court of Appeals then voted to rehear the case en banc, and the en banc panel affirmed the district court's order of dismissal. The United States Supreme Court granted certiorari to determine the appropriate standard for discovery for a selective-prosecution claim.

ISSUE: For a defendant to be entitled to discovery on a claim that he or she was singled out for prosecution on the basis of race, must the defendant make a threshold showing that the government has declined to prosecute similarly situated suspects of other races?

HOLDING AND DECISION: (Rehnquist, C.J.) Yes. For a defendant to be entitled to discovery on a claim that he or she was singled out for prosecution on the basis of race, the defendant must make a threshold showing that the government has declined to prosecute similarly situated suspects of other races. Contrary to defendants' (D) argument, Federal Rule of Criminal Procedure 16 does not mandate disclosure of material supporting a selective prosecution claim. Although Rule 16 requires disclosure of documents "material to the preparation of the defendant's defense," a selective prosecution attack is not material to the defense in the Rule 16 sense. However, under the equal protection component of the Fifth Amendment's Due Process Clause, the decision whether to prosecute may not be based on an arbitrary classification such as race or religion. In order to prove a selective-prosecution claim, the claimant must demonstrate that the prosecutorial policy had a discriminatory effect and was motivated by a discriminatory purpose. To establish a discriminatory effect of prosecution in a race case, the claimant must show that similarly situated individuals of a different race were not prosecuted. In this case, however, the "study" listing 24 defendants by race did not constitute such evidence. Reversed and remanded.

DISSENT: (Stevens, J.) The Court correctly decided that defendants' (P) showing was not strong enough to give them a right to discovery, either under Rule 16 or under the district court's inherent power to order discovery in appropriate circumstances. However, the district judge did not abuse her discretion when she concluded that the factual showing was sufficiently disturbing to require some response from the United States Attorney's Office. The brunt of the recently elevated federal penalties falls heavily on Blacks, while the majority of the persons who have used crack are Whites.

ANALYSIS

In the ordinary case, "so long as the prosecutor has probable cause to believe that the accused committed an offense defined by statute, the decision whether or not to prosecute, and what charge to file or bring before a grand jury, generally rests entirely in his [or her] discretion." *Bordenkircher v. Hayes*, 434 U.S. 357, 364 (1978). No defendant since *Yick Wo v. Hopkins*, 118 U.S. 356 (1886), has been successful in proving a race-based claim of selective prosecution. See Melissa L. Jampol, "Goodbye to the Defense of Selective Prosecution," 87 *J. Crim. Law and Criminology* 932, 965 (1997). The

Continued on next page.

Armstrong opinion will not likely change this historical trend.

Quicknotes

DUE PROCESS CLAUSE Language in the Fifth and Fourteenth Amendments to the United States Constitution providing that no person shall be deprived of "life, liberty, or property, without due process of law."

DISCOVERY Pretrial procedure during which one party makes certain information available to the other.

EN BANC The hearing of a matter by all the judges of the court, rather than only the necessary quorum.

FIFTH AMENDMENT Provides that no person shall be compelled to serve as a witness against him- or herself, be subject to trial for the same offense twice, or be deprived of life, liberty, or property without due process of law.

Costello v. United States

Accused (D) v. Federal government (P)

350 U.S. 359 (1956)

NATURE OF CASE: Petition for certiorari after conviction of income tax evasion.

FACT SUMMARY: Three investigating officers were the only witnesses before the grand jury who indicted Costello (D). They had no firsthand knowledge of the transactions upon which their computations were based. Hence, the indictment was based solely on hearsay.

RULE OF LAW

An indictment returned by a legally constituted and unbiased grand jury, if valid on its face, is enough to call for trial of the charge on the merits, regardless of the fact the only evidence before the grand jury was hearsay.

FACTS: At Costello's (D) trial the Government (P) called 144 witnesses and introduced 368 exhibits, all of which related to business transactions and expenditures by the Costellos (D). Three Government (P) agents, whose investigations had produced the evidence used against Costello (D) at trial, were also called to testify. They were allowed to summarize the evidence already introduced, and to introduce computations showing, if correct, that the Costellos (D) had received far greater income than they had reported. The three agents were the only witnesses before the grand jury. Costello (D) moved to dismiss the indictment on the ground that the only evidence before the grand jury was hearsay since the officers had no firsthand knowledge of the transactions upon which their computations were based.

ISSUE: Is an indictment returned by a legally constituted and unbiased grand jury, if valid on its face, enough to call for trial of the charge on the merits, regardless of the fact the only evidence before the grand jury was hearsay?

HOLDING AND DECISION: (Black, J.) Yes. An indictment returned by a legally constituted and unbiased grand jury, if valid on its face, is enough to call for trial of the charge on the merits, regardless of the fact the only evidence before the grand jury was hearsay. Neither the Fifth Amendment nor any other constitutional provision prescribes the kind of evidence upon which grand juries must act. The grand jury convenes as a body of lay people free from technical rules. If indictments could be challenged on the ground there was inadequate or incompetent evidence before the grand jury, a great delay would result before a trial on the merits. An accused could insist on a kind of preliminary trial to determine the adequacy and competency of the evidence before the grand jury. Perhaps most important, such a change would run counter to the whole history of the grand jury institution as a body not hampered by rigid procedural or evidential rules. Costello's (D) conviction is affirmed.

ANALYSIS

Depending upon its scope, *Costello* may (or may not) reflect the majority position among those states that regularly prosecute by indictment. In many, courts will dismiss an indictment upon a showing that there was no sworn witness or legal documentary evidence before the grand jury. In several, courts have held an indictment is also subject to attack where based solely on the testimony of an incompetent witness. Most indictment states, however, will go no further. An indictment will not be dismissed even if issued solely upon hearsay testimony; and in some jurisdictions indictments regularly are based entirely upon a summary of investigative reports presented by a single officer or the prosecuting attorney.

Quicknotes

FIFTH AMENDMENT Provides that no person shall be compelled to serve as a witness against him- or herself, be subject to trial for the same offense twice, or be deprived of life, liberty, or property without due process of law.

GRAND JURY A group summoned to investigate, inform, and accuse persons of crimes when sufficient evidence exists to do so.

HEARSAY An out-of-court statement made by a person other than the witness testifying at trial that is offered in order to prove the truth of the matter asserted.

Trump v. Vance

President of the United States (P) v. Municipal district attorney (D)

140 S. Ct. 2412 (2020)

NATURE OF CASE: Appeal from affirmance of denial of injunction in action brought by sitting President of the United States to enjoin enforcement of grand jury subpoena for records related to the President and business organizations affiliated with him.

FACT SUMMARY: After the New York County District Attorney's Office—acting on behalf of a grand jury—served a *subpoena duces tecum* on Mazars USA, LLP (Mazars) (D), the personal accounting firm of President Donald Trump (Trump) (P), for financial records relating to Trump (P) and his businesses, Trump (P) sued the district attorney (D) and Mazars (D) to enjoin enforcement of the subpoena, arguing that a sitting President enjoys absolute immunity from state criminal process under Article II and the Supremacy Clause.

RULE OF LAW

(1) A sitting President does not under Article II or the Supremacy Clause categorically have absolute immunity from a state grand jury subpoena seeking the President's private papers.

(2) Neither Article II nor the Supremacy Clause requires a heightened standard for the issuance of a state criminal subpoena seeking the private papers of a sitting President.

FACTS: The New York County District Attorney's Office—acting on behalf of a grand jury—served a *subpoena duces tecum* on Mazars USA, LLP (Mazars) (D), the personal accounting firm of sitting President Donald J. Trump (Trump) (P), for financial records relating to Trump (P) and his businesses. Trump (P), acting in his personal capacity, sued the district attorney (D) and Mazars (D) in federal district court to enjoin enforcement of the subpoena, arguing that a sitting President enjoys absolute immunity from state criminal process under Article II and the Supremacy Clause. The district court denied injunctive relief, and the court of appeals affirmed. The United States Supreme Court granted certiorari.

ISSUES:

(1) Does a sitting President under Article II or the Supremacy Clause categorically have absolute immunity from a state grand jury subpoena seeking the President's private papers?

(2) Does either Article II or the Supremacy Clause require a heightened standard for the issuance of a state criminal subpoena seeking the private papers of a sitting President?

HOLDING AND DECISION: (Roberts, C.J.)

(1) No. A sitting President does not under Article II or the Supremacy Clause categorically have absolute immunity from a state grand jury subpoena seeking the President's private papers. In 1807, Chief Justice Marshall ruled that a sitting President is not exempt from the Sixth Amendment's guarantee that those accused have compulsory process for obtaining witnesses for their defense. *United States v. Burr,* 25 F.Cas. 30 (CC Va. 1807). Marshall also concluded that the Sixth Amendment's guarantee extended to the production of documents, since the propriety of introducing any documents depends on the nature of the document and not on the character of the person who holds it, and since the court may decide whether introducing the document is appropriate after the document is produced. In the two centuries following *Burr,* successive Presidents accepted Marshall's ruling that the President is subject to subpoena, and uniformly agreed to testify when called in criminal proceedings. In 1974, the question whether to compel the disclosure of official communications over the President's objection came to a head when the Watergate Special Prosecutor secured a *subpoena duces tecum* directing President Nixon to produce, among other things, tape recordings of Oval Office meetings. The Court rejected Nixon's claim of an absolute privilege of confidentiality for all presidential communications. Recognizing that "compulsory process" was imperative for both the prosecution and the defense, the Court held that the President's "generalized assertion of privilege must yield to the demonstrated, specific need for evidence in a pending criminal trial." *United States v. Nixon,* 418 U.S. 683 (1974). President Nixon dutifully released the tapes. This history all involved federal criminal proceedings. Here, the President claims that the Supremacy Clause gives a sitting President absolute immunity from state criminal subpoenas because compliance with such subpoenas would categorically impair the performance of the President's Article II functions. Here, Trump (P) argues that state criminal subpoenas categorically impair that function and are impermissibly burdensome on grounds of diversion, stigma, and harassment. Trump (P) contends that complying with state criminal subpoenas would necessarily distract the Chief Executive

Continued on next page.

from the Executive's duties. Trump (P) grounds that concern on *Nixon v. Fitzgerald,* 457 U.S. 731 (1982), which recognized a President's absolute immunity from damages liability predicated on his official acts. However, contrary to Trump's (P) suggestion, that case did not hold that distraction was sufficient to confer absolute immunity. *Fitzgerald's* principal concern was not mere distraction but the distortion of the Executive's "decisionmaking process." The prospect that a President may become "preoccupied by pending litigation" did not ordinarily implicate constitutional concerns. Two centuries of experience likewise confirm that a properly tailored criminal subpoena will not normally hamper the performance of a President's constitutional duties. The President claims this case is different. Trump (P) believes that he is under criminal investigation and argues that the mental toll will necessarily be heavier in that circumstance. But Trump (P) is not seeking immunity from the diversion occasioned by the prospect of future criminal liability. He concedes that he may be investigated while in office. His objection is instead limited to the additional distraction caused by the subpoena itself. That argument, however, runs up against the 200 years of precedent establishing that Presidents, and their official communications, are subject to judicial process, even when the President is under investigation. Trump (P) next claims that the stigma of being subpoenaed will undermine his leadership at home and abroad. However, even if a tarnished reputation were a cognizable impairment, there is nothing inherently stigmatizing about a President performing the citizen's normal duty of furnishing information relevant to a criminal investigation. Nor can the risk of association with persons or activities under criminal investigation absolve a President of such an important public duty. The consequences for a President's public standing will likely increase if he or she is the one under investigation, but Trump (P) concedes that such investigations are permitted under Article II and the Supremacy Clause. Additionally, the receipt of a subpoena would not seem to categorically magnify the harm to Trump's (P) reputation. Additionally, in the grand jury context, longstanding secrecy rules aim to prevent the very stigma Trump (P) anticipates. Finally, Trump (P) argues that subjecting Presidents to state criminal subpoenas will make them targets for harassment. Harassing state criminal subpoenas could, under certain circumstances, threaten the independence or effectiveness of the Executive, but the law already seeks to protect against such abuse. First, grand juries are prohibited from engaging in "arbitrary fishing expeditions" or initiating investigations "out of malice or an intent to harass," and federal courts may intervene in state proceedings that are motivated by or conducted in bad faith. Second, because the Supremacy Clause prohibits state judges and prosecutors from interfering with a President's official duties, any effort to manipulate a President's policy decisions or to retaliate against a President for official acts through issuance of a subpoena would be unconstitutional. Finally, federal law allows a President to challenge any such allegedly unconstitutional influence in a federal forum. Given these safeguards and the Court's precedents, absolute immunity from a state grand jury subpoena seeking a President's private papers for a sitting President is neither necessary nor appropriate under Article II or the Supremacy Clause.

(2) No. Neither Article II nor the Supremacy Clause requires a heightened standard for the issuance of a state criminal subpoena seeking the private papers of a sitting President. First, although a President cannot be treated as an "ordinary individual" when executive communications are sought, *Burr* teaches that, with regard to private papers, a President is similarly situated to any other individual. Second, there has been no showing here that heightened protection against state subpoenas is necessary for the Executive to fulfill Article II functions. The argument in this regard favoring a heightened standard is that even if federal subpoenas to a President are warranted whenever evidence is material, state subpoenas are warranted only when the evidence is essential. However, such a double standard has no basis in law, because if the state subpoena is not issued to manipulate, and the documents themselves are not protected and the Executive is not impaired, then nothing in Article II or the Supremacy Clause supports holding state subpoenas to a higher standard than their federal counterparts. Finally, absent a need to protect the Executive, the public interest in fair and effective law enforcement cuts in favor of comprehensive access to evidence. Rejecting a heightened need standard does not leave Presidents without recourse. A President may take advantage of the same protections available to every other citizen, including the right to challenge the subpoena on any grounds permitted by state law, which usually include bad faith and undue burden or breadth. When the President invokes such protections, the high respect that is owed to the President's office should inform the conduct of the entire proceeding, including the timing and scope of discovery. In addition, a President can raise subpoena-specific constitutional challenges in either a state or a federal forum. For example, a President can challenge the subpoena as an attempt to influence the performance of the President's official duties, in violation

Continued on next page.

of the Supremacy Clause. Such a challenge would, if meritorious, would protect federal constitutional power from interference by local politics. Moreover, a President can argue that compliance with a particular subpoena would impede the President's constitutional duties. If a court is persuaded by such an argument, the court can then quash or modify the subpoena as needed to eliminate interference with the President's duties. Affirmed and remanded.

CONCURRENCE: (Kavanaugh, J.) This decision reinforces that no one is above the law, including a President. However, in light of Article II, a court may not proceed against a President as it would against an ordinary litigant. Thus, the question is how to balance a state's interests and Article II interests. *United States v. Nixon,* 418 U.S. 683 (1974), which requires that a prosecutor establish a "demonstrated, specific need" for privileged Executive Branch information, including a President's information, provides that balance. The tried-and-true *Nixon* test accommodates the interests of the criminal process and the Article II interests of the Executive, by seeking to ensure that a prosecutor's interest in subpoenaed information is sufficiently important to justify an intrusion on the Article II interests of the Presidency. The *Nixon* standard also reduces the risk of subjecting a President to unwarranted burdens, because it provides that a prosecutor may obtain a President's information only in certain defined circumstances. Regardless whether in the future the majority's standard is applied, or *Nixon's* "demonstrated, specific need" standard is used, a court will have to first delve into why the state wants the information; why and how much the state needs the information, including whether the state could obtain the information elsewhere; and whether compliance with the subpoena would unduly burden or interfere with a President's official duties.

DISSENT: (Thomas, J.) There is no dispute that a President is not entitled to absolute immunity from the issuance of a state criminal subpoena, but a President may be entitled to relief against the subpoena's enforcement, if the President can demonstrate that presidential duties require all of the President's time—until the end of the President's term or until the President is removed from office. This standard, which Chief Justice Marshall set out in *Burr* to the end that the President not be unnecessarily harassed by vexatious and unnecessary subpoenas, puts the burden on the President to show inability to comply with the subpoena at issue as a consequence of being consumed with presidential duties. However, it also requires courts to respect the demands on the President's time, especially since they are not well situated to conduct a searching review of the President's assertion of inability to comply with the subpoena. When deciding to enforce a subpoena issued against a President, courts should be guided by the understanding that the demands on the President's time and the importance of presidential tasks are extraordinary, and that the office of the President cannot be delegated to subordinates. The case should be vacated and remanded so the District Court can determine whether enforcement of the subpoena at bar should be enjoined in light of this understanding.

DISSENT: (Alito, J.) The majority's approach relegates a President to the "meager defenses" that are available to all citizens when an ordinary grand jury subpoena is challenged. Instead, the Presidency deserves greater protection. For these reasons, a prosecutor should be required (1) to provide at least a general description of the possible offenses that are under investigation, (2) to outline how the subpoenaed records relate to those offenses, and (3) to explain why it is important that the records be produced and why it is necessary for production to occur while the President is still in office. In the instant case, the district attorney should have been required to answer important questions, such as why it is important that the information be obtained from the President's records rather than some other source, and why it is necessary for those records to be produced now, rather than when the President leaves office. If there are statute of limitations concerns, those possibly can be addressed through the use of waiver. There may be other good reasons why immediate enforcement is important, such as the risk that evidence or important leads will be lost, but if a prosecutor believes that immediate enforcement is needed for such a reason, the prosecutor should be required to provide a reasonably specific explanation why that is so and why alternative means, such as measures to preserve evidence and prevent spoliation, would not suffice. The prosecutor's response must be detailed and specific, and must address concerns for the President's ability to carry out the President's official duties, before a subpoena will be enforced during the President's term. In sum, the Court's decision threatens to impair the functioning of the Presidency and provides the Presidency no real protection against the use of the subpoena power by the Nation's 2,300+ local prosecutors.

ANALYSIS

The assertion that President Trump (P) made in this case was extraordinary. Had his claim of absolute immunity from criminal process prevailed, there potentially would have been limitless immunity from criminal process not only for a President during the President's term of office, but also for the President's family members and associates. As the district court observed, presidential immunity would stretch to cover every phase of criminal proceedings, including investigations, grand jury

Continued on next page.

proceedings and subpoenas, indictment, prosecution, arrest, trial, conviction, and incarceration. Such immunity presumably would encompass any conduct, at any time, in any forum, whether federal or state, and whether the President acted alone or in concert with other individuals. The President's exemption from criminal proceedings would extend not only to matters arising from performance of the President's duties and functions in the President's official capacity, but also to ones arising from the President's private affairs, financial transactions, and all other conduct undertaken by the President as an ordinary citizen, both during and before the President's tenure in office. The practical implications and actual effects of such categorical immunity could be far reaching. In some circumstances, applicable statutes of limitations could run, barring further investigation and prosecution of serious criminal offenses, thus potentially enabling both the President and any accomplices to escape being brought to justice. Temporally, such immunity would operate to frustrate the administration of justice by insulating from criminal law scrutiny and judicial review, whether by federal or state courts, not only matters occurring during the President's tenure in office, but potentially also records relating to transactions and illegal actions the President and others may have committed before the President assumed the Presidency. However, Trump's (P) claim did not prevail. All the courts that reviewed the claim, as well as all the Supreme Court Justices, agreed that there is nothing in the Constitution, in the constitutional balance of power between the respective branches of government, or in the Supreme Court's precedents that absolutely immunizes a sitting President from criminal process during the President's term. As Chief Justice Roberts notes in the majority opinion, the Founders shunned the concept of the inviolability of the King of England and the bounds of the monarch's protective screen covering the Crown's actions from legal scrutiny, and, therefore, disclaimed any notion that the Constitution generally conferred similarly all-encompassing immunity upon the President. The wisdom of that view has been tested before the courts on various occasions and has been roundly and consistently reaffirmed by the Supreme Court and lower courts, which, in numerous rulings, have circumscribed claims of presidential immunity in multiple ways. As the district court put it, the proposition advanced by Trump (P) is "repugnant to the nation's governmental structure and constitutional values." *Trump v. Vance*, 395 F. Supp. 3d 283, 290 (S.D.N.Y. 2019).

Quicknotes

STATUTE OF LIMITATIONS A law prescribing the period in which a legal action may be commenced.

SUBPOENA DUCES TECUM A court mandate compelling the production of documents under a witness's control.

SUPREMACY CLAUSE Article VI, ¶ 2 of the U.S. Constitution, which provides that federal action must prevail over inconsistent state action.

CHAPTER 7

Bail and Preventive Detention

Quick Reference Rules of Law

	PAGE
1. *United States v. Salerno.* The Bail Reform Act allowing for the denial of bail upon a showing that the defendant presents a risk of danger is constitutional.	*118*

United States v. Salerno

Federal government (P) v. Accused criminal (D)

481 U.S. 739 (1987)

NATURE OF CASE: Appeal from denial of bail.

FACT SUMMARY: Salerno (D) contended the Bail Reform Act violated his constitutional rights by allowing a denial of bail based on his potentially dangerous activities.

RULE OF LAW

The Bail Reform Act allowing for the denial of bail upon a showing that the defendant presents a risk of danger is constitutional.

FACTS: Salerno (D) was charged with violation of the criminal Racketeer Influenced and Corrupt Organizations (RICO) statute. He was denied bail after a hearing resulted in a finding that no release conditions would reasonably assure the safety of any person and the community. He appealed, contending the statute allowing for such denial violated due process and excessive bail prohibitions and was thus unconstitutional on its face. The court of appeals reversed, and the United States Supreme Court granted certiorari.

ISSUE: Is the Bail Reform Act allowing for the denial of bail upon a showing that the defendant presents a risk of danger constitutional?

HOLDING AND DECISION: (Rehnquist, C.J.) Yes. The Bail Reform Act (the Act) allowing for the denial of bail upon a showing that the defendant presents a risk of danger is constitutional. Detention is not punishment. This Act is regulatory, not punitive. The regulatory goal was to protect the public and people close to a trial from potentially harmful individuals. Thus, the regulatory goal was directly related to its means. The Government's (P) interest in preserving safety may outweigh an individual's right to freedom. Thus, some circumstances exist wherein application of the Act is constitutional. Thus, it is not invalid on its face. Reversed.

DISSENT: (Marshall, J.) This statute punishes a person for the commission of a perceived future crime. Incarceration is punishment. Thus, the statute is unconstitutional.

ANALYSIS

The traditional basis for determining if bail is available is whether there is a risk of flight, that is, whether there is a risk the defendant will not show up for court proceedings. The higher the possibility for flight, usually based on the severity of the crime, the higher the bail. A person is considered innocent until proven guilty; thus, pretrial detention walks a thin constitutional line.

Quicknotes

DUE PROCESS The constitutional mandate requiring the courts to protect and enforce individuals' rights and liberties consistent with prevailing principles of fairness and justice and prohibiting the federal and state governments from such activities that deprive its citizens of life, liberty, or property interest.

RICO Racketeer Influenced and Corrupt Organization laws; federal and state statutes enacted for the purpose of prosecuting organized crime.

CHAPTER 8

Discovery

Quick Reference Rules of Law

		PAGE
1.	*United States v. Agurs.* A prosecutor need not reveal evidence to the defense without a request unless such evidence clearly would have swayed the jury's decision.	*120*
2.	*Williams v. Florida.* The constitutional privilege against self-incrimination is not violated by a requirement that the defendant give notice of an alibi defense and disclose his or her alibi witnesses.	*121*
3.	*United States v. Nobles.* Prosecutorial discovery may allow the court to order the defense to produce its evidence where such is unprivileged and does not violate the Fifth Amendment.	*122*

United States v. Agurs

Federal government (P) v. Convicted murderer (D)

427 U.S. 97 (1976)

NATURE OF CASE: Appeal from grant of new trial following conviction for murder.

FACT SUMMARY: The court of appeals reversed the district court and held the prosecutor's failure to reveal evidence showing Sewell's violent nature denied Agurs (D) a fair trial, as she could not strengthen her self-defense argument without it.

RULE OF LAW

A prosecutor need not reveal evidence to the defense without a request unless such evidence clearly would have swayed the jury's decision.

FACTS: Sewell was discovered on top of Agurs (D), struggling for the knife Agurs (D) was holding. Sewell was apparently attempting to stab Agurs (D). Sewell subsequently died of knife wounds, and Agurs (D) was charged with murder. Agurs (D) pleaded self-defense but was convicted. She appealed, contending the prosecution had denied her a fair trial by failing to reveal Sewell's arrest record. Such record arguably showed Sewell's violent nature, yet the defense never requested its production. The court of appeals reversed, and the United States Supreme Court granted certiorari.

ISSUE: Must a prosecutor reveal evidence to the defense without a request unless such evidence clearly would have swayed the jury's decision?

HOLDING AND DECISION: (Stevens, J.) No. A prosecutor need not reveal evidence to the defense without a request unless such evidence clearly would have swayed the jury's decision. In this case, Agurs (D) had already shown Sewell's violent nature through other evidence. Thus, introduction of the arrest record would have added nothing to the case and could not have swayed the jury. As a result, the right to a fair trial was not abridged. Reversed.

DISSENT: (Marshall, J.) The majority's rule creates little, if any, incentive for the prosecutor conscientiously to determine whether his or her files contain evidence helpful to the defense. Indeed, the rule reinforces the natural tendency of the prosecutor to overlook evidence favorable to the defense and creates an incentive for the prosecutor to resolve close questions of disclosure in favor of concealment.

ANALYSIS

In this case, the United States Supreme Court seems to give with one hand and take with the other. It recognizes that in some cases prosecutors have a constitutional duty to reveal evidence even where such has not been requested. However, it limits this duty to evidence that is so material as to clearly affect the jury verdict. Thus, the duty is a very narrow one.

Quicknotes

EXCULPATORY EVIDENCE A statement or other evidence that tends to excuse, justify, or absolve the defendant from alleged fault or guilt.

Williams v. Florida

Convicted robber (D) v. State (P)

399 U.S. 78 (1970)

NATURE OF CASE: Appeal from conviction of robbery.

FACT SUMMARY: Florida law requires that a defendant submit to a limited form of pretrial discovery by the state whenever he or she intends to rely at trial on the defense of alibi.

RULE OF LAW

The constitutional privilege against self-incrimination is not violated by a requirement that the defendant give notice of an alibi defense and disclose his or her alibi witnesses.

FACTS: Williams (D) was charged with robbery. Prior to his trial, Williams (D) sought a protective order to be excused from complying with a Florida law that requires a defendant, on written demand of the prosecution, to give notice in advance of trial if the defendant intends to claim an alibi, and to furnish the prosecution with information as to the place he or she claims to have been and with the names and addresses of the alibi witnesses he or she intends to use. Williams (D) wanted to declare his intent to use an alibi but objected to further disclosure on the ground that the rule would compel him to be a witness against himself in violation of the Fifth and Fourteenth Amendments. The rule also obligated the state to notify a defendant of any rebuttal witnesses to the alibi defense the state will call. Failure to comply by either side results in the exclusion of the defendant's alibi evidence or the state's rebuttal evidence. When Williams's (D) motion for the protective order was denied, he complied with the rule. On the morning of his trial, the State (P) interviewed a Mrs. Scotty, Williams's (D) chief alibi witness. At trial, Mrs. Scotty gave testimony that contradicted her pretrial statements. The State (P) also furnished a rebuttal witness. Williams (D) was convicted.

ISSUE: Is a notice-of-alibi rule violative of the Fifth and Fourteenth Amendments by compelling a defendant to be a witness against him- or herself?

HOLDING AND DECISION: (White, J.) No. The rule is fair to both the defendant and state in permitting liberal discovery. The state has a legitimate interest in protecting itself against eleventh hour defenses; although based on an adversary system, a trial is not yet a poker game in which players may conceal their cards at will. No pretrial statements of Mrs. Scotty were introduced at trial; her pretrial testimony was only used to find rebuttal witnesses. A defendant is always in a dilemma whether to remain silent or present a defense that may prove disastrous. Nothing in the rule obligates the defendant to rely on an alibi or prevents him or her from abandoning it as a defense. The rule requires only that a defendant accelerate the timing of his or her disclosure of information he or she would have revealed at trial anyway. A defendant is not entitled to await the end of the prosecution's case before announcing the nature of his or her defense any more than he or she can await the jury's verdict on the state's case before deciding to take the stand him- or herself. Absent the rule, the prosecution would be entitled to a continuance at trial on the grounds of surprise. The rule thus serves to prevent a disrupted trial. Affirmed.

CONCURRENCE AND DISSENT: (Black, J.) The decision goes to more than just "timing." The majority's decision opens the way to compel complete pretrial discovery of a defendant's case, and any defenses defendant might raise.

ANALYSIS

At the time *Williams* was decided, 15 states other than Florida had notice-of-alibi requirements of varying kinds. One such rule, in *Wardius v. Oregon*, 412 U.S. 470 (1973), was struck down because it failed to provide reciprocal discovery rights to the defendant. The United States Supreme Court found this omission violative of the Due Process Clause of the Fourteenth Amendment. Because exclusion of the testimony of alibi witnesses is a drastic sanction for failure on the defendant's part to comply with the rule's disclosure requirements, other sanctions have been suggested. These include: (1) granting a continuance to the prosecution; (2) allowing the prosecution or court to comment on the defendant's failure to the jury; and (3) placing the defense counsel in contempt when the failure was not in "good faith."

Quicknotes

FOURTEENTH AMENDMENT DUE PROCESS CLAUSE Provides that protections mandated by the U.S. Constitution and observed by the federal government are equally applicable, and therefore must be observed by the states.

United States v. Nobles

Federal government (P) v. Convicted bank robber (D)

422 U.S. 225 (1975)

NATURE OF CASE: Appeal from conviction for robbery.

FACT SUMMARY: The Court of Appeals for the Ninth Circuit held that a federal trial court cannot compel a criminal defendant to reveal the relevant portions of his investigator's report on prosecution witnesses.

RULE OF LAW

Prosecutorial discovery may allow the court to order the defense to produce its evidence where such is unprivileged and does not violate the Fifth Amendment.

FACTS: Nobles (D) was put on trial for bank robbery and attempted to have his investigator testify to discredit the prosecution's witnesses. When Nobles (D) refused to reveal the contents of his investigator's report on the witnesses, the judge refused to allow the investigator's testimony. Nobles (D) appealed from his subsequent conviction on the basis that the report was not discoverable by the prosecution. The Court of Appeals for the Ninth Circuit reversed, and the United States Supreme Court granted certiorari.

ISSUE: Is defense evidence discoverable by the prosecution?

HOLDING AND DECISION: (Powell, J.) Yes. Defense evidence is discoverable if it is unprivileged and if its discovery would not violate the Fifth Amendment. Criminal discovery is not a one-way street. The purpose of trial is to ascertain truth without violating the defendant's constitutional rights. Thus, where the defense possesses evidence that would aid the trier of fact in making a determination, such is discoverable. Reversed.

ANALYSIS

The United States Supreme Court also discussed the role of the work product limitation on discovery. This rule stems from the decision in *Hickman v. Taylor*, 329 U.S. 495 (1947). It creates a privilege for documents that are the work product of the attorney or his agent. This privilege is qualified and may be waived. In this case, had the investigator testified, the privilege would have been waived.

Quicknotes

ATTORNEY WORK PRODUCT DOCTRINE A doctrine excluding from discovery work performed by an attorney in preparation of litigation.

FIFTH AMENDMENT Provides that no person shall be compelled to serve as a witness against him- or herself, be subject to trial for the same offense twice, or be deprived of life, liberty, or property without due process of law.

CHAPTER 9

Guilty Pleas and Bargaining

Quick Reference Rules of Law

	PAGE
1. *United States v. Ruiz.* The Fifth and Sixth Amendments do not require prosecutors, before entering a plea bargain, to disclose impeachment information relating to any informants or other witnesses.	*124*

United States v. Ruiz

Federal government (P) v. Drug possessor (D)

536 U.S. 622 (2002)

NATURE OF CASE: Appeal by Government (P) from the vacating of a sentencing determination.

FACT SUMMARY: Angela Ruiz (D) argued that the Constitution prohibits a defendant from waiving the right to impeachment information before they can enter into a plea agreement.

RULE OF LAW

The Fifth and Sixth Amendments do not require prosecutors, before entering a plea bargain, to disclose impeachment information relating to any informants or other witnesses.

FACTS: After immigration agents found 30 kilograms of marijuana in Angela Ruiz's (D) luggage, federal prosecutors offered her a so-called "fast track" plea bargain in return for which the Government (P) agreed to recommend a more lenient sentence than otherwise would have been mandated. Such plea bargain agreement contained detailed terms, including that the defendant waive the right to receive impeachment information relating to any informants or other witnesses. Because Ruiz (D) would not agree to this waiver, the prosecutors withdrew their bargaining offer. Despite the absence of a plea agreement, Ruiz (D) pleaded guilty and requested that the sentencing judge grant her the same reduced sentence she would have received if she had accepted the "fast track" plea. The judge refused, however, and the Court of Appeals for the Ninth Circuit vacated the district judge's sentencing determination, taking the position that the Constitution prohibits defendants from waiving their right to impeachment information before they enter into a plea agreement. The Government (P) appealed.

ISSUE: Do the Fifth and Sixth Amendments require prosecutors, before entering a plea bargain, to disclose impeachment information relating to any informants or other witnesses?

HOLDING AND DECISION: (Breyer, J.) No. The Fifth and Sixth Amendments do not require prosecutors, before entering a plea bargain, to disclose impeachment information relating to any informants or other witnesses. Impeachment information is special in relation to the fairness of a trial, not in respect to whether a plea is voluntary ("knowing," "intelligent," and "sufficiently aware"). Of course, the more information the defendant has, the more aware he or she is of the likely consequences of a plea, waiver, or decision, and the wiser that decision will likely be. However, the Constitution does not require the prosecutor to share all useful information with the defendant. The law ordinarily considers a waiver knowing, intelligent, and sufficiently aware if the defendant fully understands the nature of the right and how it would likely apply in general in the circumstances—even though the defendant may not know the specific detailed consequences of invoking it. It is particularly difficult to characterize impeachment information as critical information of which the defendant must always be aware prior to pleading guilty given the random way in which such information may, or may not, help a particular defendant. The degree of help that impeachment information can provide will depend upon the defendant's own independent knowledge of the prosecution's potential case, a matter that the Constitution does not require prosecutors to disclose. Furthermore, since the proposed plea agreement provides that the Government (P) will provide any information establishing the factual innocence of the defendant, that fact along with other guilty-plea safeguards diminishes the force of Ruiz's (D) concern that, in the absence of impeachment information, innocent individuals, accused of crimes, will plead guilty. Reversed.

ANALYSIS

In *Ruiz*, the United States Supreme Court found no decisional authority to support the Ninth Circuit position of required disclosure of impeachment witnesses. To the contrary, noted the Court, it would be difficult to distinguish, in terms of importance, (1) a defendant's ignorance of grounds for impeachment of potential witnesses at a possible future trial from (2) the varying forms of ignorance that could be at issue in any particular case.

Quicknotes

FIFTH AMENDMENT Provides that no person shall be compelled to serve as a witness against him- or herself, be subject to trial for the same offense twice, or be deprived of life, liberty, or property without due process of law.

IMPEACHMENT The discrediting of a witness by offering evidence to show that the witness lacks credibility.

SIXTH AMENDMENT Provides the right to a speedy and public trial by impartial jury, the right to be informed of the accusation, the right to confront witnesses, and the right to have the assistance of counsel in all criminal prosecutions.

CHAPTER 10

Trial and Trial-Related Rights

Quick Reference Rules of Law

CHAPTER 10

16. *Missouri v. Frye.* Counsel for criminal defendants has the duty to communicate formal offers from the prosecution with terms and conditions that may be favorable to the defendants. *147*

17. *Lafler v. Cooper.* When claiming ineffective assistance of counsel based on erroneous advice to reject a plea offer, a defendant must show there was a reasonable probability that the court would have accepted the plea agreement and that the conviction and sentence would have been less severe than those that were in fact imposed. *149*

18. *Caplin & Drysdale v. United States.* Federal forfeiture laws do not deny a defendant right to counsel. *151*

19. *Luis v. United States.* Criminal defendants have a Sixth Amendment right to use their own untainted or innocent property to pay for the assistance of defense counsel. *152*

20. *Faretta v. California.* There is a constitutional right to represent oneself in a criminal proceeding. *154*

United States v. Marion

Federal government (P) v. Accused (D)

404 U.S. 307 (1971)

NATURE OF CASE: Government's appeal from the dismissal of an indictment.

FACT SUMMARY: Marion (D) contended that his Sixth Amendment right to a speedy trial was violated by a delay of three years between the end of his alleged criminal scheme and the return of the indictment.

RULE OF LAW

The Sixth Amendment speedy trial provision has no application until the putative defendant in some way becomes an accused.

FACTS: Marion (D) was indicted approximately three years after the end of the criminal scheme charged. The lower court dismissed the indictment for lack of speedy prosecution, and the Government (P) appealed.

ISSUE: Does the Sixth Amendment speedy trial provision apply before the putative defendant in some way becomes an accused?

HOLDING AND DECISION: (White, J.) No. The Sixth Amendment speedy trial provision has no application until the putative defendant in some way becomes an accused. Inordinate delay between arrest, indictment, and trial may impair a defendant's ability to present an effective defense. However, the major evils protected against by the speedy trial guarantee exist quite apart from actual or possible prejudice to an accused's defense. Arrest is a public act that may seriously interfere with the defendant's liberty, whether he or she is free on bail or not, and that may disrupt his or her employment, drain his or her financial resources, curtail his or her associations, subject him or her to public obloquy, and create anxiety in the defendant, his or her family, and his or her friends. So viewed, it is readily understandable that it is either a formal indictment or information or else the actual restraints imposed by arrest and holding to answer a criminal charge that engage the particular protections of the speedy trial provision of the Sixth Amendment. This Court declines to extend the reach of the Sixth Amendment to the period prior to arrest. Until this event occurs, a citizen suffers no restraints on his or her liberty and is not the subject of public accusation; his or her situation does not compare with that of a defendant who has been arrested and held to answer. The mere possibility of prejudice at trial is not itself sufficient reason to wrench the Sixth Amendment from its proper context. Possible prejudice is inherent in any delay, however short; it may also even weaken the government's case. Reversed.

ANALYSIS

In *Marion*, the United States Supreme Court noted that the law has provided other mechanisms to guard against possible, as distinguished from actual, prejudice resulting from the passage of time between crime and arrest or charge. The applicable statute of limitations is the primary guarantee against bringing overly stale criminal charges. These statutes provide predictability by specifying a limit beyond which there is an irrebuttable presumption that a defendant's right to a fair trial would be prejudiced.

Quicknotes

SIXTH AMENDMENT Provides the right to a speedy and public trial by impartial jury, the right to be informed of the accusation, the right to confront witnesses, and the right to have the assistance of counsel in all criminal prosecutions.

United States v. Lovasco

Federal government (P) v. Accused (D)

431 U.S. 783 (1977)

NATURE OF CASE: Appeal from dismissal of an indictment.

FACT SUMMARY: Lovasco (D) contended the indictment should be dismissed because the 18-month delay in filing it prejudiced his defense.

RULE OF LAW

A court cannot dismiss an indictment merely because the delay in filing prejudiced the defense.

FACTS: Lovasco (D) was indicted for possessing stolen firearms. The indictment was filed 18 months after the crimes were alleged to have occurred. In the interim, two defense witnesses died. Lovasco (D) successfully moved to dismiss the indictment on the basis that the delay had prejudiced the defense. The court of appeals affirmed, and the United States Supreme Court granted certiorari.

ISSUE: Can a court dismiss an indictment merely because the delay in filing prejudiced the defense?

HOLDING AND DECISION: (Marshall, J.) No. A court cannot dismiss an indictment merely because the delay in filing prejudiced the defense. It is in the prosecutor's prerogative to decide when to seek charges against a suspect. A court may not violate the separation of powers doctrine and abort a criminal prosecution. Such would encroach on the prosecutor's role. As a result, the indictment was improperly dismissed. Reversed.

ANALYSIS

In cases such as *United States v. Marion*, 404 U.S. 307 (1971), and *United States v. MacDonald*, 632 F.2d 258 (4th Cir. 1980), courts have dismissed indictments for unreasonable delay in filing. In these cases, prejudice is a necessary, yet not dispositive, element in dismissing the indictment. Due process requires inquiry into the reasons for the delay.

Quicknotes

DUE PROCESS The constitutional mandate requiring the courts to protect and enforce individuals' rights and liberties consistent with prevailing principles of fairness and justice and prohibiting the federal and state governments from such activities that deprive its citizens of life, liberty, or property interest.

SEPARATION OF POWERS The system of checks and balances preventing one branch of government from infringing upon exercising the powers of another branch of government.

Barker v. Wingo

Convicted murderer (D) v. State (P)

407 U.S. 514 (1972)

NATURE OF CASE: Petition for certiorari of a murder conviction.

FACT SUMMARY: Although Willie Barker (D) made no objections during the first four years of a five-year delay between his arrest and conviction for murder, he subsequently claimed that his right to a speedy trial had been violated.

RULE OF LAW

The determination of whether a defendant has been deprived of his or her Sixth Amendment right to a speedy trial must be made on a case-by-case basis by balancing the following four factors: (1) length of delay, (2) reason for delay, (3) the defendant's assertion of his or her right, and (4) prejudice to the defendant.

FACTS: On July 20, 1958, an elderly couple was murdered. Shortly afterward, Silas Manning and Willie Barker (D) were arrested as suspects. On September 15 they were indicted, on September 17 counsel was appointed, and Barker's (D) trial was set for October 21. However, Barker (D) was not brought to trial for more than five years after his arrest due to numerous continuances by the prosecution. Initially the continuances were for purpose of first convicting Manning, against whom the Commonwealth had a stronger case, to assure his testimony at Barker's (D) trial (i.e., to eliminate problems of self-incrimination). However, Manning was not convicted until 1962. Afterward, Barker's (D) trial was delayed another seven months due to the illness of the chief investigating officer in the case. During these continuances, Barker (D) was free for all but ten months in jail, and he made no objections during the first four years of delay. However, Barker (D) objected to the last few continuances, and, at his trial, he moved for dismissal on the basis that his Sixth Amendment right to a speedy trial had been violated. This motion was denied and Barker (D) was convicted of murder. Upon appeal to the Kentucky Court of Appeals, the conviction was affirmed. Barker (D) then petitioned for habeas corpus in the United States District Court. Upon denial of that petition, he appealed to the Sixth Circuit Court of Appeals. Upon affirmance of his conviction, Barker (D) brought a petition for certiorari.

ISSUE: Must the determination of whether a defendant has been deprived of his or her Sixth Amendment right to a speedy trial be made on a case-by-case basis by balancing the following four factors: (1) length of delay, (2) reason for delay, (3) the defendant's assertion of his or her right, and (4) prejudice to the defendant.

HOLDING AND DECISION: (Powell, J.) Yes. The determination of whether a defendant has been deprived of his or her Sixth Amendment right to a speedy trial must be made on a case-by-case basis by balancing the following four factors: (1) length of delay, (2) reason for delay, (3) the defendant's assertion of his or her right, and (4) prejudice to the defendant. Since the deprivation of the right to a speedy trial does not per se prejudice the ability of an accused to defend himself, it is impossible to state "with precision" when the right has been denied. Each factor, therefore, must be separately analyzed. First, it is true that a long delay before trial is more likely to be justified for a serious, complex crime (e.g., murder) than for a simple one. Here, however, the delay of over five years was extreme by any standard. Second, it is true that a delay in bringing an accused to trial may be justified by a showing of some strong reason for it. Here, however, there was a strong reason for delay (i.e., illness of the chief investigator) for only seven months of the five-year delay. Although some additional delay might also have been necessary to acquire Manning as a witness, over four years was clearly unreasonable. Third, it is true that failure to assert the right to a speedy trial will not constitute a waiver of that right, unless it is found to be an "intentional relinquishment or abandonment of a known right." Here, however, it is obvious that Barker (D) did not want a trial at all, hoping, rather, that the delays would ultimately result in dismissal of the charges against him. Fourth, it is true that the prejudice that results from a delay of a defendant's trial must be evaluated in the light of those interests that a speedy trial was designed to protect (i.e., prevention of "oppressive pretrial incarceration," minimization of anxiety and concern of the accused, and limitation on the possibility that the defense will be "impaired"). Here, however, prejudice was minimal. Although Barker (D) was prejudiced to some extent by spending some time in jail and by living for years under "a cloud of suspicion," none of his witnesses died or became unavailable. In conclusion, the fact that Barker (D) did not want a trial and was not prejudiced by the delay outweighs the unjustified length of delay. Judgment affirmed.

Continued on next page.

CONCURRENCE: (White, J.) Barker's (D) acquiescence to the delays in this case was the dispositive factor in the denial of the speedy trial issue.

ANALYSIS

This case illustrates the discretion available (through the balancing test) to the courts in determining when the right to a speedy trial has been violated, and the emphasis on the desire of an accused to have a speedy trial. Note that an accused "waives" the right to a speedy trial if he or she flees the state after arraignment or requests postponement of his or her trial. Note also, that the right to a speedy trial attaches only after a person is accused (i.e., indicted or arrested), so that it is not violated by police delay in filing charges. However, if such a delay was purposeful, due process requires dismissal of the charges.

Quicknotes

HABEAS CORPUS A proceeding in which a defendant brings a writ to compel a judicial determination of whether he or she is lawfully being held in custody.

SIXTH AMENDMENT Provides the right to a speedy and public trial by impartial jury, the right to be informed of the accusation, the right to confront witnesses, and the right to have the assistance of counsel in all criminal prosecutions.

Apprendi v. New Jersey

Convicted accused (D) v. State (P)

530 U.S. 466 (2000)

NATURE OF CASE: Appeal from sentence.

FACT SUMMARY: Apprendi (D) contended that any fact that increases the penalty for a crime beyond the statutory maximum must be submitted to a jury and proved beyond a reasonable doubt.

RULE OF LAW

The Due Process Clause of the Fourteenth Amendment requires that any fact that increases the penalty for crime beyond the statutory maximum be submitted to a jury and proved beyond a reasonable doubt.

FACTS: Apprendi (D) pled guilty to a shooting, and at sentencing the Government (P) produced evidence that the shooting was racially motivated. The sentencing judge found evidence of racial bias by a preponderance of the evidence and imposed an enhanced sentence on the basis of the hate crime law. That sentence was well above what Apprendi (D) could have received for the crime to which he pled guilty. The sentence was upheld by the New Jersey appellate court, which concluded that the state had the authority to define racial motivation as a "sentencing factor" rather than as "an element of the crime." Apprendi (D) appealed.

ISSUE: Does the Due Process Clause of the Fourteenth Amendment require that any fact that increases penalty for crime beyond the statutory maximum be submitted to a jury and proved beyond a reasonable doubt?

HOLDING AND DECISION: (Stevens, J.) Yes. The Due Process Clause of the Fourteenth Amendment requires that any fact that increases penalty for crime beyond the statutory maximum be submitted to a jury and proved beyond a reasonable doubt. The New Jersey procedure here challenged is an unacceptable departure from the jury tradition that is an indispensable part of our criminal justice system. At stake in this case are constitutional protections of surpassing importance: the proscription of any deprivation of liberty without due process of law and the guarantee, inter alia, of public trial by an impartial jury. Taken together, these rights indisputably entitle a criminal defendant to a jury determination that he or she is guilty of every element of the crime with which charged, beyond a reasonable doubt. In this regard, this Court does not recognize any distinction between an "element" of a felony offense and a "sentencing factor." This Court has previously made clear that due process and associated jury protections extend, to some degree, to determinations that go not to a defendant's guilt or innocence, but simply to the length of his or her sentence. Reversed.

CONCURRENCE: (Scalia, J.) The founders of the American Republic were not prepared to leave it to the states to design a fair and efficient criminal justice system, which is why the jury-trial guarantee was one of the least controversial provisions of the Bill of Rights.

CONCURRENCE: (Thomas, J.) Sentencing elements may be new creatures, but the question that they create is not. The original understanding of which "facts" are "elements" of a crime was even broader than the rule that the Court here adopts. Authority establishes that a "crime" includes every fact that is by law a basis for imposing or increasing punishment (in contrast with a fact that mitigates punishment).

DISSENT: (O'Connor, J.) This Court has long recognized that not every fact that bears on a defendant's punishment need be charged in an indictment, submitted to a jury, and proved by the government beyond a reasonable doubt. Rather, the legislature's definition of the elements of the offense is usually dispositive.

DISSENT: (Breyer, J.) There are, to put it simply, far too many potentially relevant sentencing factors to permit submission of all (or even many) of them to a jury. Even the Federal Sentencing Guidelines themselves note that a sentencing system tailored to fit every conceivable wrinkle of each case can become unworkable and seriously compromise the certainty of punishment and its deterrent effect. To ask a jury to consider all, or many, such matters would do the same.

ANALYSIS

As the United States Supreme Court makes clear in *Apprendi*, the historic link between verdict and judgment and the consistent limitations of judges' discretion to operate within the limits of the legal penalties highlight the novelty of a legislative scheme, such as that of New Jersey, that removes the jury from the determination of a fact that, if found, exposes the criminal defendant to a penalty exceeding the maximum he or she would receive if punished according to the facts reflected in the jury verdict alone. It is for this articulated reason that the Court emphasizes that the "reasonable doubt" requirement has such a vital role in American criminal procedure for cogent reasons. Hence, the Court

Continued on next page.

requires, among other things, procedural protections in order to provide concrete substance for the presumption of innocence and to reduce the risk of imposing such deprivations erroneously.

Quicknotes

DUE PROCESS CLAUSE Language in the Fifth and Fourteenth Amendments to the United States Constitution providing that no person shall be deprived of "life, liberty, or property, without due process of law."

FOURTEENTH AMENDMENT Declares that no state shall make or enforce any law that shall abridge the privileges and immunities of citizens of the United States; no state shall deny to any person within its jurisdiction the equal protection of the laws.

REASONABLE DOUBT Enough doubt on the part of jurors to acquit a defendant based on the absence of evidence.

County Court v. Allen

County (P) v. Convicted felon (D)

442 U.S. 140 (1979)

NATURE OF CASE: Appeal from conviction for possession of firearms.

FACT SUMMARY: Allen (D) contended that a New York statute that created a presumption of possession of a firearm by all in a car was unconstitutional.

RULE OF LAW

Statutory presumptions are not subject to constitutional attack on their face.

FACTS: Allen (D) was present in an automobile in which the police found firearms. There were three other people in the car and all were charged with possession of the firearms. At trial, Allen (D) contended that the New York law that created a statutory presumption that all people in a car in which firearms are found are in possession of the firearms was unconstitutional on its face. The trial court instructed the jury as to this presumption, and Allen (D) was convicted. The court of appeals affirmed, and the United States Supreme Court granted certiorari.

ISSUE: Are statutory presumptions subject to attack as unconstitutional on their face?

HOLDING AND DECISION: (Stevens, J.) No. Statutory presumptions are not subject to attack as being unconstitutional on their face. The presumption in this case gave rise to a permissive inference from certain established facts to certain inferred facts. The presumption was not a mandatory inference. As a result, it did not lighten the prosecution's burden of proof; it merely added to its case. As a result, the presumption could not be held unconstitutional on its face. Affirmed.

DISSENT: (Powell, J.) The presumption charged in this case encouraged the jury to draw a particular factual inference regardless of any other evidence presented. The presumption thus charged was unconstitutional because it did not fairly reflect what common sense and experience tell us about passengers in automobiles and the possession of handguns. People present in automobiles where there are weapons simply are not "more likely than not" the possessors of those weapons.

ANALYSIS

There are two types of presumptions: rebuttable and irrebuttable. A defendant need only produce some evidence that the inference is not valid in order to successfully attack a rebuttable presumption. An irrebuttable presumption withstands any contrary showing.

Quicknotes

REBUTTABLE PRESUMPTION A rule of law, inferred from the existence of a particular set of facts, that is conclusive in the absence of contrary evidence.

Duncan v. Louisiana

Accused (D) v. State (P)

391 U.S. 145 (1968)

NATURE OF CASE: Appeal from conviction for battery.

FACT SUMMARY: Duncan (D) contended the Sixth Amendment right to jury trial applied to the states through the Due Process Clause of the Fourteenth Amendment.

RULE OF LAW

A right guaranteed by the Sixth Amendment that is fundamental to the American scheme of justice applies to the states through the Fourteenth Amendment.

FACTS: Duncan (D) was charged with battery by the state of Louisiana (P). He demanded and was refused a trial by jury and was convicted by the court. He appealed, contending the Sixth Amendment right to jury trial applied to the states through the Due Process Clause of the Fourteenth Amendment. He contended the failure to honor his request for a jury trial denied him liberty without due process of law.

ISSUE: Does a right guaranteed by the Sixth Amendment that is fundamental to the American scheme of justice apply to the states through the Fourteenth Amendment?

HOLDING AND DECISION: (White, J.) Yes. A right guaranteed by the Sixth Amendment that is fundamental to the American scheme of justice applies to the states through the Fourteenth Amendment. The jury trial, in cases wherein that right would be available in a federal court, is fundamental to the scheme of American justice. Thus Duncan (D) was denied due process and his conviction cannot stand. Reversed.

ANALYSIS

The United States Supreme Court has adopted several tests to be used in determining what rights guaranteed by the Bill of Rights apply to the several states through the Due Process Clause of the Fourteenth Amendment. In *Powell v. Alabama*, 287 U.S. 45 (1932), the test was whether the right was a fundamental principle of liberty. In *Gideon v. Wainwright*, 372 U.S. 335 (1963), the test followed was whether the right was essential to a fair trial.

Quicknotes

DUE PROCESS CLAUSE Language in the Fifth and Fourteenth Amendments to the United States Constitution providing that no person shall be deprived of "life, liberty, or property without due process of law."

FOURTEENTH AMENDMENT No person shall be deprived of life, liberty, or property, without the due process of law.

RIGHT TO JURY TRIAL The right guaranteed by the Sixth Amendment to the federal Constitution that in all criminal prosecutions the accused has a right to a trial by an impartial jury of the state and district in which the crime was allegedly committed.

SIXTH AMENDMENT Provides the right to a speedy trial by impartial jury, the right to be informed of the accusation, the right to confront witnesses, and the right to have the assistance of counsel in all criminal prosecutions.

Williams v. Florida

Convicted robber (D) v. State (P)

399 U.S. 78 (1970)

NATURE OF CASE: Appeal from conviction for robbery.

FACT SUMMARY: Williams (D) contended he had a constitutional right to a twelve-person jury.

RULE OF LAW

There is no constitutional requirement that criminal juries contain twelve members.

FACTS: Williams (D) was arrested for robbery. He made a pre-trial motion for a twelve-member jury, even though Florida law required only six. The motion was denied and Williams (D) was convicted. He appealed, contending the Constitution required a twelve-person jury. The United States Supreme Court granted certiorari.

ISSUE: Is there a constitutional requirement that criminal juries contain twelve members?

HOLDING AND DECISION: (White, J.) No. There is no constitutional requirement that a criminal jury contain twelve members. From known history, the number twelve holds no magical connotation and, more likely, was arrived at by accident rather than by reason and logic. As a result, a lesser number is acceptable so long as the basic ingredients of the right to jury trial are maintained. States are therefore free to adopt a number less than twelve. Affirmed.

ANALYSIS

The case illustrates that, although the Sixth Amendment right applies against the states, the procedural rules applicable in federal court do not extend to state prosecutions. In *Ballew v. Georgia*, 435 U.S. 223 (1977), the United States Supreme Court held that the six-person jury is the minimum allowed by the Constitution.

Quicknotes

SIXTH AMENDMENT Provides the right to a speedy and public trial by impartial jury, the right to be informed of the accusation, the right to confront witnesses, and the right to have the assistance of counsel in all criminal prosecutions.

Ballew v. Georgia

Misdemeanor convict (D) v. State (P)

435 U.S. 223 (1978)

NATURE OF CASE: Appeal from conviction for distributing obscene material.

FACT SUMMARY: Ballew (D) contended his conviction by a jury of five people was unconstitutional.

RULE OF LAW

The constitutional minimum size of a criminal jury is six.

FACTS: Ballew (D) appealed his conviction for distributing obscene material on the basis that the Georgia law allowing five-member juries was unconstitutional. Georgia (P) argued it had the power to determine the size of the juries. The court of appeals affirmed, and the United States Supreme Court granted certiorari.

ISSUE: Is the constitutional minimum size of a criminal jury six?

HOLDING AND DECISION: (Blackmun, J.) Yes. The constitutional minimum size of a criminal jury is six. A jury was meant to represent the community in a criminal trial. A number below six jeopardizes this representation and undermines the reliability of the findings of fact. As a result, the Constitution requires a minimum of six people. Reversed.

CONCURRENCE: (White, J.) A jury of five does not represent the community.

CONCURRENCE: (Powell, J.) A line must be drawn that, although arbitrary, upholds basic requirements of fairness.

CONCURRENCE: (Brennan, J.) The Sixth and Fourteenth Amendments require juries in criminal trials to contain more than five persons.

ANALYSIS

This case modifies the United States Supreme Court's earlier decisions in *Duncan v. Louisiana*, 391 U.S. 145 (1968), and *Williams v. Florida*, 399 U.S. 78 (1970). In the former case, the right to jury trial was held to apply to state prosecutions through the Fourteenth Amendment. In the latter, it was held that a jury need not consist of twelve persons. Thus, a constitutional jury must contain somewhere between six and twelve members.

Quicknotes

FOURTEENTH AMENDMENT Declares that no state shall make or enforce any law that shall abridge the privileges and immunities of citizens of the United States; no state shall deny to any person within its jurisdiction the equal protection of the laws.

SIXTH AMENDMENT Provides the right to a speedy and public trial by impartial jury, the right to be informed of the accusation, the right to confront witnesses, and the right to have the assistance of counsel in all criminal prosecutions.

Ramos v. Louisiana

Individual convicted of a "serious" crime (D) v. State (P)

140 S. Ct. 1390 (2020)

NATURE OF CASE: Appeal from conviction for a "serious" crime. [The procedural posture of the case is not presented in the casebook extract.]

FACT SUMMARY: Evangelisto Ramos (Ramos) (D), who was convicted of a serious crime by a 10-to-2 nonunanimous jury and sentenced to life in prison without parole, contended that his conviction by a nonunanimous jury was an unconstitutional denial of the Sixth Amendment right to a jury trial.

RULE OF LAW

The Sixth Amendment right to a jury trial—as incorporated against the states by way of the Fourteenth Amendment—requires a unanimous verdict to convict a defendant of a serious offense.

FACTS: Evangelisto Ramos (Ramos) (D) was convicted in Louisiana (P) of a serious crime by a 10-to-2 nonunanimous jury and sentenced to life in prison without parole. Louisiana (P) and Oregon were the only two states that permitted such a nonunanimous conviction for a serious crime. Ramos (D) challenged his nonunanimous conviction, contending that it constituted an unconstitutional denial of his Sixth Amendment right to a jury trial. The United States Supreme Court granted certiorari. [The procedural posture of the case is not presented in the casebook extract.]

ISSUE: Does the Sixth Amendment right to a jury trial—as incorporated against the states by way of the Fourteenth Amendment—require a unanimous verdict to convict a defendant of a serious offense?

HOLDING AND DECISION: (Gorsuch, J.) Yes. The Sixth Amendment right to a jury trial—as incorporated against the states by way of the Fourteenth Amendment—requires a unanimous verdict to convict a defendant of a serious offense. The Constitution's text and structure clearly indicate that the Sixth Amendment term "trial by an impartial jury" carries with it some meaning about the content and requirements of a jury trial. One such requirement is that a jury must reach a unanimous verdict in order to convict. Juror unanimity emerged as a vital common-law right in 14th-century England, appeared in the early American state constitutions, and provided the backdrop against which the Sixth Amendment was drafted and ratified. By the time of ratification, unanimous verdicts had been required for about 400 years, and if the term "trial by an impartial jury" carried any meaning at all, it surely included a requirement as long and widely accepted as unanimity. Postadoption treatises and 19th-century American legal treatises confirm this understanding. Moreover, this is not a case where the original public meaning of that phrase was lost to time and only recently recovered, given that the Court has commented on the Sixth Amendment's unanimity requirement no fewer than 13 times over more than 120 years, and has also explained that the Sixth Amendment right to a jury trial is incorporated against the states under the Fourteenth Amendment. Thus, if the jury trial right requires a unanimous verdict in federal court, it requires no less in state court. Louisiana's (P) and Oregon's unconventional schemes were first confronted *in Apodaca v. Oregon,* 406 U.S. 404 (1972), and *Johnson v. Louisiana,* 406 U.S. 356 (1972), in a badly fractured set of opinions. A four-Justice plurality, questioning whether unanimity serves an important "function" in "contemporary society," concluded that unanimity's costs outweighed its benefits. Four dissenting Justices recognized that the Sixth Amendment requires unanimity, and that the guarantee is fully applicable against the States under the Fourteenth Amendment. The remaining Justice, Justice Powell, adopted a "dual-track" incorporation approach. He agreed that the Sixth Amendment requires unanimity but believed that the Fourteenth Amendment does not render this guarantee fully applicable against the States—even though the dual-track incorporation approach had been rejected by the Court nearly a decade earlier. The best Louisiana (P) can suggest is that all of the Court's prior statements that the Sixth Amendment does require unanimity are dicta, but even if that were so, Louisiana (P) offers no explanation as to why the Court would walk away from those statements now and does not dispute that 400 years of common law required unanimity. Louisiana's (P) argument that the drafting history of the Sixth Amendment left unanimity behind is unsupported, and its argument that unanimity is not important enough to be read as part of the Sixth Amendment is unpersuasive. Similarly rejected is the dissent's argument that stare decisis requires adherence to *Apodaca,* because factors traditionally considered by the Court when determining whether to preserve precedent on stare decisis grounds do not favor upholding *Apodaca*. When it revisits a precedent, the Court has traditionally considered the quality of the decision's reasoning, its consistency with related decisions, legal developments since the decision,

Continued on next page.

and reliance on the decision. In this case, each factor weighs against upholding *Apodaca*. [Reversed.]

CONCURRENCE: (Sotomayor, J.) This is an instance where it is acceptable to depart from precedent and principles of stare decisis because the precedent at issue (*Apodaca*) goes to a fundamental constitutional protection, in the face of which the strength of stare decisis is at its lowest, and because it was wrongly decided. To be clear, *Apodaca* is not being set aside merely because a majority of this Court disagrees with it as a matter of interpretational mode (the majority here uses an originalist mode of interpretation, whereas the *Apodaca* Court applied a functionalist analysis), given that reasonable minds have disagreed over time—and continue to disagree—about the best mode of constitutional interpretation.

CONCURRENCE: (Kavanaugh, J.) Regarding stare decisis, it is sometimes appropriate for the Court to overrule erroneous decisions. Going forward, when considering whether to depart from precedent, the Court should use a consistent methodology that inquires whether the precedent was grievously or egregiously wrong, whether the prior decision caused significant negative jurisprudential or real-world consequences, and whether overruling the prior decision would unduly upset reliance interests.

CONCURRENCE: (Thomas, J.) This case should be decided on the grounds that the Privileges or Immunities Clause of the Fourteenth Amendment, not the Due Process Clause, made all the Bill of Rights provisions enforceable against the states, so that the unanimity requirement is also enforceable against the states.

DISSENT: (Alito, J.) The majority errs because it departs from binding precedent and disregards principles of stare decisis.

ANALYSIS

Stare decisis has been a fundamental part of the Court's jurisprudence since the founding, and the Court generally adheres to its prior decisions, even if it questions their soundness, because doing so promotes the evenhanded, predictable, and consistent development of legal principles; fosters reliance on judicial decisions; and contributes to the actual and perceived integrity of the judicial process. The doctrine reflects respect for the accumulated wisdom of judges who have previously tried to solve the same problem. As this case clearly illustrates, however, stare decisis has never been treated as an inexorable command, and the doctrine is at its weakest when the Court interprets the Constitution – as opposed to a statute – because a mistaken judicial interpretation of that supreme law is often practically impossible to correct through other means.

Quicknotes

FOURTEENTH AMENDMENT Declares that no state shall make or enforce any law that shall abridge the privileges and immunities of citizens of the United States; no state shall deny to any person within its jurisdiction the equal protection of the laws.

SIXTH AMENDMENT Provides the right to a speedy and public trial by impartial jury, the right to be informed of the accusation, the right to confront witnesses, and the right to have the assistance of counsel in all criminal prosecutions.

STARE DECISIS Doctrine whereby courts follow legal precedent unless there is good cause for departure.

Taylor v. Louisiana

Convicted kidnapper (D) v. State (P)

419 U.S. 522 (1975)

NATURE OF CASE: Appeal from criminal conviction on the basis that the jury was unconstitutionally constituted.

FACT SUMMARY: Louisiana (P) had a statute that provided that women would be exempt from jury duty unless they specifically requested to serve.

RULE OF LAW

The exclusion of a segment of society from jury duty is sufficient to establish a per se violation of a defendant's constitutional right to a trial by jury of his or her peers guaranteed under the Sixth Amendment.

FACTS: Louisiana (P) enacted a statute that provided that women should not be selected for jury duty unless they filed a specific request to serve. The practical effect of this provision was that women (constituting 53 percent of potential jurors) were virtually unrepresented on juries within Louisiana (P). Taylor (D) was convicted of aggravated kidnapping. He moved to quash the conviction on the basis that no women were available to sit on the jury that tried him. Taylor (D) claimed that this violated his rights to a trial by a jury of his peers (i.e., a fair cross-segment of the community). This was violative of the Sixth Amendment, which was made applicable to the states under the Fourteenth Amendment to the U.S. Constitution. The motion was denied by the trial court.

ISSUE: Is the exclusion of a segment of society from jury duty sufficient to establish a per se violation of a defendant's constitutional right to a trial by jury of his or her peers guaranteed under the Sixth Amendment?

HOLDING AND DECISION: (White, J.) Yes. The exclusion of a segment of society from jury duty is sufficient to establish a per se violation of a defendant's constitutional right to a trial by jury of his or her peers guaranteed under the Sixth Amendment. A defendant is entitled to be tried by a representative cross-section of his community. The failure to provide such a cross section is violative of the Sixth Amendment's constitutional guarantee of a trial by jury. The blanket exemption for women has the effect of practically excluding them from jury panels. The role of women in society (i.e., mothers) is insufficient grounds for the issuance of a blanket exemption. Liberal specific exemptions are allowed where individual facts warrant. Reversed.

ANALYSIS

In *Hamlin v. U.S.*, 418 U.S. 87 (1974), the United States Supreme Court held that exclusion of the young through a failure to update the master jury wheel for four years was not a per se violation of the defendant's Sixth Amendment guarantees. It would require a showing of prejudice to require a reversal of the conviction. The mere fact that persons who have become eligible for jury duty have been excluded is insufficient to establish purposeful discrimination. This last fact is what differentiates *Hamlin* from *Taylor*.

Quicknotes

FOURTEENTH AMENDMENT No person shall be deprived of life, liberty, or property, without the due process of law.

SIXTH AMENDMENT Provides the right to a speedy trial by impartial jury, the right to be informed of the accusation, the right to confront witnesses, and the right to have the assistance of counsel in all criminal prosecutions.

Batson v. Kentucky

Convicted burglar (D) v. State (P)

476 U.S. 79 (1986)

NATURE OF CASE: Review of burglary conviction.

FACT SUMMARY: Batson (D) contended that the prosecution's use of peremptory challenges to exclude jurors of his race itself constituted an infringement of equal protection.

RULE OF LAW

The use of peremptory challenges by the prosecution on voir dire may, itself, prove an infringement of equal protection.

FACTS: Batson (D), an African American, was charged with burglary. At trial, the prosecution exercised peremptory challenges on all Black veniremen, resulting in an all-White jury. The trial court rejected Batson's (D) objection that this violated equal protection. He was convicted. The Kentucky Supreme Court affirmed, and the United States Supreme Court granted review.

ISSUE: May the use of peremptory challenges by the prosecution on voir dire itself prove an infringement of equal protection?

HOLDING AND DECISION: (Powell, J.) Yes. The use of peremptory challenges by the prosecution on voir dire may, itself, prove an infringement of equal protection. This Court has long held that the prosecution may not systematically exclude from a petit jury members of a defendant's own race. This constitutes an infringement of the equal protection rights of the defendant and veniremen alike. An accused makes a prima facie case if he or she shows that peremptories were used to exclude veniremen of the defendant's own race. When this showing is made, the burden then shifts to the prosecution to offer racially neutral explanations for the use of the peremptories. Here, the matter must be remanded for such determination. Reversed and remanded.

CONCURRENCE: (Marshall, J.) The only sure cure of the evil of discrimination in jury selection is to abolish peremptory challenges.

DISSENT: (Burger, C.J.) Analytically, there can be only two types of challenges, with cause and without. By permitting inquiry into the basis for peremptory challenges, the majority creates an indefinable middle ground that will ultimately collapse and eliminate the category of peremptory challenges. (Rehnquist, J.) As long as peremptories are not used against any race in particular, the use of peremptories to exclude members of a defendant's race does not offend equal protection.

DISSENT: (Rehnquist, J.) There is nothing unequal in permitting peremptory challenges to strike Blacks from the jury in cases involving Black defendants so long as such challenges are permitted to strike Whites in cases involving White defendants, Hispanics in cases involving Hispanic defendants, and Asians in cases involving Asian defendants. The basis for the strikes likely is crudely stereotypical instincts and may be hopelessly mistaken. So long as they are applied across-the-board, their use does not violate the Equal Protection Clause.

ANALYSIS

The present case, as Justice White observed, left a lot of interstices to be filled. It applied in its context only to Black people but probably applied to other races as well. Also, it was unclear whether a defendant could exclude from a jury members of other races, or whether it applies to civil cases.

Quicknotes

PEREMPTORY CHALLENGE Challenge brought by a party to a lawsuit of a prospective juror without the need to specify a particular reason.

VENIREMAN A juror who has been impaneled.

VOIR DIRE Examination of potential jurors on a case.

Chandler v. Florida

Police officer (D) v. State (P)

449 U.S. 560 (1981)

NATURE OF CASE: Appeal from conviction for burglary.

FACT SUMMARY: Chandler (D) contended the presence of the news media at trial over his objection denied him a fair trial per se.

RULE OF LAW

There is no per se constitutional prohibition against allowing the news media to broadcast portions of a criminal trial.

FACTS: Chandler (D), a police officer, was charged with burglary, and his arrest caused a flurry of publicity. He moved the trial court to deny the news media the right to broadcast portions of the trial, arguing that such broadcast, absent his consent was per se unconstitutional. The motion was denied, and Chandler (D) was convicted. The court of appeals affirmed, and the United States Supreme Court granted certiorari.

ISSUE: Is there a per se constitutional prohibition against allowing the news media to broadcast portions of a criminal trial over the objection of the accused?

HOLDING AND DECISION: (Burger, C.J.) No. There is no per se constitutional prohibition against allowing the news media to broadcast portions of a criminal trial. Merely because in selected cases broadcasting would present the likelihood of prejudice to the defense does not justify the recognition of a per se rule banning the broadcasting of all criminal trials. The presence of the news media ensures that judges will be aware of their obligation to protect the fundamental rights of the accused. The defendant retains the right to appeal on the basis the conduct of the media in that particular case deprived him of a fair trial. This right of review adequately protects him or her while causing a less intrusive encumbrance on the First Amendment rights of the media. As a result, the conviction was proper. Affirmed.

ANALYSIS

The precedent referred to was *Estes v. Texas*, 381 U.S. 532 (1965). In that case the defendant, Estes, who had been linked to President Lyndon Johnson, was on trial for swindling. Because of the presidential connection, the trial was covered extensively by all types of broadcast and print media. Estes (D) successfully argued that the press had encroached upon his right to a fair trial. In *Chandler*, the United States Supreme Court refused to extend the *Estes* holding to formulate a per se rule of exclusion.

Quicknotes

FIRST AMENDMENT RIGHTS Rights conferred by the First Amendment to the U.S. Constitution prohibiting Congress from enacting any law respecting an establishment of religion or prohibiting the free exercise of religion; abridging freedom of speech or of the press; the right of peaceful assembly; and the right to petition for a redress of grievances.

PER SE By itself; without more; taken alone; not requiring additional evidence for proof, as a matter of law.

Illinois v. Allen

State (P) v. Disruptive defendant (D)

397 U.S. 337 (1970)

NATURE OF CASE: Appeal from issuance of writ of habeas corpus.

FACT SUMMARY: Allen (P) contended he was denied his right to confront witnesses when he was removed from court for disruptive behavior.

RULE OF LAW

A defendant may be removed from the courtroom without violating his or her right to confrontation where such is done to preserve order.

FACTS: Allen (P) petitioned for a writ of habeas corpus, contending he was denied his right to confront witnesses when the judge had him taken from the courtroom for disruptive behavior. The district court granted the petition and the court of appeals affirmed, holding a defendant could never be removed from court without violating his or her right to confront witnesses. The United States Supreme Court granted certiorari.

ISSUE: May a defendant be removed from the courtroom without violating his or her right to confrontation where such is done to preserve order?

HOLDING AND DECISION: (Black, J.) Yes. A defendant may be removed from the courtroom without violating his or her right to confrontation where such is done to preserve order. The decorum in court is essential to the proper conduct of trial, and the defendant may be removed if he or she disrupts it. As a result, the removal was not improper. Reversed.

ANALYSIS

The United States Supreme Court suggested that binding and gagging a defendant might be a viable alternative to removal. However, the adverse connotations communicated to the jury and the inability of the defendant to communicate with counsel suggest some disadvantages to this technique.

Quicknotes

CONFRONTATION CLAUSE A provision in the Sixth Amendment to the United States Constitution that an accused in a criminal action has the right to confront the witnesses against him or her, including the right to attend the trial and to cross-examine witnesses called on behalf of the prosecution.

WRIT OF HABEAS CORPUS A proceeding in which a defendant brings a writ to compel a judicial determination of whether he or she is lawfully being held in custody.

Strickland v. Washington

Defense counsel (D) v. Defendant client (P)

466 U.S. 668 (1984)

NATURE OF CASE: Appeal from decision establishing new standards for analyzing ineffective counsel claims in sentencing proceedings.

FACT SUMMARY: Strickland (D) appealed from a decision of the court of appeals in which the court developed its own framework for analyzing ineffective assistance claims and remanded the case to the district court to determine whether Strickland (D) had provided ineffective counsel to Washington (P) at his sentencing proceeding.

RULE OF LAW

A defendant has not received ineffective assistance of counsel in violation of the Sixth Amendment requiring reversal of a death sentence unless counsel's representation falls below an objective standard of reasonableness, and the defendant has been sufficiently prejudiced such that there is a reasonable doubt in the reliability of the sentence.

FACTS: Washington (P) planned and engaged in three groups of crimes, including kidnappings, assaults, torture, and brutal murders. He confessed to the third set of crimes, was indicted for kidnapping and murder, and was appointed an experienced criminal lawyer to represent him. Strickland (D) actively pursued the defense but experienced a sense of hopelessness about the case when he learned that Washington (P), against his advice, had also confessed to the first two murders. Washington (P) was charged with all three murders, and again against Strickland's (D) advice, he pleaded guilty to all three charges, including three capital murder charges. At the plea colloquy, Washington (P) told the judge that he accepted responsibility for the crimes and that he was under emotional and financial stress. He rejected Strickland's (D) advice to have an advisory jury present at his capital sentencing hearing. Strickland (D) based his strategy at the hearing on the judge's remarks at the plea colloquy and his reputation, choosing not to introduce evidence concerning Washington's (P) character or emotional state. He did not seek out any character witnesses and did not request a psychiatric evaluation. The trial judge found the aggravating circumstances surrounding the murders outweighed the mitigating circumstances, and Washington (P) was sentenced to death. These convictions were affirmed on direct appeal. Washington (P) sought collateral relief in state court on a number of grounds, including ineffective assistance of counsel at the sentencing hearing. The state courts denied relief. Washington (P) then filed a writ of habeas corpus in federal district court. The district court did not disturb the state court findings and denied relief. The court of appeals en banc reversed the district court and remanded. From this decision, Strickland (D) appealed.

ISSUE: Has a defendant received ineffective assistance of counsel in violation of the Sixth Amendment requiring reversal of a death sentence if counsel's representation has not fallen below an objective standard of reasonableness, and the defendant has not been sufficiently prejudiced such that there is a reasonable doubt in the reliability of the sentence?

HOLDING AND DECISION: (O'Connor, J.) No. A defendant has not received ineffective assistance of counsel in violation of the Sixth Amendment requiring reversal of a death sentence unless counsel's representation falls below an objective standard of reasonableness, and the defendant has been sufficiently prejudiced such that there is a reasonable doubt in the reliability of the sentence. Effective assistance of counsel is critical to our adversarial system of justice in order to ensure just results. This assurance of a fair trial must serve as the guide to developing standards for evaluating ineffective assistance claims. Capital sentencing proceedings need not be distinguished from ordinary trials in this respect. In determining the reasonableness of the assistance, the assistance rendered must be considered in light of all circumstances. Counsel has a reasonable duty to investigate. His or her decisions may be substantially influenced by the defendant's own actions or statements. Judicial scrutiny of counsel's performance must be highly deferential. Even if counsel's assistance is professionally unreasonable, the death sentence need not be set aside if the ineffective counsel had no effect on the judgment. Excluding conflict of interest cases, the defendant in ineffective assistance cases must ordinarily affirmatively prove prejudice, a showing that the proceeding would probably have been different. If there is a reasonable probability sufficient to undermine confidence in the outcome, judgment reversal is warranted. The assessment of prejudice proceeds on the assumption that the decision-maker will be reasonable and impartial. The focus of the entire inquiry into ineffective counsel on the fundamental fairness of the proceeding is particularly appropriate since fundamental is a central concern in writs of habeas corpus. Applying these principles to the present case, there is nothing in the record to indicate that the hopelessness felt by Strickland (D) in any way affected his representation of Washington (P).

Continued on next page.

His strategy choice in light of all the circumstances was well within the range of professionally reasonable judgments. Reversed.

DISSENT: (Marshall, J.) Today's adoption of the objective standard of reasonableness is too ambiguous to provide the Court guidance in this area. Many areas of criminal defense work are subject to judicial oversight. The prejudice standard adopted by the Court relies too much on hindsight to ascertain effect and ignores the Sixth Amendment function of ensuring that convictions are obtained only through fundamentally fair procedures. Today's opinion can be read as imposing an impermissibly heavy burden of persuasion in ineffective assistance cases. Further, capital sentencing proceedings should be distinguished from ordinary trials, given the severity and irrevocability of the sanctions at stake. Strickland's (D) representation may have involved reasonable strategy choices had he properly investigated the array of choices available to him, which he did not. The circumstances more than make out sufficient case of ineffective counsel in violation of the Sixth Amendment.

ANALYSIS

Justice Marshall's dissent seems to be highly concerned with the lack of guidance the Court's opinion gives as to what is the objectively reasonable standard of competence. There is some question as to what this standard might be, whether it will be local or national, or determined by whether counsel is retained or appointed. It seems clear, however, given the differences in the standards between locales as to what constitutes effective counsel, it would be difficult to provide a nationwide standard of competence more along the lines that Justice Marshall seems to desire.

Quicknotes

SIXTH AMENDMENT Provides the right to a speedy trial by impartial jury, the right to be informed of the accusation, the right to confront witnesses, and the right to have the assistance of counsel in all criminal prosecutions.

WRIT OF HABEAS CORPUS A proceeding in which a defendant brings a writ to compel a judicial determination of whether he or she is lawfully being held in custody.

Padilla v. Kentucky

Individual (P) v. State (D)

559 U.S. 356 (2010)

NATURE OF CASE: Appeal from state court decision finding that plaintiff did not have a valid claim of ineffective assistance of counsel.

FACT SUMMARY: After being charged with trafficking in marijuana, Padilla (P), a permanent resident of the United States, was informed by his attorney that a guilty plea would not lead to deportation. After pleading guilty, Padilla (P) faced deportation.

RULE OF LAW

A criminal defense attorney has an obligation to advise his or her clients that pleading guilty to a charge may lead to deportation, and a failure to so advise will provide grounds for a claim of ineffective assistance of counsel.

FACTS: Jose Padilla (P), a permanent resident of the United States for more than 40 years, was charged with trafficking in marijuana. His attorney informed him that pleading guilty to the charge would not affect his immigration status. After pleading guilty, Padilla (P) faced deportation. After his conviction, Padilla (P) filed a petition for post-conviction relief in Kentucky state court. After a series of appeals, the Kentucky Supreme Court finally held that Padilla (P) had not stated a claim for ineffective assistance of counsel because the ramifications of a guilty plea on one's immigration status were collateral to advice relating to the criminal matter. The United States Supreme Court granted Padilla's (P) petition for review.

ISSUE: Does a criminal defense attorney have an obligation to advise his or her clients that pleading guilty to a charge may lead to deportation, and will a failure to so advise provide grounds for a claim of ineffective assistance of counsel?

HOLDING AND DECISION: (Stevens, J.) Yes. A criminal defense attorney has an obligation to advise his or her clients that pleading guilty to a charge may lead to deportation, and a failure to so advise will provide grounds for a claim of ineffective assistance of counsel. Changes to federal immigration law over the last 90 years have raised the stakes for a noncitizen's criminal conviction. For many crimes, the most important consideration is the effect of a guilty plea or conviction on one's immigration status. Recent changes to federal law have made removal an automatic result for a broad class of crimes. To state a claim for ineffective assistance of counsel, a plaintiff must show that a counsel's representation fell below the objective standard of reasonableness. The second step is to determine whether the result of the criminal matter would have been different but for the errors of the counsel. Almost all bar associations require that defense counsel advise their clients as to the risk of deportation. Moreover, a simple review of the relevant statute in this case would have made Padilla's (P) counsel aware that a conviction would lead to deportation. Accordingly, Padilla (P) has stated a claim for ineffective assistance of counsel based on his attorney's incorrect assertions that a guilty plea would not affect his immigration status. However, Padilla (P) must still prove that the ineffective assistance he received was prejudicial to him. Reversed and remanded.

CONCURRENCE: (Alito, J.) The judgment correctly determines an attorney provides ineffective assistance of counsel if he or she fails to advise a noncitizen client of the removal risks of a conviction. The criminal defense attorney, however, should not have to advise the client of those consequences but rather advise the client to seek the advice of an immigration attorney. Immigration law is complex and specialized. Unreasonable and inaccurate advice about removal consequences could give rise to an ineffective assistance of counsel claim. The Sixth Amendment is satisfied if the criminal defense attorney advises the noncitizen client that conviction may have removal consequences, immigration law is a specialized field, the defense attorney is not an immigration lawyer, and the client should seek the advice of an immigration lawyer.

DISSENT: (Scalia, J.) No constitutional text or principle requires counsel to advise beyond those matters germane to the criminal prosecution at hand. The Sixth Amendment has no application here because the subject of the misadvice was not the prosecution for which Padilla (P) was entitled to effective assistance of counsel. The majority prevents legislation that could address this issue in a more targeted fashion.

ANALYSIS

In state courts across the country, for a noncitizen criminal defendant, the ramifications of a guilty plea on his or her immigration status is paramount. The possibility of deportation plays a large role in the plea negotiations between prosecutors and defense counsel. Often, criminal defendants will accept guilty pleas to lesser, misdemeanor charges that will not result in deportation.

Continued on next page.

Quicknotes

INEFFECTIVE ASSISTANCE OF COUNSEL A claim brought by an accused in which it must be determined whether the attorney's rendering of representation was such that the ultimate disposition of the case may not be relied upon as fair.

SIXTH AMENDMENT Provides the right to a speedy and public trial by impartial jury, the right to be informed of the accusation, the right to confront witnesses, and the right to have the assistance of counsel in all criminal prosecutions.

■▬▬■

Missouri v. Frye

State (P) v. Convicted individual claiming ineffective assistance of counsel (D)

566 U.S. 134 (2012)

NATURE OF CASE: State's (P) appeal from state appellate court's decision to grant plaintiff post-conviction relief.

FACT SUMMARY: Frye's (D) attorney failed to communicate to him a formal plea-offer from the prosecution that included more favorable terms than the terms to which Frye (D) eventually pleaded guilty.

RULE OF LAW

Counsel for criminal defendants has the duty to communicate formal offers from the prosecution with terms and conditions that may be favorable to the defendants.

FACTS: In August 2007, Frye (D) was charged with driving with a revoked license. He had been convicted of the same offence on three other occasions. Under Missouri law, the fourth charge allowed the State (P) to charge him with a Class D felony. The felony charge carried a possible four-year prison term. In November, the prosecution sent a formal written plea offer to Frye's (D) counsel with two choices. First, the prosecutor offered a three-year sentence if Frye (D) plead guilty to the felony charge, without a recommendation for probation but a requirement that Frye (D) spend ten days "shock" time in jail. The second offer was to reduce the charge to a misdemeanor and have Frye (D) serve 90 days in jail. The misdemeanor charge had a possible one-year maximum sentence. The letter stated the offer would expire on December 28. Frye's (D) counsel never communicated the offer to him and the plea offers expired. A week before his preliminary hearing on the August 2007 charge, Frye (D) was again arrested for driving with a revoked license. At a subsequent hearing, Frye (D) eventually pleaded guilty to the felony charge and the trial court sentenced him to three years in prison. Following the conviction, Frye (D) filed for post-conviction relief in state court on the grounds his attorney's failure to inform him of the plea offers constituted actionable ineffective assistance of counsel. The state trial court denied his petition, but the Missouri Court of Appeals reversed, finding that Frye (D) received ineffective assistance of counsel and that Frye (D) was prejudiced thereby. The United States Supreme Court granted the State of Missouri's (D) petition for review.

ISSUE: Does counsel for criminal defendants have the duty to communicate formal offers from the prosecution with terms and conditions that may be favorable to the defendants?

HOLDING AND DECISION: (Kennedy, J.) Yes. Counsel for criminal defendants has the duty to communicate formal offers from the prosecution with terms and conditions that may be favorable to the defendants. When a defense counsel fails to communicate a plea offer to his or her client, that failure constitutes actionable ineffective assistance of counsel under the Constitution. This holding is supported by the reality that more than 94 percent of state criminal convictions are the result of guilty pleas. That is only one part of the analysis. The convicted defendant must also show the ineffective assistance of counsel caused him or her prejudice in the criminal proceedings. To show prejudice when an attorney fails to communicate a plea offer, the defendant must demonstrate a reasonable probability that he or she would have accepted the earlier plea offer had he or she been aware of it. Significantly, defendants must also show that the prosecution would not have canceled the plea deal or that the trial court would not have rejected the agreement. This is relevant because some states allow prosecutors the discretion to cancel a plea agreement up to the moment the agreement is accepted by the court. This further showing is also important because a defendant has no constitutional right to be offered a plea agreement and no right that the judge accepts the agreement. In the instant case, Frye (D) can show he would have accepted the offer to plead guilty to the lesser misdemeanor charge. However, Frye's (D) subsequent arrest for the same offense one week prior to his hearing complicates matters for him. It is not entirely clear that the prosecution would not have canceled the agreement based on that new arrest. Nor is it clear that the trial court would have agreed to the plea deal. Accordingly, it is appropriate to remand the case to the Missouri Court of Appeals for it to consider whether the prosecution and the trial court would have agreed to the plea offer of the lesser misdemeanor charge in light of Frye's (D) new arrest for the same offence. Vacated and remanded for consideration of state-law questions.

DISSENT: (Scalia, J.) The majority improperly constitutionalizes the plea-bargaining process in criminal cases. While it is clear Frye (D) received ineffective assistance of counsel, it is not entirely clear he was prejudiced thereby. The majority's reasonable probability test is nothing more than crystal ball gazing masquerading as legal analysis. There are no cases that discuss the standard for a prosecutor's withdrawal from a plea agreement or a trial court's authority to accept or reject a plea deal. In

Continued on next page.

most states, the trial court has broad discretion to accept or reject such agreements. The judicial branch should not create precedents based upon what prosecutors and judges might have done in the past. State legislatures are better equipped to regulate the plea-bargain process, starting by imposing punishments upon a defense counsel's right to practice when they fail to communicate valid plea offers to their clients. However, in this case, Frye (D) was not prejudiced because he pleaded guilty to the felony charge after the usual colloquy with the trial court judge that assured his guilty plea was voluntary and truthful.

ANALYSIS

The majority's decision was based on the prevalent use of plea bargains in criminal prosecutions, both at the state and federal level. In addition to the 94 percent of convictions in state cases resulting from plea bargains, 97 percent of convictions in federal court are similarly the result of plea negotiations. Note that the majority's holding is narrow: where a plea offer is made, the defense counsel must communicate it to their clients. The Court refrained from adjudicating on any strategic decisions defense counsel may make during those plea negotiations.

Quicknotes

INEFFECTIVE ASSISTANCE OF COUNSEL A claim brought by an accused in which it must be determined whether the attorney's rendering of representation was such that the ultimate disposition of the case may not be relied upon as fair.

PLEA BARGAIN An agreement between a prosecutor and a criminal defendant that is submitted to the court for approval, generally involves the defendant's pleading guilty to a lesser charge or count in exchange for a more lenient sentence.

Lafler v. Cooper

State (P) v. Convicted individual seeking relief due to ineffective counsel (D)

566 U.S. 156 (2012)

NATURE OF CASE: State's (P) appeal from Sixth Circuit Court of Appeals' decision upholding plaintiff's post-conviction relief.

FACT SUMMARY: After the State (P) charged Anthony Cooper (D) with intent to murder and related charges, the State (P) offered a favorable plea agreement to Cooper (D). Cooper's (D) counsel advised him not to take it and proceed to trial. A jury convicted Cooper (D) and he received a sentence greater than that offered in the plea agreement.

RULE OF LAW

When claiming ineffective assistance of counsel based on erroneous advice to reject a plea offer, a defendant must show there was a reasonable probability that the court would have accepted the plea agreement and that the conviction and sentence would have been less severe than those that were in fact imposed.

FACTS: On March 25, 2003, Anthony Cooper (D) shot Kali Mundy multiple times, but Mundy survived. The State of Michigan (P) charged Cooper (D) with intent to murder, possession of a firearm by a felon, possession of a firearm in the commission of a felony, and for being a habitual offender. Prior to trial, the prosecution offered to dismiss two of the charges and to recommend a sentence of 51 to 85 months in prison in exchange for a guilty plea. Cooper's (D) counsel advised him to reject the offer because he felt the State (P) would be unable to prove intent at the trial. A jury convicted Cooper (D) of all charges. The trial court then sentenced him to 185 to 360 months in prison. Cooper (D) then filed a petition for habeas relief in federal district court. The basis for the petition was that the advice of Cooper's (D) counsel to reject the plea offer constituted ineffective assistance of counsel. The district court granted the writ and ordered the State (P) to impose a sentence consistent with the original plea offer. The Sixth Circuit Court of Appeals affirmed. The United States Supreme Court granted the State's (P) petition for review.

ISSUE: When claiming ineffective assistance of counsel based on erroneous advice to reject a plea offer, must a defendant show there was a reasonable probability that the court would have accepted the plea agreement and that the conviction and sentence would have been less severe than those that were in fact imposed?

HOLDING AND DECISION: (Kennedy, J.) Yes. When claiming ineffective assistance of counsel based on erroneous advice to reject a plea offer, a defendant must show there was a reasonable probability that the court would have accepted the plea agreement and that the conviction and sentence would have been less severe than those that were in fact imposed. In this appeal, all parties agree the advice of Cooper's (D) attorney constituted ineffective assistance of counsel. The issue here is whether that ineffective assistance prejudiced Cooper (D). The State (P) essentially argues that Cooper (D) and his counsel validly rejected the plea offer in the hopes the jury would return a verdict of not guilty. The State (P) argues that Cooper (D) went on to receive a full and fair trial and his subsequent conviction rendered the ineffective assistance of counsel moot. When examining ineffective assistance of counsel claims in the context of plea bargaining, the defendant must show a reasonable probability the court would have accepted the agreement. The defendant must also show the prosecutor would not have withdrawn the offer prior to trial. The State's (P) view of the protections of the Sixth Amendment is too narrow. The Sixth Amendment requires effective assistance of counsel at all critical stages of the criminal proceeding, especially including the plea-bargaining process. If a plea bargain is offered, the defendant has the right to effective counsel when considering whether to accept the offer. Cooper (D) has shown that he did not receive effective assistance of counsel and was prejudiced because he received a greater sentence than the sentence included in the plea offer. The task now is to determine the appropriate remedy. The Sixth Amendment requires that remedies should be tailored to the injuries suffered and should not infringe on competing interests. The remedy should not grant a windfall to the defendant. Essentially, the trial court has the discretion to review the matter and impose the sentence offered as part of the plea agreement or to retain the sentence imposed after the jury verdict. Courts should consider a defendant's willingness or unwillingness to accept responsibility for their actions. Here, the State (P) should reoffer the plea agreement to Cooper (D). The court can then exercise its discretion to accept the agreement, retain the sentence imposed post-conviction, or something between those two options. Vacated and remanded.

DISSENT: (Scalia, J.) Cooper (D) received a full and fair trial and received a sentence that the law prescribed. This Court has never held that a defendant is entitled to competent counsel when deciding to reject a plea

Continued on next page.

offer. The Court effectively creates a new constitutional right to effective plea bargaining. Moreover, the Sixth Amendment's focus is to ensure a fair trial. The inquiry is to determine if the ineffective assistance of counsel undermined the adversarial process and failed to produce a just result. Here, the error of Cooper's (D) attorney was unfortunate, but it was not of constitutional significance. The Court's remedy is also absurd. It is extraordinary that a trial judge has discretion to create a remedy where there is a constitutional violation and even more extraordinary that the judge has discretion to issue no remedy at all.

ANALYSIS

This decision expands on the companion case of *Missouri v. Frye*, 566 U.S. 134 (2012). In *Frye*, the United States Supreme Court held that defense counsel has the duty to communicate plea offers to their clients. The *Cooper* decision goes further and essentially constitutionalizes the entire plea-bargaining process. Both decisions are based on the reality that well over 90 percent of convictions in state and federal court are the result of plea bargains.

Quicknotes

INEFFECTIVE ASSISTANCE OF COUNSEL A claim brought by an accused in which it must be determined whether the attorney's rendering of representation was such that the ultimate disposition of the case may not be relied upon as fair.

PLEA BARGAIN An agreement between a prosecutor and a criminal defendant that is submitted to the court for approval; generally involves the defendant's pleading guilty to a lesser charge or count in exchange for a more lenient sentence.

SIXTH AMENDMENT Provides the right to a speedy and public trial by impartial jury, the right to be informed of the accusation, the right to confront witnesses, and the right to have the assistance of counsel in all criminal prosecutions.

WRIT OF HABEAS CORPUS A proceeding in which a defendant brings a writ to compel a judicial determination of whether he or she is lawfully being held in custody.

Caplin & Drysdale v. United States

Law firm (P) v. Federal government (D)

491 U.S. 617 (1989)

NATURE OF CASE: Review of order of forfeiture under 21 U.S.C. § 848.

FACT SUMMARY: Caplin & Drysdale (P), attorneys for convicted drug dealer Reckmeyer (D), contended that federal forfeiture laws denied a defendant right to counsel.

RULE OF LAW

Federal forfeiture laws do not deny a defendant right to counsel.

FACTS: Reckmeyer (D) was charged with narcotics violations. Pursuant to 21 U.S.C. § 848, providing for forfeiture of ill-gotten assets from criminals, the Government (D) obtained an order freezing Reckmeyer's (D) assets. Reckmeyer (D) contended that this prevented him from using an attorney of his choice, in violation of the Sixth Amendment. Caplin & Drysdale (P), his attorneys, also raised this objection on its own behalf. Reckmeyer (D) eventually pleaded guilty, and his assets were declared forfeited. Caplin & Drysdale (P), which contended that its fees were payable from those assets, made a claim against the assets. The district court granted the firm's claim for a share of the assets. The court of appeals reversed, and the United States Supreme Court granted review.

ISSUE: Do federal forfeiture laws deny a defendant right to counsel?

HOLDING AND DECISION: (White, J.) No. Federal forfeiture laws do not deny a defendant right to counsel. The effect of the forfeiture law is limited. It does not prevent an accused from using assets not subject to forfeiture to pay for counsel, nor does it prevent an attorney from representing the defendant in hope of an acquittal, which could unfreeze the assets. To the extent that the statute prevents the accused from using funds subject to forfeiture, a defendant has no Sixth Amendment right to spend money not lawfully his. Since 21 U.S.C. § 848 freezes only money unlawfully in a defendant's possession, no Sixth Amendment principle is violated. Further, the government has powerful interests at stake: confiscated money is used for public purposes, those with rightful claims are paid, and criminals' excessive influence due to illegitimate wealth is circumscribed. With respect to due process, it is foreseeable that some instances of Fifth Amendment violations could occur. However, none are alleged here, and this Court will not make any sweeping announcement in this area. Affirmed.

DISSENT: (Blackmun, J.) This decision allows the government to beggar those it prosecutes in order to disable their defense at trial. This goes to the heart of our adversarial system of justice.

ANALYSIS

The law in question does, of course, allow for release of the assets after trial in the event of an acquittal. However, the freezing makes acquittal much less likely. This was the heart of the due process argument, and the United States Supreme Court never really addressed this issue.

Quicknotes

RIGHT TO COUNSEL Right conferred by the Sixth Amendment that the accused shall be provided effective legal assistance in a criminal proceeding.

SIXTH AMENDMENT Provides the right to a speedy and public trial by impartial jury, the right to be informed of the accusation, the right to confront witnesses, and the right to have the assistance of counsel in all criminal prosecutions.

Luis v. United States

Individual (D) v. Federal government (P)

578 U.S. 5 (2016)

NATURE OF CASE: Appeal from lower court decision in favor of the federal Government.

FACT SUMMARY: The Government (P) charged Sila Luis (D) with a number of crimes related to health care fraud, including fraudulently obtaining $45 million. Prior to trial, the Government(P) sought an order freezing all her assets, including funds that she did not obtain from her alleged criminal activity. The district court granted the order.

RULE OF LAW

Criminal defendants have a Sixth Amendment right to use their own untainted or innocent property to pay for the assistance of defense counsel.

FACTS: The Government (P) charged Sila Luis (D) with a number of crimes related to health care fraud, including fraudulently obtaining $45 million. 18 U.S.C. Section 1345 allows a court to freeze prior to trial certain assets of a criminal defendant in order to preserve funds for restitution for victims or payment of penalties to the government after a conviction. The statute allows the court to freeze (1) property obtained as a result of the crime, (2) property traceable to the crime, and (3) other property of equal value. While the Government (P) conceded the funds were untainted, the district court agreed with the Government (P) that Luis's (D) untainted funds fell into this third category and could thus be seized. Luis (D) argued the order violated her Sixth Amendment right to pay for defense counsel. The district court issued the order and Luis (D) appeals.

ISSUE: Do criminal defendants have a Sixth Amendment right to use their own untainted or innocent property to pay for the assistance of defense counsel?

HOLDING AND DECISION: (Breyer, J.) Yes. Criminal defendants have a Sixth Amendment right to use their own untainted or innocent property to pay for the assistance of defense counsel. This case is unlike past decisions where the defendant sought to use funds that were garnered through their criminal activities. There is no dispute among any party that the funds frozen by the court order belong to Luis (D). In other cases, the funds belonged to the victims or to the government. Typically, title to property used to commit a crime passes to the government at the time the crime is committed. Here, Luis (D) can reasonably claim that the property was and always has been hers. The Government (P) does not have a substantial property interest in those funds at the pretrial stage. At the pretrial stage, the defendant's constitutional, Sixth Amendment right to counsel outweighs the victims' interests in obtaining payment from these assets. Freezing these assets would force criminal defendants like Luis (D) to use public defenders who are already overworked and underpaid. This would erode the Sixth Amendment right to effective counsel. In addition, any concerns over the fungibility of assets will be alleviated by courts' use of tracing rules employed in similar fraud or bankruptcy related matters. Reversed.

CONCURRENCE: (Thomas, J.) The plurality is correct that the pretrial freeze of untainted assets violates the criminal defendant's Sixth Amendment's right to counsel. My reasoning is based not on the governing statute but the common law. At common law, only tainted assets could be seized at the pretrial stage.

DISSENT: (Kennedy, J.) This decision rewards criminal defendants who quickly spend, dissipate, or otherwise conceal stolen funds after their arrest, confident in the knowledge they will be able to use their own funds to pay for counsel. In addition, the decision is not reasonable because of the fungible nature of funds in cases involving fraud, embezzlement, or other type of theft.

DISSENT: (Kagan, J.) This Court has previously, and correctly, held that a criminal defendant who has been convicted of a crime has no Sixth Amendment rights to use forfeited funds to pay for counsel. Following conviction, those funds garnered as a result of the crimes become the property of the federal government. Respectfully, I disagree with the notion that the government may seize any funds prior to trial, simply based on probable cause to believe that the property in question will become forfeitable. However, Luis (D) has not asked this Court to overrule any prior decisions. Accordingly, because we are bound by precedent, I agree with the dissent that the Government (P) has shown that it will likely recover the untainted funds after a conviction. Accordingly, under prior case law, Luis (D) has no right to use them to pay for an attorney.

ANALYSIS

The decision Justice Kagan struggled with was *United States v. Monsanto*, 109 S. Ct. 2657 (1989), which upheld the government's ability to freeze assets at the pretrial

Continued on next page.

stage. Analyzing a different statute, it held essentially that there was no exemption from an order to freeze for property that could be used to pay for defense counsel.

Quicknotes

ARREST WARRANT An order issued by a court directing an officer to arrest a particular individual.

INVESTIGATORY STOP A brief, non-intrusive stop, requiring the police officer to have a reasonable suspicion that a crime has been committed based on specific and articulable facts.

SIXTH AMENDMENT Provides the right to a speedy and public trial by impartial jury, the right to be informed of the accusation, the right to confront witnesses, and the right to have the assistance of counsel in all criminal prosecutions.

Faretta v. California

Convicted thief (D) v. State (P)

422 U.S. 806 (1975)

NATURE OF CASE: Appeal from conviction for grand theft.

FACT SUMMARY: The trial court held Faretta (D) incompetent to represent himself and appointed counsel over his objection.

RULE OF LAW

There is a constitutional right to represent oneself in a criminal proceeding.

FACTS: Faretta (D) was tried for grand theft and moved to represent himself. After granting the motion, the trial court subsequently determined Faretta (D) was not qualified to represent himself and appointed counsel. Faretta (D) was convicted and appealed, contending he had a constitutional right to represent himself. His conviction was affirmed, and the United States Supreme Court granted certiorari.

ISSUE: Is there a constitutional right to represent oneself in a criminal proceeding?

HOLDING AND DECISION: (Stewart, J.) Yes. There is a constitutional right to represent oneself in a criminal proceeding. Forcing a lawyer on an unwilling client violates the basic tenets of justice. All Sixth Amendment rights of confrontation and information accrue to the defendant, not his or her appointed counsel. As a result, it is the defendant who has the constitutional right to present his or her defense. Therefore, Faretta (D) was denied his right to self-representation. Conviction vacated and case remanded.

DISSENT: (Burger, C.J.) There is no advantage either to justice or to an accused to create a constitutional right to represent oneself.

ANALYSIS

The United States Supreme Court in this case indicated that the defendant's apparent lack of technical legal knowledge was immaterial. He had a right to represent himself and made a knowing exercise of such right. Therefore, the trial court was bound to allow the self-representation.

Quicknotes

SIXTH AMENDMENT Provides the right to a speedy and public trial by impartial jury, the right to be informed of the accusation, the right to confront witnesses, and the right to have the assistance of counsel in all criminal prosecutions.

CHAPTER 11

Sentencing

Quick Reference Rules of Law

Ewing v. California

Convicted thief (D) v. State (P)

538 U.S. 11 (2003)

NATURE OF CASE: Appeal from conviction for theft.

FACT SUMMARY: When Gary Ewing (D) was sentenced, under California's Three Strikes Law, to 25 years to life for theft of golf clubs valued at $1,197, he argued that the sentence constituted cruel and unusual punishment prohibited by the Eighth Amendment.

RULE OF LAW

A Three Strikes Law is not so grossly disproportionate as to constitute cruel and unusual punishment under the Eighth Amendment.

FACTS: Under the California Three Strikes Law, when a defendant is convicted of a felony, and he or she has previously been convicted of one or more prior felonies defined as "serious" or "violent," the defendant must receive an indeterminate prison term of 25 years to life. Gary Ewing (D) walked into a pro shop and left with golf clubs valued at $1,197 concealed in his pants leg. He was caught, tried, and convicted of the crime. He had previously committed several felony robberies and burglaries, making him eligible for sentencing under the Three Strikes Law; he was sentenced, accordingly, to a prison term of 25 years to life. Ewing (D) appealed, arguing that the sentence was so disproportionate to the $1,197 theft as to constitute prohibited cruel and unusual punishment under the Eighth Amendment. The California Court of Appeal affirmed the sentence, and the Supreme Court of California denied Ewing's (D) petition to hear the case. Ewing (D) appealed to the United States Supreme Court.

ISSUE: Is a Three Strikes Law so grossly disproportionate as to constitute cruel and unusual punishment under the Eighth Amendment?

HOLDING AND DECISION: (O'Connor, J.) No. A Three Strikes Law is not so grossly disproportionate as to constitute cruel and unusual punishment under the Eighth Amendment. In weighing the gravity of Ewing's (D) offense, we must place on the scales not only his current felony, but also his long history of felony recidivism. Recidivism has long been recognized as a legitimate basis for increased punishment. Any other approach would fail to accord proper deference to the policy judgments that find expression in the legislature's choice of sanctions. Four years after the passage of California's Three Strikes Law, the recidivism rate of parolees returned to prison for the commission of a new crime dropped by nearly 25 percent. Ewing's (D) sentence is justified by the state's public-safety interest in incapacitating and deterring recidivist felons, and amply supported by his own long, serious criminal record. His prior "strikes" were serious felonies, including robbery and three residential burglaries. To be sure, Ewing's (D) sentence is a long one; however, it reflects a rational legislative judgment, entitled to deference, that offenders who have committed serious or violent felonies and who continue to commit felonies must be incapacitated. Here, therefore, Ewing's (D) situation does not constitute "the rare case" in which a threshold comparison of the crime committed and the sentence imposed leads to an inference of gross disproportionality. The Eighth Amendment does not require strict proportionality between crime and sentence. Rather, it forbids only extreme sentences that are grossly disproportionate to the crime. Affirmed.

CONCURRENCE: (Scalia, J.) The notion that the punishment should fit the crime is inherently a concept tied to the penological goal of retribution. Perhaps the plurality should revise its terminology so that what it reads into the Eighth Amendment is the unstated proposition that all punishment should reasonably pursue the multiple purposes of the criminal law.

CONCURRENCE: (Thomas, J.) The proportionality test is incapable of precise judicial application, hence, although I here concur, I do not feel "compelled" by stare decisis to apply it.

DISSENT: (Stevens, J.) It is anomalous indeed to suggest that the Eighth Amendment makes proportionality review applicable in the context of bail and fines but not in the context of other forms of punishment, such as imprisonment.

DISSENT: (Breyer, J.) Ewing's (D) sentence on its face imposes one of the most severe punishments available—25 years to life—for the theft of golf clubs valued at $1,197. Here, the "sentence-triggering behavior" ranks well toward the bottom of the criminal conduct scale.

ANALYSIS

As the United States Supreme Court notes in its *Ewing* decision, the Eighth Amendment, which forbids cruel and unusual punishment, contains a "narrow proportionality principle" that applies to noncapital sentences. The essential four principles of proportionality review, according to the Supreme Court, are: (1) the primacy

Continued on next page.

of the legislature, (2) the variety of legitimate penological schemes, (3) the nature of the federal system, and (4) the requirement that proportionality review be guided by objective factors.

Quicknotes

CRUEL AND UNUSUAL PUNISHMENT Punishment that is excessive or disproportionate to the offense committed; it is prohibited by the Eighth Amendment to the U.S. Constitution.

EIGHTH AMENDMENT Prohibits the imposition of excessive bail, fines, and cruel and unusual punishment.

Kimbrough v. United States

Individual (D) v. Federal government (P)

552 U.S. 85 (2007)

NATURE OF CASE: Appeal from Fourth Circuit Court of Appeals decision in favor of the Government (P).

FACT SUMMARY: After Kimbrough (D) pled guilty to possession with intent to distribute crack cocaine, a federal court judge deviated from the sentencing guidelines that mandated much higher sentences for possession of crack cocaine than cocaine in powder form.

RULE OF LAW

A criminal sentence outside of the sentencing guidelines range is not per se unreasonable because it is based on a disagreement with the sentencing disparity for crack and powder cocaine offenses.

FACTS: Kimbrough (D) pled guilty to several charges, including possession to distribute crack cocaine as well as powder cocaine. At the time of his arrest, Kimbrough (D) possessed 56 grams of crack cocaine and 92.1 grams of powder cocaine. The district court judge contrasted Kimbrough's (D) sentencing guideline range of 228 to 270 months for possession of the crack cocaine with the much lower sentence of 97 to 106 months if Kimbrough's (D) crack cocaine had been in powder form. The district court judge stated this was one of those cases that exemplified the disproportionate and unjust effect of the sentencing guidelines. The judge, therefore, found that a sentence applying the sentencing guidelines for crack cocaine would have been "greater than necessary" and applied a lower sentence, giving Kimbrough (D) a total of 15 years in prison, or 180 months. The Fourth Circuit vacated the decision on the grounds the sentencing guidelines for crack cocaine is mandatory and the judge is not free to lower the sentence imposed by the guidelines. Kimbrough (D) appealed.

ISSUE: Is a criminal sentence outside of the sentencing guidelines range per se unreasonable because it is based on a disagreement with the sentencing disparity for crack and powder cocaine offenses?

HOLDING AND DECISION: (Ginsburg, J.) No. A criminal sentence outside of the sentencing guidelines range is not per se unreasonable because it is based on a disagreement with the sentencing disparity for crack and powder cocaine offenses. In *United States v. Booker*, 543 U.S. 220 (2005), the Court held the sentencing guidelines were advisory only. *Booker* is controlling here. The judge must consider the cocaine portion of the guidelines during sentencing, but the guidelines are not mandatory. A judge is free to determine a particular sentence pursuant to the guidelines is "greater than necessary" to serve the objectives of sentencing generally. A judge may properly consider the disparity in length of sentences for crack cocaine offenses versus powder offenses. The Sentencing Commission has stated in several reports that the disparity has led to anomalous results whereby major drug dealers who handle powder cocaine get shorter sentences than local distributors who convert the powder into crack cocaine form. Accordingly, the district court's 180-month sentence was appropriate. The court considered the guidelines, the nature of the offense, and the defendant's criminal history. The ultimate determination is whether the sentence was reasonable. We conclude that it was. The Fourth Circuit's decision is vacated.

DISSENT: (Thomas, J.) *Booker* was mistakenly decided. This Court's obligation is not to make policy considerations but to apply the law as stated in the governing federal statutes regarding sentencing. While the mandatory nature of the guidelines may have led to a Sixth Amendment violation, the remedy was not to do away with the guidelines, but rather to submit all facts supporting a given sentence to the jury. *Booker* has forced this Court into a legislative role by creating a new sentencing scheme that has no basis in any federal statute.

ANALYSIS

The disparity in sentences for crack cocaine versus powder cocaine was one of the driving forces to make the sentencing guidelines advisory only. Statutory minimum sentences still apply for crack cocaine offenses. Judges now have the discretion to raise or lower the length of the sentence when the sentencing guidelines suggest a sentence above the statutory minimums.

Quicknotes

SIXTH AMENDMENT Provides the right to a speedy and public trial by impartial jury, the right to be informed of the accusation, the right to confront witnesses, and the right to have the assistance of counsel in all criminal prosecutions.

Rita v. United States

Individual (D) v. Federal government (P)

551 U.S. 338 (2007)

NATURE OF CASE: Appeal from the Fourth Circuit's decision against the defendant.

FACT SUMMARY: After Rita (D) was convicted of perjury, a district court judge imposed a sentence of 33 months, which was within the suggested sentencing guidelines range.

RULE OF LAW

Federal courts of appeal may presume that a sentence imposed within the properly calculated sentencing guidelines range is a reasonable sentence.

FACTS: A jury convicted Rita (D) of perjury, making false statements, and obstructing justice. At sentencing, the judge reviewed a pre-sentence report from a probation officer that recommended a sentence of 33 to 41 months. This sentence was derived from an application of the sentencing guidelines. Rita (D) argued for a downward departure within the guidelines' framework based on his prior criminal government work as an immigration officer, his past military duty of 25 years, and his poor physical condition. The district court judge denied the request for a downward departure and imposed a sentence of 33 months, which was at the low end of the suggested sentence derived from the guidelines. The Fourth Circuit Court of Appeals held that a sentence imposed within the guidelines was presumptively reasonable. Rita (D) appealed.

ISSUE: May federal courts of appeal presume that a sentence imposed within the properly calculated sentencing guidelines range is a reasonable sentence?

HOLDING AND DECISION: (Breyer, J.) Yes. Federal courts of appeal may presume that a sentence imposed within the properly calculated sentencing guidelines range is a reasonable sentence. The presumption is not binding. However, it is a reflection that by the time the case reaches the appeals court, the sentencing judge specifically and the Sentencing Commission generally have reached the same conclusion as to the correct sentence for a particular crime. A sentencing judge who imposes a sentence within the guidelines thus makes a decision that is consistent with the Sentencing Commission's overall assessment as to the proper sentence. The presumption at the appellate stage does not violate the Sixth Amendment. Our prior cases do not forbid a sentencing judge from taking into account factual matters not considered by a jury to possibly increase a sentence. Moreover, the presumption of reasonableness at the appellate stage does not require the sentencing judge to impose the sentence suggested by the sentencing guidelines. In this case, the sentencing judge's reasons in support of the sentence were sufficient. The Fourth Circuit's application of the presumption of reasonableness of the sentence was also proper. Affirmed.

CONCURRENCE: (Scalia, J.) *Booker*, 543 U.S. 220 (2005), which made the guidelines advisory as opposed to mandatory, was properly decided. However, the precise contours of what a reasonableness review includes were not explained in *Booker*. The majority's opinion may run afoul of *Apprendi v. New Jersey*, 530 U.S. 466 (2000), which held any fact in support of a sentence must be found by a jury or admitted by the defendant. This opinion, which allows for a presumption of reasonableness for all within guidelines sentences, may allow for constitutional violations where a judge, as opposed to a jury, has found facts in support of a sentence given within the guidelines.

DISSENT: (Souter, J.) The majority's opinion is inconsistent with *Apprendi's* rule that facts in support of a sentence be found by the jury or admitted by the defendant. This opinion may allow for judges to find facts that will support a sentence at the higher range of the suggested sentencing guidelines. District court judges will read this opinion and conclude that their judicial factfinding in support of longer sentences will be allowed, as long as that longer sentence is within the suggested range from the sentencing guidelines.

ANALYSIS

This decision does not modify sentencing practices in place since the United States Supreme Court decided *Booker*, 543 U.S. 220 (2005). However, a case may reach the court where a judge increases a sentence within the guidelines' suggested range based upon a judicial finding of fact. It is clear several of the justices have Sixth Amendment concerns around such a scenario.

Quicknotes

PRESUMPTION A rule of law requiring the court to presume certain facts to be true based on the existence of other facts, thereby shifting the burden of proof to the party against whom the presumption is asserted.

SIXTH AMENDMENT Provides the right to a speedy and public trial by impartial jury, the right to be informed of the accusation, the right to confront witnesses, and the right to have the assistance of counsel in all criminal prosecutions.

Williams v. New York

Convicted murderer (D) v. State (P)

337 U.S. 241 (1949)

NATURE OF CASE: Appeal from trial judge's discretionary imposition of death penalty on convicted murderer.

FACT SUMMARY: Williams (D) was convicted of first-degree murder. The jury recommended a life sentence. The judge, under a New York (P) statute, substituted the death penalty. His decision was based upon a probation report and Williams's (D) past criminal record—both of which would not be admissible at trial on the issue of guilt.

RULE OF LAW

Due process is not denied where a judge, on the basis of probation reports, substitutes a more stringent sentence on a convicted defendant than that recommended by the jury.

FACTS: Williams (D), after being found guilty in a concededly fair trial, was sentenced to death by the judge. The murder conviction was handed down by a jury that recommended life imprisonment. The judge substituted the more stringent sentence upon Williams (D) on the basis of a New York (P) statute permitting additional information about the defendant obtained from the probation department and other sources. Williams (D) claimed the statute is a denial of due process in that the information was supplied by witnesses without an opportunity for him to cross-examine or confront them. The court of appeals affirmed the death penalty against a due process challenge, and the Supreme Court then considered the case.

ISSUE: Is due process denied where a judge, on the basis of probation reports, substitutes a more stringent sentence on a convicted defendant than that recommended by the jury?

HOLDING AND DECISION: (Black, J.) No. Due process is not denied where a judge, on the basis of probation reports, substitutes a more stringent sentence on a convicted defendant than that recommended by the jury. After a criminal defendant has been fairly convicted of a crime, there are several reasons for allowing a state to broaden the scope of information to be used for purposes of imposing a sentence. First, the issue of guilt has been resolved by the sentencing stage of the prosecution, so there is no need to confine a judge to information relevant only to that issue. A probation report would be irrelevant and prejudicial when considering the type and extent of punishment to be imposed. Second, our judicial history has always recognized that a sentencing judge has wide discretion on the sources and types of evidence used to assist him or her in determining the sentence to be imposed. Third, the prevalent modern philosophy of penology asserts that the punishment should fit the offender and not merely the crime. To that end, a judge must know the offender's background when imposing a sentence. For these reasons, we cannot conclude that due process requirements forbid the age-old practice of seeking information from out-of-court sources to guide judicial determination of the sentence to be imposed. Affirmed.

ANALYSIS

The majority opinion states the dominant view today under state constitutions as well as the binding rule of federal constitutional law. The flaw in Justice Murphy's dissent is his focus on the rights of an "accused." He fails to recognize that once guilt has been found, the procedural safeguards against an improper finding of guilt are no longer relevant. An out-of-court statement, like a probation report, while prejudicial against an accused on the issue of his or her guilt, cannot be said to affect the accused's procedural rights after guilt has been fairly established. At that point, the defendant is no longer technically an accused, but rather a convict, guilty of the offense charged.

Quicknotes

DUE PROCESS The constitutional mandate requiring the courts to protect and enforce individuals' rights and liberties consistent with prevailing principles of fairness and justice and prohibiting the federal and state governments from such activities that deprive its citizens of life, liberty, or property interest.

Morrissey v. Brewer

Convicted forger (D) v. State (P)

408 U.S. 471 (1972)

NATURE OF CASE: On certiorari after denial of petition for writ of habeas corpus.

FACT SUMMARY: Morrissey (D) claimed that he was denied due process because his parole was revoked without a hearing.

RULE OF LAW

The Due Process Clause of the Fourteenth Amendment requires that a state afford a person some opportunity to be heard before revoking his or her parole. Due process requires that two hearings occur during course of a parole revocation: a hearing to determine whether there is reasonable ground to believe that a parole violation has occurred, and a revocation hearing. Both hearings must be conducted by an impartial officer within a reasonable time of the parolee's arrest. The parolee must be given written notice of the alleged violations and must be allowed to present evidence and cross-examine the adverse witnesses, and the officer must state the reasons for revoking parole.

FACTS: Seven months after his parole, Morrissey (D) was arrested as a parole violator, and his parole was revoked without a hearing. Morrissey (D) claimed that the revocation of his parole without a hearing violated his right to due process.

ISSUE: Does the Due Process Clause of the Fourteenth Amendment require that a state afford a person some opportunity to be heard before revoking his parole?

HOLDING AND DECISION: (Burger, C.J.) Yes. The Due Process Clause of the Fourteenth Amendment requires that a state afford a person some opportunity to be heard before revoking his parole. It is true that revocation of parole is not part of a criminal prosecution and so the full panoply of rights due a defendant in such a proceeding does not apply. However, the Due Process Clause does protect interests that fall within the "liberty or property" language of the Fourteenth Amendment. Whether procedural protections are due in a given situation depends on the extent to which an individual will suffer a grievous loss. Parole revocation terminates a parolee's liberty. Liberty is an interest protected by the Fourteenth Amendment, and its termination does certainly inflict a grievous loss. Hence, some procedural safeguards must be applied. Due process requires that an informal inquiry by an impartial officer be conducted within a reasonable time of an arrest of an alleged parole violator to determine if there is reasonable ground to believe that a parole condition has been violated. Due process also requires that, in addition to the preliminary hearing, a revocation hearing must be conducted reasonably soon after the parolee's arrest. The minimum due process requirements for these hearings are written notice to the parolee of the alleged violations, an opportunity for the parolee to be heard and to present witnesses and evidence, the right to confront and cross-examine adverse witnesses (unless good cause is found for not allowing confrontation), a neutral and detached hearing body and a written statement by the fact finders as to the evidence relied on, and the reasons for revoking parole. In addition, at the revocation hearing the parolee is entitled to disclosure of the evidence against him or her. The court does not decide the question of whether the parolee is entitled to the assistance of counsel or to appointed counsel if he or she is indigent.

ANALYSIS

In *Menechino v. Oswald*, 430 F.2d 403 (1970), it was held that due process did not guarantee legal representation to New York state prisoners when they appeared at a hearing to determine whether they would be released on parole. In a later decision *United States ex rel. John Bey v. Connecticut State Board of Parole*, 443 F.2d 1079 (2d Cir. 1971), the same court distinguished "release on parole" from "revocation of parole." Calling the latter "a liberty akin to a private interest," it held that parolees must be afforded legal assistance at parole revocation hearings. The court stressed, however, that a lawyer's participation was to merely be in the form of assistance and that it was not in any way restricting the parole board's power to limit counsel's participation, so that parole hearings do not become legal battles.

Quicknotes

DUE PROCESS The constitutional mandate requiring the courts to protect and enforce individuals' rights and liberties consistent with prevailing principles of fairness and justice and prohibiting the federal and state governments from such activities that deprive its citizens of life, liberty, or property interest.

FOURTEENTH AMENDMENT Declares that no state shall make or enforce any law that shall abridge the privileges and immunities of citizens of the United States; no state

Continued on next page.

shall deny to any person within its jurisdiction the equal protection of the laws.

FOURTEENTH AMENDMENT DUE PROCESS CLAUSE Provides that protections mandated by the U.S. Constitution and observed by the federal government are equally applicable, and therefore must be observed by the states.

PAROLE The release of a prisoner from jail for the remainder of his or her sentence if he or she complies with certain conditions.

CHAPTER 12

Double Jeopardy

Quick Reference Rules of Law

United States v. Scott

Federal government (P) v. Indicted drug dealer (D)

437 U.S. 82 (1978)

NATURE OF CASE: Appeal from dismissals of two counts of a criminal indictment.

FACT SUMMARY: Two of the three counts in the indictment against Scott (D) were dismissed on the ground his defense had been prejudiced by pre-indictment delay, and the Government (P) sought to appeal.

RULE OF LAW

There is no violation of the Double Jeopardy Clause if the government appeals when the defendant has successfully sought to have his or her trial terminated without any submission to either judge or jury as to his or her guilt or innocence, whether it be by dismissal of the count or otherwise.

FACTS: Scott (D) successfully moved to have two of the three counts in his indictment for distributing narcotics dismissed on the ground his defense had been prejudiced by pre-indictment delay. The offense allegedly occurred in September 1974, and the indictment was issued on March 5, 1975. A guilty verdict as to the third count was returned, but the Government (P) sought to appeal the dismissal of the first two counts. Concluding that any further prosecution on those counts was barred by the Double Jeopardy Clause, the court dismissed the appeal and the Government (P) then sought review of that decision only as to the first count.

ISSUE: Is there a violation of the Double Jeopardy Clause if the government appeals when the defendant has successfully sought to have his or her trial terminated without any submission to either judge or jury as to his or her guilt or innocence, whether it be by dismissal of the count or otherwise?

HOLDING AND DECISION: (Rehnquist, J.) No. There is no violation of the Double Jeopardy Clause if the government appeals when the defendant has successfully sought to have his or her trial terminated without any submission to either judge or jury as to his or her guilt or innocence, whether it be by dismissal of the count or otherwise. The Double Jeopardy Clause looks askance at the government repeatedly seeking to try a person, but it does not come into play when the government is quite willing to continue a trial to conclusion but the defendant elects to seek termination of the trial on grounds unrelated to guilt or innocence. Unlike an insanity or entrapment defense, dismissal of a charge for pre-indictment delay represents a legal judgment that a defendant, although criminally culpable, may not be punished because of a supposed constitutional violation. It is a termination of a trial on grounds unrelated to guilt or innocence, and the Double Jeopardy Clause is not offended when such a dismissal is appealed by the government. In such a case, it is the government that has lost its rights to "one complete opportunity to convict those who have violated its laws"; the defendant has voluntarily given up, as opposed to being deprived of, his or her valued right to go to the jury first. Judgment reversed.

DISSENT: (Brennan, J.) The basic purpose of the Double Jeopardy Clause is to protect the accused from the agony of two criminal trials for the same alleged offense. Because a defendant should be protected from the agony of a second trial, all acquittals, whether due to unconstitutional delay or a finding of innocence from the evidence, should not be subject to appeal by the government. Finally, any distinction between acquittals based on innocence and technical acquittals based on procedural errors by the prosecution unnecessarily complicates the law.

ANALYSIS

Prior to this case, the United States Supreme Court had determined that an appeal by the government is barred by double jeopardy considerations when there is a pre-verdict judgment of acquittal based on the trial court's determination of the sufficiency of the evidence. Since the same result could be obtained by dismissing the indictment for failure to charge an offense, which would be more like a mistrial and would make appeal possible in certain circumstances, the trial court would be left with two options how to treat a particular case. One option would bar government appeal and the other would not. Regarding this situation, Wright, Miller and Cooper, 15 *Federal Practice and Procedure* § 3919 (1975 pocket part) states: "If this conclusion is correct, it means that the trial court has discretion to control the double jeopardy consequences of its ruling. It also means that the government must be astute to argue for a disposition that leaves it free to appeal or start over. Although it is troubling that trial judges should be left free of appellate review, procedural punctilio at least has the advantage of helping the defendant to know whether further proceedings may be possible. Even this virtue may be reduced, however, until the 'manifest necessity' standard that limits retrials after a mistrial or

Continued on next page.

dismissal without the defendant's consent is elaborated in the context of defective indictments."

Quicknotes

DOUBLE JEOPARDY CLAUSE A prohibition against a second prosecution for the same offense after an acquittal or conviction for that offense in a prior proceeding or against multiple punishments for the same offense.

Illinois v. Somerville

State (P) v. Convicted thief (D)

410 U.S. 458 (1973)

NATURE OF CASE: Appeal of a judgment granting a petition for habeas corpus.

FACT SUMMARY: The judge declared a mistrial of Somerville's (P) first trial, and Somerville (P) claimed that the second trial amounted to double jeopardy.

RULE OF LAW

If a trial judge grants a mistrial over the objections of the defendant because there is a manifest necessity to grant a mistrial or in order to meet the ends of public justice, a second trial for the same offense does not amount to double jeopardy.

FACTS: During the trial of Somerville (P) for theft, subsequent to the swearing of the jury but prior to the presentation of evidence, the trial court granted a mistrial motion by the state over Somerville's (P) objection, because the indictment was fatally defective for failure to allege the requisite criminal intent. Somerville (P) was retried and convicted. He then sought a writ of habeas corpus, arguing that the new trial violated his rights under the Double Jeopardy Clause.

ISSUE: If a trial judge grants a mistrial over the objections of the defendant because there is a manifest necessity to grant a mistrial or in order to meet the ends of public justice, does a second trial for the same offense amount to double jeopardy?

HOLDING AND DECISION: (Rehnquist, J.) No. If a trial judge grants a mistrial over the objections of the defendant because there is a manifest necessity to grant a mistrial or in order to meet the ends of public justice, a second trial for the same offense does not amount to double jeopardy. The court must consider all the circumstances in making its decision. In this case it would have been useless to complete the first trial under the defective indictment because on appeal the decision would have been reversed and the case would have had to be retried. By declaring a mistrial, all parties were saved considerable time and expense. The court also pointed out that the public has an interest in seeing all trials end in either a conviction or an acquittal. The court held that even though a defendant has a valued right to have his trial completed by a particular tribunal, that right must in some instances be subordinated to the public's interest in fair trials ending in just judgments. Since the declaration of a mistrial implemented a reasonable state policy, Somerville's (P) interest in proceeding to verdict was outweighed by the competing and equally legitimate demand for public justice.

ANALYSIS

This case illustrates one of the situations in which a second trial is permissible, even though jeopardy would normally have been held to have attached at the first trial. Jeopardy attaches when the jury has been sworn in a jury trial or when the first witness has been sworn in a trial without a jury. Usually, once jeopardy has attached, a second trial would constitute double jeopardy. Note, however, that there are several other situations in which a second trial is permissible after jeopardy has attached: (1) after a successful appeal by the defendant, (2) where a jury is unable to reach a verdict due to some "evident necessity" (e.g., death of judge or juror), (3) where there is a "hung jury," or (4) where "misconduct of a witness or a defendant" personally causes a mistrial.

Quicknotes

DOUBLE JEOPARDY CLAUSE A prohibition against a second prosecution for the same offense after an acquittal or conviction for that offense in a prior proceeding or against multiple punishments for the same offense.

MISTRIAL An erroneous or invalid trial.

WRIT OF HABEAS CORPUS A proceeding in which a defendant brings a writ to compel a judicial determination of whether he or she is lawfully being held in custody.

Arizona v. Washington

State (P) v. Convicted murderer (D)

434 U.S. 497 (1978)

NATURE OF CASE: Appeal from grant of writ of habeas corpus.

FACT SUMMARY: Washington (D) contended he could not be retried after the prosecution's motion for a mistrial was granted.

RULE OF LAW

A defendant may be retried following the granting of the prosecution's motion for mistrial where the mistrial is "manifestly necessary."

FACTS: Washington's (D) attorney made a statement on voir dire alleging prosecutorial misconduct. The court granted the prosecution's motion for a mistrial. Washington (D) petitioned for a writ of habeas corpus, contending he could not be retried on the basis of double jeopardy. The district court issued the writ on the basis that the trial court had not made a finding on the issue of whether the mistrial was "manifestly necessary." The court of appeals affirmed, and the United States Supreme Court granted certiorari.

ISSUE: May a defendant be retried following the granting of the prosecution's motion for mistrial where the mistrial is "manifestly necessary"?

HOLDING AND DECISION: (Stevens, J.) Yes. A defendant may be retried following the granting of the prosecution's motion for a mistrial where the mistrial is "manifestly necessary." It is not necessary that the trial court find the mistrial to be of manifest necessity. The granting of a motion for mistrial is essentially based on a factual finding. Thus, unless clearly erroneous, it should be upheld. The holding in this case was based on the court's discretion and must be upheld. Reversed.

ANALYSIS

There are instances in which a defendant may not be retried after successfully moving for a mistrial. In *Oregon v. Kennedy*, 456 U.S. 667 (1982), the United States Supreme Court held that this was true where the conduct giving rise to the motion was intended to induce the motion for a mistrial. Thus, a finding of prosecutorial overreaching is required to trigger double jeopardy in this case.

Quicknotes

DOUBLE JEOPARDY CLAUSE A prohibition against a second prosecution for the same offense after an acquittal or conviction for that offense in a prior proceeding or against multiple punishments for the same offense.

MISTRIAL An erroneous or invalid trial.

VOIR DIRE Examination of potential jurors for a trial.

WRIT OF HABEAS CORPUS A proceeding in which a defendant brings a writ to compel a judicial determination of whether he or she is lawfully being held in custody.

Burks v. United States

Defendant successful on appeal (D) v. Federal government (P)

437 U.S. 1 (1978)

NATURE OF CASE: Appeal from conviction for bank robbery.

FACT SUMMARY: Burks (D) contended he could not be retried after his appeal was successful, on grounds of lack of sufficient evidence.

RULE OF LAW

The Double Jeopardy Clause precludes a retrial where an appeal is successful based on a holding that the conviction was supported by insufficient evidence.

FACTS: Burks (D) pleaded insanity to a federal bank robbery charge. He was convicted and appealed on the basis that the verdict was not supported by sufficient evidence. The court of appeals reversed and remanded, and Burks (D) argued he could not be retried because the basis for the successful appeal was the insufficiency of the evidence. The United States Supreme Court granted certiorari.

ISSUE: Does the Double Jeopardy Clause preclude a retrial where an appeal is successful based on a holding that the conviction was supported by insufficient evidence?

HOLDING AND DECISION: (Burger, C.J.) Yes. The Double Jeopardy Clause precludes a retrial where an appeal is successful based on a holding that the conviction was supported by insufficient evidence. Where an appeal is successful based on trial error, it does not require an evaluation of the prosecutor's substantive case. However, where evidence is found to be insufficient, the prosecution should not be given a second chance. As a result, no retrial may be had. Reversed.

ANALYSIS

In *United States v. Ball*, 163 U.S. 662 (1896), the United States Supreme Court held that a retrial following a reversal of a conviction does not violate the Double Jeopardy Clause. The present case limits the application of *Ball* to cases of trial error. Other cases extending *Ball* were specifically overruled.

Quicknotes

DOUBLE JEOPARDY CLAUSE A prohibition against a second prosecution for the same offense after an acquittal or conviction for that offense in a prior proceeding or against multiple punishments for the same offense.

United States v. Dixon

Federal government (P) v. Convicted contemnor (D)

509 U.S. 688 (1993)

NATURE OF CASE: Consolidated appeals cases from ruling barring subsequent criminal prosecution in one and allowing it in the other.

FACT SUMMARY: Both Dixon (D) and Foster (D), who were convicted of criminal contempt in connection with alleged underlying criminal conduct, argued that the Double Jeopardy Clause barred any subsequent criminal prosecution on charges arising out of the same criminal conduct.

RULE OF LAW

The Double Jeopardy Clause does not permit subsequent prosecution of an offense that has already been the basis of criminal contempt proceedings.

FACTS: Dixon (D) had been arrested for second-degree murder. The form by which he was released on bond specified that he was not to commit "any criminal offense" and warned that any violation of the conditions of release would subject him "to revocation of release, an order of detention, and prosecution for contempt of court." While awaiting trial, Dixon (D) was arrested and indicted for possession of cocaine with intent to distribute. He was found guilty of criminal contempt and sentenced to 180 days in jail. The trial court later granted Dixon's (D) motion to dismiss the cocaine indictment on double jeopardy grounds. Foster (D) violated a civil protection order (CPO) requiring that he not "molest, assault, or in any manner threaten or physically abuse" his wife. He was held in contempt for numerous violations of the CPO. The court found Foster (D) guilty beyond a reasonable doubt of four counts of criminal contempt, acquitted him on the other counts, and sentenced him to 600 days' imprisonment. The U.S. Attorney's office later obtained an indictment charging Foster (D) with simple assault, threatening to injure another, and assault with intent to kill. Foster (D) moved to dismiss, claiming a double jeopardy bar to all counts. The trial court denied the double jeopardy claim. The Government (P) appealed in *Dixon*, while Foster (D) appealed the trial court's denial of his motion. After consolidating the two cases, the court of appeals ruled that both subsequent prosecutions were barred by the Double Jeopardy Clause. The Government (P) appealed.

ISSUE: Does the Double Jeopardy Clause permit subsequent prosecution of an offense that has already been the basis of criminal contempt proceedings?

HOLDING AND DECISION: (Scalia, J.) No. The Double Jeopardy Clause does not permit subsequent prosecution of an offense that has already been the basis of criminal contempt proceedings. This applies both to successive punishments and to successive prosecutions for the same criminal offense. This Court has concluded that where the two offenses for which the defendant is punished or tried cannot survive the "same-elements" test, the double jeopardy bar applies. The same-elements test inquires whether each offense contains only elements contained in the other; if so, they are the "same offense," and double jeopardy bars additional punishment and successive prosecution. If not, they are not the same offense, and there is no double jeopardy bar. Dixon's (D) cocaine possession, although an offense under the D.C. Code, was not an offense under the contempt statute until a judge incorporated the statutory drug offense into his release order. Here, where the contempt sanction was imposed for violating the order through commission of the incorporated drug offense, the later attempt to prosecute Dixon (D) for the drug offense resembles the double jeopardy situation. Criminal contempt, at least in its nonsummary form, "is a crime in every fundamental respect." Because Dixon's (D) drug offense did not include any element not contained in his previous contempt offense, his subsequent prosecution violated the Double Jeopardy Clause. The foregoing analysis obviously applies to the indictment against charging Foster (D) with assault, based on the same event that was the subject of his prior contempt conviction for violating the provision of the civil protection order forbidding him to commit simple assault. Thus, the subsequent prosecution for assault is barred. However, the remaining four counts of assault with intent to kill and threats to injure or kidnap are not barred. Each of those offenses contained a separate element, and the test for double jeopardy was not met. Thus, Dixon's (D) subsequent prosecution for cocaine possession, as well as Foster's (D) subsequent prosecution for simple assault, violate the Double Jeopardy Clause and are barred. We overrule our decision in *Grady v. Corbin*, 495 U.S. 508 (1990), which prohibited subsequent prosecutions if, to establish an essential element of an offense charged in that prosecution, the government will prove conduct that constitutes an offense for which the defendant has already been prosecuted. *Grady* lacks constitutional roots; the "same conduct" rule it announced is wholly inconsistent with earlier Supreme Court precedent and with the clear common-law understanding of double jeopardy. Furthermore, *Grady* has already proved

Continued on next page.

unstable in application. Affirmed [as to *Dixon*]. Affirmed in part; reversed in part [as to *Foster*].

CONCURRENCE AND DISSENT: (Rehnquist, C.J.) A defendant who is guilty of possession with intent to distribute cocaine or of assault has not necessarily satisfied any statutory element of criminal contempt. Nor can it be said that a defendant who is held in criminal contempt has necessarily satisfied any element of those substantive crimes. The offenses for which Dixon (D) and Foster (D) were prosecuted in this case cannot be analogized to greater and lesser included offenses; hence, they are separate and distinct for double jeopardy purposes.

CONCURRENCE AND DISSENT: (Souter, J.) If a separate prosecution were permitted for every offense arising out of the same conduct, the government could manipulate the definitions of offenses, creating fine distinctions among them and permitting a zealous prosecutor to try a person again and again for essentially the same criminal conduct. Clearly, when one has already been tried for a crime comprising certain conduct, as here, a subsequent prosecution seeking to prove the same conduct is barred by the Double Jeopardy Clause.

ANALYSIS

The same-elements test was first enunciated by the United States Supreme Court in *Blockburger v. United States*, 284 U.S. 299 (1932), and is commonly referred to as the "*Blockburger*" test. In arriving at its ruling in the instant case, the majority overruled its recent decision in *Grady v. Corbin*, 495 U.S. 508 (1990), which held that in addition to passing the *Blockburger* test, a subsequent prosecution must satisfy a "same conduct" test to avoid the double jeopardy bar. The *Grady* test provided that if, to establish an essential element of an offense charged in that prosecution, the government would prove conduct that constituted an offense for which the defendant had already been prosecuted, a second prosecution may not be had. In the majority's view, *Grady* was not only wrong in principle but had already proved inconsistent in application.

Quicknotes

DOUBLE JEOPARDY CLAUSE A prohibition against a second prosecution for the same offense after an acquittal or conviction for that offense in a prior proceeding or against multiple punishments for the same offense.

Ashe v. Swenson

Convicted robber (D) v. State (P)

397 U.S. 436 (1970)

NATURE OF CASE: Appeal from conviction for robbery.

FACT SUMMARY: Ashe (D) was acquitted of robbing a participant in a poker game but was later convicted of the same offense against a different participant in the same card game.

RULE OF LAW

Collateral estoppel is part of the Fifth Amendment's guarantee against double jeopardy.

FACTS: Four armed men robbed six men who were playing poker. Ashe (D) was tried for robbery of Knight, one of the card players. At trial, persuasive evidence was not given as to Ashe's (D) guilt and he was acquitted. Six weeks later, Ashe (D) was tried for robbery of another participant in the same poker game. Ashe's (D) motion to dismiss based on his previous acquittal was overruled. Witnesses were substantially the same but gave substantially stronger testimony on Ashe's (D) identity. One weak witness from the first trial was not called. Ashe (D) was convicted and sentenced to 35 years imprisonment. Ashe (D) appealed, urging that the determination that he was not present at the robbery by the first jury collaterally estops, under the guarantee against double jeopardy, a retrial of that issue.

ISSUE: Is collateral estoppel part of the Fifth Amendment's guarantee against double jeopardy?

HOLDING AND DECISION: (Stewart, J.) Yes. Collateral estoppel is part of the Fifth Amendment's guarantee against double jeopardy. When an issue of ultimate fact has once been determined by a valid and final judgment, the issue cannot again be litigated between the same parties in any future lawsuits. In criminal cases, collateral estoppel is not to be applied with the hypertechnical and archaic approach of a nineteenth century pleading book, but with realism and rationality. Where there has been a general verdict of acquittal, the court must examine the record of the prior proceeding and conclude whether the jury could have grounded its verdict upon an issue other than that which the defendant seeks to foreclose from consideration. The single rationally conceivable issue in dispute before the jury was whether Ashe (D) had been one of the robbers. The jury found Ashe (D) was not. Under double jeopardy, that issue cannot be relitigated. Reversed.

ANALYSIS

The Double Jeopardy Clause is a guarantee that repeated attempts to convict an individual for an alleged offense, thereby subjecting him or her to embarrassment, expense, and ordeal, and compelling him or her to live in a continual state of insecurity, shall not be allowed. The Model Penal Code suggests that all offenses arising out of one criminal transaction should be tried at one time. Limited circumstances where that would be excused would be where the police, despite diligent effort, did not discover the crime or offense until afterward. Collateral estoppel will not prevent multiple prosecutions when the first trial ends with a guilty verdict.

Quicknotes

COLLATERAL ESTOPPEL A doctrine whereby issues litigated and determined in a prior proceeding are binding upon all subsequent litigation between the parties regarding that issue.

DOUBLE JEOPARDY CLAUSE A prohibition against a second prosecution for the same offense after an acquittal or conviction for that offense in a prior proceeding or against multiple punishments for the same offense.

FIFTH AMENDMENT Provides that no person shall be compelled to serve as a witness against him- or herself, be subject to trial for the same offense twice, or be deprived of life, liberty, or property without due process of law.

Gamble v. United States

Convicted felon (D) v. Federal government (P)

139 S. Ct. 1960 (2019)

NATURE OF CASE: Appeal from affirmance of denial of motion to dismiss an indictment for a federal felon-in-possession-of-a-firearm offense.

FACT SUMMARY: Terance Gamble (Gamble) (D), who had been convicted by a state for possessing a firearm as a felon, contended that it would violate the constitutional prohibition on double jeopardy to be prosecuted by the United States (P) under a federal felon-in-possession law for the identical conduct that underlay the state conviction.

RULE OF LAW

Pursuant to the dual-sovereignty doctrine, the Double Jeopardy Clause allows successive prosecutions by separate sovereigns for the same underlying conduct by a defendant, even where one of the sovereigns is a state and the other sovereign is the federal government.

FACTS: Terance Gamble (Gamble) (D), who had been convicted of second-degree robbery, was found by a local police officer to be in the possession of a gun and convicted under state law for the crime of possessing a firearm as a felon. Thereafter, federal prosecutors indicted him under a United States' (P) felon-in-possession law for the same instance of possession of the gun. Gamble (D) moved to dismiss the federal indictment on the ground that because the federal indictment was for the same offense as the one at issue in his state conviction, he would be subject to double jeopardy in violation of the Constitution's Fifth Amendment. The federal district court denied this motion, invoking the dual-sovereignty doctrine, according to which two offenses are not considered the same offence for double jeopardy purposes if prosecuted by different sovereigns. The circuit court affirmed, and the United States Supreme Court granted certiorari.

ISSUE: Pursuant to the dual-sovereignty doctrine, does the Double Jeopardy Clause allow successive prosecutions by separate sovereigns for the same underlying conduct by a defendant, even where one of the sovereigns is a state and the other sovereign is the federal government?

HOLDING AND DECISION: (Alito, J.) Yes. Pursuant to the dual-sovereignty doctrine, the Double Jeopardy Clause allows successive prosecutions by separate sovereigns for the same underlying conduct by a defendant, even where one of the sovereigns is a state and the other sovereign is the federal government. The dual-sovereignty doctrine is not an exception to the double jeopardy right but follows from the Fifth Amendment's text. The Double Jeopardy Clause protects individuals from being "twice put in jeopardy" "for the same offence." As originally understood, an "offence" is defined by a law, and each law is defined by a sovereign. Thus, where there are two sovereigns, there are two laws and two "offences." This understanding is embodied in the Court's precedents, which not only honor the formal difference between two distinct criminal codes, but also honor the substantive differences between the interests that two sovereigns can have in punishing the same act; Gamble (D) provides no convincing reason to depart from those precedents. Regarding the dissents' objections to this analysis, first, although the Constitution rests on the principle that the people are sovereign, that does not mean that they have conferred all the attributes of sovereignty on a single government. Instead, the people, by adopting the Constitution, have split sovereignty among the federal and state governments, which have different interests and rights. The United States is a federal republic, not a unitary state like the United Kingdom. Because of this, the powers of the federal government and state governments often overlap, with a resulting overlap in regulation, which often has a state layer and a federal layer. This system, while fundamental to the protection of liberty, does not always maximize individual liberty at the expense of other interests. That is why the argument propounded by the dissent and Gamble (D), that the division of federal and state power was meant to promote liberty, and, therefore, cannot support a rule that exposes Gamble (D) to a second sentence for the same conduct, is not convincing. Gamble's (D) attempts to blunt the force of stare decisis here also do not succeed. Gamble (D) contends that the recognition of the Double Jeopardy Clause's incorporation against the states washed away any theoretical foundation for the dual-sovereignty rule. However, the rule rests on the fact that only same-sovereign prosecutions can involve the "same offence," and that is just as true after incorporation as before. Gamble (D) also argues that the proliferation of federal criminal laws has raised the risk of successive prosecutions under state and federal law for the same criminal conduct, thus compounding the harm inflicted by precedent. This objection assumes that precedent was erroneous from the start, so it is only as strong as the historical arguments that have already been found wanting. In any case, eliminating the dual-sovereignty rule would do little to trim the reach of federal criminal law or prevent

Continued on next page.

many successive state and federal prosecutions for the same criminal conduct—unless the long-settled rule that an "offence" for double jeopardy purposes is defined by statutory elements, not by what might be described in a looser sense as a unit of criminal conduct, were overruled. Affirmed.

CONCURRENCE: (Thomas, J.) The founding generation foresaw very limited potential for overlapping criminal prosecutions by the states and the federal government, and therefore had no reason to address the double jeopardy question before the Court. Given the framer's understanding of Congress' limited criminal jurisdiction and the absence of an analogous dual-sovereign system in England, it is difficult to know whether the founders understood the Constitution to prohibit prosecution by a state and the federal government for the same offense.

DISSENT: (Ginsburg, J.) The majority uses a flawed syllogism in reaching its decision. That syllogism centers on the word "offence": An "offence," the argument runs, is the violation of a sovereign's law, the United States and each state are separate sovereigns, ergo successive state and federal prosecutions do not place a defendant in "jeopardy... for the same offence." The flaw inherent in the argument is that the United States (P) and its constituent states, unlike foreign nations, make up "ONE WHOLE." Within that "WHOLE," the federal and state governments should be disabled from accomplishing together what neither government could do alone—prosecute an ordinary citizen twice for the same offence. The notion that the federal government and the states are separate sovereigns overlooks a basic tenet of U.S. federalism, namely, that ultimate sovereignty resides in the governed people, and that the division of governmental authority between the federal government and the state governments was meant to function as a "double security" for the people's rights. However, in the hands of the majority, the separate-sovereign doctrine is used not to shore up people's rights, but instead to withhold liberty. Accordingly, the use of the dual-sovereign doctrine is an erroneous means for giving effect to the Double Jeopardy Clause, which is meant to safeguard the "person" and restrain the government. As a matter of historical constitutional interpretation, the majority discounts incorporation as material to the analysis on the ground that the application of the Double Jeopardy Clause to the states did not affect comprehension of the word "offence" to mean the violation of one sovereign's law. However, prior to incorporation, the Court attributed a separate-sovereigns meaning to "offence" at least in part because the Double Jeopardy Clause did not apply to the states. Therefore, incorporation of the Clause against the states should prompt the Court to consider the protection against double jeopardy from the defendant's perspective and to ask why each of two governments within the United States should be permitted to try a defendant once for the same offense when neither could try the defendant twice. Additionally, the expansion of federal criminal law has exacerbated the problems created by the separate-sovereigns doctrine—which, for these reasons, should be abandoned in the double-jeopardy context.

DISSENT: (Gorsuch, J.) A free society does not allow its government to try the same individual for the same crime until it's happy with the result. Unfortunately, the majority's decision endorses a colossal exception to this ancient rule against double jeopardy. The consequence of the majority's rule is that by considering the federal government and each state to be "separate sovereigns," entitled to try the same person for the same crime, if all the might of one of these "sovereigns" cannot succeed against the presumptively free individual, another "sovereign" may insist on the chance to try again. If both so-called sovereigns succeed, the result is that they can add one punishment on top of the other. A key problem with this approach, however, is that it finds no meaningful support in the text of the Constitution, its original public meaning, structure, or history. Instead, the Constitution promises all Americans that they will never suffer double jeopardy. First, there is no evidence that the framers conceived of the term "same offense" in a technical, lawyerly sovereign-specific way as referring merely to the same statute. Thus, given that double jeopardy prevents one government from prosecuting a defendant multiple times for the same offense under the banner of separate statutory labels, there should be no difference when many governments collectively seek to do the same thing. Imagining the majority's rule from a defendant's perspective, the rule says: "Yes, you were sentenced to state prison for being a felon in possession of a firearm. And don't worry—the State can't prosecute you again. But a federal prosecutor can send you to prison again for exactly the same thing. What's more, that federal prosecutor may work hand-in-hand with the same state prosecutor who already went after you. They can share evidence and discuss what worked and what didn't the first time around. And the federal prosecutor can pursue you even if you were acquitted in the state case." Does none of that offend the Constitution's plain words protecting a person from being placed "twice... in jeopardy of life or limb" for "the same offence?" According to the majority, none of that matters. In effect, the majority reframes the Constitution's protections against double jeopardy to make prosecutors' jobs easier, but that is not for the Court to do. Moreover, there is no doubt that the benefits the framers saw in prohibiting double prosecutions remain real, and maybe more vital than ever. "When governments may unleash all their might in multiple prosecutions against an individual, exhausting themselves only when those who hold

Continued on next page.

the reins of power are content with the result, it is 'the poor and the weak,' and the unpopular and controversial, who suffer first—and there is nothing to stop them from being the last. The separate sovereigns exception was wrong when it was invented, and it remains wrong today."

ANALYSIS

Arguably, incorporation of the Double Jeopardy Clause as a restraint on action by the states has rendered obsolete the rationale for retaining the separate-sovereign doctrine, given that the Clause originally restrained only the federal government and did not bar successive state prosecutions. Before incorporation was effected by the Court in *Benton v. Maryland*, 395 U.S. 784 (1969), without the separate-sovereigns doctrine and its carve-out for successive prosecutions by separate sovereigns, the Double Jeopardy Clause would have barred the federal government from prosecuting a defendant previously tried by a state, but would not have prevented a state from prosecuting a defendant previously tried by the federal government. Because incorporation changed this, so that the double jeopardy proscription now applies equally to the federal government and the states alike, it is arguable that the only purpose the separate-sovereigns doctrine now serves is to enable federal and state prosecutors, proceeding one after the other, to expose defendants to double jeopardy.

Quicknotes

DOUBLE JEOPARDY A prohibition against a second prosecution for the same offense after an acquittal or conviction for that offense in a prior proceeding or against multiple punishments for the same offense.

DUAL-SOVEREIGNTY DOCTRINE The doctrine that state and federal governments (sovereignties) may both prosecute an individual without violating the U.S. Constitution's prohibition against double jeopardy if the individual's act breaks the laws of each sovereignty.

FIFTH AMENDMENT Provides that no person shall be compelled to serve as a witness against him- or herself, be subject to trial for the same offense twice, or be deprived of life, liberty, or property without due process of law.

STARE DECISIS Doctrine whereby courts follow legal precedent unless there is good cause for departure.

North Carolina v. Pearce

State (P) v. Convicted rapist (D)

395 U.S. 711 (1969)

NATURE OF CASE: Appeal from grant of writ of habeas corpus.

FACT SUMMARY: Rice (D) and Pearce (D) contended they could not be sentenced more harshly on retrial than they had been when originally tried.

RULE OF LAW

The guarantee against double jeopardy imposes no restrictions upon the length of sentence upon reconviction for the same crime.

FACTS: In separate cases, Rice (D) and Pearce (D) obtained reversals on their convictions for burglary and rape, respectively. They were granted new trials. On retrial, they were sentenced to a longer sentence than when originally convicted. They appealed, contending this sentence violated the Double Jeopardy Clause. The United States Supreme Court granted certiorari to review the granting of habeas corpus.

ISSUE: Does the guarantee against double jeopardy impose any restrictions upon the length of sentence upon reconviction for the same crime?

HOLDING AND DECISION: (Stewart, J.) No. The guarantee against double jeopardy imposes no restrictions upon the length of sentence upon reconviction for the same crime. In this case, the original conviction was set aside at the defendants' request. Thus, the slate has been wiped clean and no sentencing restrictions exist. As a result, a harsher sentence could validly be imposed. However, in order to avoid any vindictiveness against a defendant who successfully challenges his or her sentence or conviction, when a harsher sentence is imposed, the court must affirmatively show the reasons therefor. As this was not done in this case, the writ of habeas corpus must issue.

ANALYSIS

The United States Supreme Court decided this case on due process grounds, holding due process required findings on the reasons for the harsher sentencing. It was not decided on double jeopardy grounds. This led to subsequent decisions such as *Colten v. Kentucky*, 407 U.S. 104 (1972), which narrowed the application of the present case based on due process grounds where such narrowing could not have occurred under the double jeopardy provisions. The Court there held that a second sentence, handed down by a higher court in a two-tiered trial system, was not subject to this case and could not be harsher than the original sentence.

Quicknotes

DOUBLE JEOPARDY A prohibition against a second prosecution for the same offense after an acquittal or conviction for that offense in a prior proceeding or against multiple punishments for the same offense.

DUE PROCESS The constitutional mandate requiring the courts to protect and enforce individuals' rights and liberties consistent with prevailing principles of fairness and justice and prohibiting the federal and state governments from such activities that deprive its citizens of a life, liberty, or property interest.

WRIT OF HABEAS CORPUS A proceeding in which a defendant brings a writ to compel a judicial determination of whether he or she is lawfully being held in custody.

CHAPTER 13

Post-Conviction Challenges

Quick Reference Rules of Law

Chapman v. California

Convicted felon (D) v. State (P)

386 U.S. 18 (1967)

NATURE OF CASE: Constitutional challenge against a state that permits comments and inferences to be made about why the defendants failed to testify on their own behalf.

FACT SUMMARY: Chapman (D) and Teale (D) refused to take the stand on their own behalf during their trial for kidnapping and murder.

RULE OF LAW

An error is not deemed harmless if there is a reasonable possibility that the evidence complained of might have contributed to the conviction.

FACTS: Chapman (D) and Teale (D) were tried for robbery, kidnapping, and murder. Each (D) refused to testify at trial. Under a California statute, this failure could be commented on by the court and counsel and could be considered by the jury and the judge. Both the prosecutor and the judge commented on Chapman (D) and Teale's (D) failure to testify and the jury was instructed that it could draw inferences from it. Chapman (D) and Teale (D) were both found guilty. After the trial, but prior to appeal, *Griffin v. California*, 380 U.S. 609 (1965), was decided. It held that the California statute violated the Fifth and Fourteenth Amendments. The California Supreme Court held that the comments and instructions were harmless error in *Chapman* and affirmed the conviction. Chapman (D) and Teale (D) appealed, contending that the denial of a federal constitutional right should automatically result in a reversal.

ISSUE: Is an error deemed harmless if there is a reasonable possibility that the evidence complained of might have contributed to the conviction?

HOLDING AND DECISION: (Black, J.) No. An error is not deemed harmless if there is a reasonable possibility that the evidence complained of might have contributed to the conviction. The constitutional standard was set out in *Fahy v. Connecticut*, 375 U.S. 85 (1963). The question is whether there is a reasonable possibility that the evidence complained of might have contributed to the conviction. If the error affects substantial rights, it is never deemed harmless. Before a federal constitutional error can be deemed harmless, the court must be able to declare a belief that it was harmless beyond a reasonable doubt. Here, while California (P) presented a strong circumstantial case, there is no question that the repeated comments and instructions by the judge and prosecutor were highly prejudicial. The error was not harmless. Reversed.

ANALYSIS

Where the evidence of guilt is overwhelming, the United States Supreme Court has declined to reverse for a violation of the right of confrontation. *Harrington v. California*, 395 U.S. 250 (1969). This decision settled the question of automatic reversals for the violation of federal constitutional rights. The Court held if, on their own reading of the record, the violation would not have altered the decision of an average jury, the error was harmless.

Quicknotes

FIFTH AMENDMENT Provides that no person shall be compelled to serve as a witness against him- or herself, be subject to trial for the same offense twice, or be deprived of life, liberty, or property without due process of law.

FOURTEENTH AMENDMENT Declares that no state shall make or enforce any law that shall abridge the privileges and immunities of citizens of the United States; no state shall deny to any person within its jurisdiction the equal protection of the laws.

Wainwright v. Sykes

State (P) v. Convicted murderer (D)

433 U.S. 72 (1977)

NATURE OF CASE: Appeal from issuance of writ of habeas corpus.

FACT SUMMARY: Sykes (D) sought federal review of his conviction even though he failed to object at trial to the things serving as the basis for his federal petition.

RULE OF LAW

Federal habeas corpus relief will not be granted where the petitioner fails to honor state contemporaneous objection rules.

FACTS: Sykes (D) confessed to homicide after being given *Miranda* warnings. He (D) petitioned for a federal writ of habeas corpus on the basis that he was intoxicated and could not understand the *Miranda* warnings. He (D) had not raised this objection at trial, yet the district court issued the writ. The court of appeals affirmed, holding the contemporaneous objection rule did not bar the relief sought.

ISSUE: Will federal habeas corpus relief be granted where the petitioner fails to honor state contemporaneous objection rules?

HOLDING AND DECISION: (Rehnquist, J.) No. Federal habeas corpus relief will not be granted where the petitioner fails to honor state contemporaneous objection rules. If federal relief were granted, defense attorneys would have no inducement to litigate all possible defenses at trial in hopes of federal review. This would lead to costly and duplicitous litigation. As a result, the failure to raise this issue at or before trial constituted a waiver and barred federal collateral relief. Reversed.

DISSENT: (Brennan, J.) Inadvertent procedural defaults should be subject to cure by federal habeas corpus relief.

ANALYSIS

This case requires that cause and prejudice be shown prior to the granting of federal habeas relief. It is believed that collateral review is costly and duplicitous and should be extended only where cause is shown for failure to object at trial and where state procedures prejudiced rights.

Quicknotes

HABEAS CORPUS A proceeding in which a defendant brings a writ to compel a judicial determination of whether he is lawfully being held in custody.

***MIRANDA* WARNINGS** Specified warnings that must be communicated to a person prior to a custodial interrogation; in the absence of the communication of such warnings, any communications made during the interrogation are inadmissible at trial. See *Miranda v. Arizona*, 384 U.S. 436 (1966).

Glossary

Common Latin Words and Phrases Encountered in the Law

A FORTIORI: Because one fact exists or has been proven, therefore a second fact that is related to the first fact must also exist.

A PRIORI: From the cause to the effect. A term of logic used to denote that when one generally accepted truth is shown to be a cause, another particular effect must necessarily follow.

AB INITIO: From the beginning; a condition that has existed throughout, as in a marriage that was void ab initio.

ACTUS REUS: The wrongful act; in criminal law, such action sufficient to trigger criminal liability.

AD VALOREM: According to value; an ad valorem tax is imposed upon an item located within the taxing jurisdiction calculated by the value of such item.

AMICUS CURIAE: Friend of the court. Its most common usage takes the form of an amicus curiae brief, filed by a person who is not a party to an action but is nonetheless allowed to offer an argument supporting his legal interests.

ARGUENDO: In arguing. A statement, possibly hypothetical, made for the purpose of argument is one made arguendo.

BILL QUIA TIMET: A bill to quiet title (establish ownership) to real property.

BONA FIDE: True, honest, or genuine. May refer to a person's legal position based on good faith or lacking notice of fraud (such as a bona fide purchaser for value) or to the authenticity of a particular document (such as a bona fide last will and testament).

CAUSA MORTIS: With approaching death in mind. A gift causa mortis is a gift given by a party who feels certain that death is imminent.

CAVEAT EMPTOR: Let the buyer beware. This maxim is reflected in the rule of law that a buyer purchases at his own risk because it is his responsibility to examine, judge, test, and otherwise inspect what he is buying.

CERTIORARI: A writ of review. Petitions for review of a case by the United States Supreme Court are most often done by means of a writ of certiorari.

CONTRA: On the other hand. Opposite. Contrary to.

CORAM NOBIS: Before us; writs of error directed to the court that originally rendered the judgment.

CORAM VOBIS: Before you; writs of error directed by an appellate court to a lower court to correct a factual error.

CORPUS DELICTI: The body of the crime; the requisite elements of a crime amounting to objective proof that a crime has been committed.

CUM TESTAMENTO ANNEXO, ADMINISTRATOR (ADMINISTRATOR C.T.A.): With will annexed; an administrator c.t.a. settles an estate pursuant to a will in which he or she is not appointed.

DE BONIS NON, ADMINISTRATOR (ADMINISTRATOR D.B.N.): Of goods not administered; an administrator d.b.n. settles a partially settled estate.

DE FACTO: In fact; in reality; actually. Existing in fact but not officially approved or engendered.

DE JURE: By right; lawful. Describes a condition that is legitimate "as a matter of law," in contrast to the term "de facto," which connotes something existing in fact but not legally sanctioned or authorized. For example, de facto segregation refers to segregation brought about by housing patterns, etc., whereas de jure segregation refers to segregation created by law.

DE MINIMUS: Of minimal importance; insignificant; a trifle; not worth bothering about.

DE NOVO: Anew; a second time; afresh. A trial de novo is a new trial held at the appellate level as if the case originated there and the trial at a lower level had not taken place.

DICTA: Generally used as an abbreviated form of obiter dicta, a term describing those portions of a judicial opinion incidental or not necessary to resolution of the specific question before the court. Such nonessential statements and remarks are not considered to be binding precedent.

DUCES TECUM: Refers to a particular type of writ or subpoena requesting a party or organization to produce certain documents in their possession.

EN BANC: Full bench. Where a court sits with all justices present rather than the usual quorum.

EX PARTE: For one side or one party only. An ex parte proceeding is one undertaken for the benefit of only one party, without notice to, or an appearance by, an adverse party.

EX POST FACTO: After the fact. An ex post facto law is a law that retroactively changes the consequences of a prior act.

EX REL.: Abbreviated form of the term "ex relatione," meaning upon relation or information. When the state brings an action in which it has no interest against an individual at the instigation of one who has a private interest in the matter.

FORUM NON CONVENIENS: Inconvenient forum. Although a court may have jurisdiction over the case, the action should be tried in a more conveniently located court, one to which parties and witnesses may more easily travel, for example.

GUARDIAN AD LITEM: A guardian appointed by the court to represent a minor or incompetent person in a legal action.

HABEAS CORPUS: You have the body. The modern writ of habeas corpus is a writ directing that a person (body) being detained (such as a prisoner) be brought before the court so that the legality of his detention can be judicially ascertained.

IN CAMERA: In private, in chambers. When a hearing is held before a judge in his or her chambers or when all spectators are excluded from the courtroom.

IN FORMA PAUPERIS: In the manner of a pauper. A party who proceeds in forma pauperis because of his poverty is one who is allowed to bring suit without liability for costs.

INFRA: Below, under. A word referring the reader to a later part of a book. (The opposite of supra.)

IN LOCO PARENTIS: In the place of a parent.

IN PARI DELICTO: Equally wrong; a court of equity will not grant requested relief to an applicant who is in pari delicto, or as much at fault in the transactions giving rise to the controversy as is the opponent of the applicant.

IN PARI MATERIA: On like subject matter or upon the same matter. Statutes relating to the same person or things are said to be in pari materia. It is a general rule of statutory construction that such statutes should be construed together, i.e., looked at as if they together constituted one law.

IN PERSONAM: Against the person. Jurisdiction over the person of an individual.

IN RE: In the matter of. Used to designate a proceeding involving an estate or other property.

IN REM: A term that signifies an action against the res, or thing. An action in rem is basically one that is taken directly against property, as distinguished from an action in personam, i.e., against the person.

INTER ALIA: Among other things. Used to show that the whole of a statement, pleading, list, statute, etc., has not been set forth in its entirety.

INTER PARTES: Between the parties. May refer to contracts, conveyances, or other transactions having legal significance.

INTER VIVOS: Between the living. An inter vivos gift is a gift made by a living grantor, as distinguished from bequests contained in a will, which pass upon the death of the testator.

IPSO FACTO: By the mere fact itself.

JUS: Law or the entire body of law.

LEX LOCI: The law of the place; the notion that the rights of parties to a legal proceeding are governed by the law of the place where those rights arose.

MALUM IN SE: Evil or wrong in and of itself; inherently wrong. This term describes an act that is wrong by its very nature, as opposed to one which would not be wrong but for the fact that there is a specific legal prohibition against it (malum prohibitum).

MALUM PROHIBITUM: Wrong because prohibited, but not inherently evil. Used to describe something that is wrong because it is expressly forbidden by law but that is not in and of itself evil, e.g., speeding.

MANDAMUS: We command. A writ directing an official to take a certain action.

MENS REA: A guilty mind; a criminal intent. A term used to signify the mental state that accompanies a crime or other prohibited act. Some crimes require only a general mens rea (general intent to do the prohibited act), but others, like assault with intent to murder, require the existence of a specific mens rea.

MODUS OPERANDI: Method of operating; generally refers to the manner or style of a criminal in committing crimes, admissible in appropriate cases as evidence of the identity of a defendant.

NEXUS: A connection to.

NISI PRIUS: A court of first impression. A nisi prius court is one where issues of fact are tried before a judge or jury.

N.O.V. (NON OBSTANTE VEREDICTO): Notwithstanding the verdict. A judgment n.o.v. is a judgment given in favor of one party despite the fact that a verdict was returned in favor of the other party, the justification being that the verdict either had no reasonable support in fact or was contrary to law.

NUNC PRO TUNC: Now for then. This phrase refers to actions that may be taken and will then have full retroactive effect.

PENDENTE LITE: Pending the suit; pending litigation underway.

PER CAPITA: By head; beneficiaries of an estate, if they take in equal shares, take per capita.

PER CURIAM: By the court; signifies an opinion ostensibly written "by the whole court" and with no identified author.

PER SE: By itself, in itself; inherently.

PER STIRPES: By representation. Used primarily in the law of wills to describe the method of distribution where a person, generally because of death, is unable to take that which is left to him by the will of another, and therefore his heirs divide such property between them rather than take under the will individually.

PRIMA FACIE: On its face, at first sight. A prima facie case is one that is sufficient on its face, meaning that the evidence supporting it is adequate to establish the case until contradicted or overcome by other evidence.

PRO TANTO: For so much; as far as it goes. Often used in eminent domain cases when a property owner receives partial payment for his land without prejudice to his right to bring suit for the full amount he claims his land to be worth.

QUANTUM MERUIT: As much as he deserves. Refers to recovery based on the doctrine of unjust enrichment in those cases in which a party has rendered valuable services or furnished materials that were accepted and enjoyed by another under circumstances that would reasonably notify the recipient that the rendering party expected to be paid. In essence, the law implies a contract to pay the reasonable value of the services or materials furnished.

QUASI: Almost like; as if; nearly. This term is essentially used to signify that one subject or thing is almost analogous to another but that material differences between them do exist. For example, a quasi-criminal proceeding is one that is not strictly criminal but shares enough of the same characteristics to require some of the same safeguards (e.g., procedural due process must be followed in a parole hearing).

QUID PRO QUO: Something for something. In contract law, the consideration, something of value, passed between the parties to render the contract binding.

RES GESTAE: Things done. In evidence law, this principle justifies the admission of a statement that would otherwise be hearsay when it is made so closely to the event in question as to be said to be a part of it, or with such spontaneity as not to have the possibility of falsehood.

RES IPSA LOQUITUR: The thing speaks for itself. This doctrine gives rise to a rebuttable presumption of negligence when the instrumentality causing the injury was within the exclusive control of the defendant, and the injury was one that does not normally occur unless a person has been negligent.

RES JUDICATA: A matter adjudged. Doctrine which provides that once a court of competent jurisdiction has rendered a final judgment or decree on the merits, that judgment or decree is conclusive upon the parties to the case and prevents them from engaging in any other litigation on the points and issues determined therein.

RESPONDEAT SUPERIOR: Let the master reply. This doctrine holds the master liable for the wrongful acts of his servant (or the principal for his agent) in those cases in which the servant (or agent) was acting within the scope of his authority at the time of the injury.

STARE DECISIS: To stand by or adhere to that which has been decided. The common law doctrine of stare decisis attempts to give security and certainty to the law by following the policy that once a principle of law as applicable to a certain set of facts has been set forth in a decision, it forms a precedent that will subsequently be followed, even though a different decision might be made were it the first time the question had arisen. Of course, stare decisis is not an inviolable principle and is departed from in instances where there is good cause (e.g., considerations of public policy led the Supreme Court to disregard prior decisions sanctioning segregation).

SUPRA: Above. A word referring a reader to an earlier part of a book. (The opposite of infra.)

ULTRA VIRES: Beyond the power. This phrase is most commonly used to refer to actions taken by a corporation that are beyond the power or legal authority of the corporation.

Addendum of French Derivatives

CHATTEL: Tangible personal property.

CY PRES: Doctrine permitting courts to apply trust funds to purposes not expressed in the trust but necessary to carry out the settlor's intent.

IN PAIS: Not pursuant to legal proceedings.

PER AUTRE VIE: For another's life; during another's life. In property law, an estate may be granted that will terminate upon the death of someone other than the grantee.

PROFIT A PRENDRE: A license to remove minerals or other produce from land.

VOIR DIRE: Process of questioning jurors as to their predispositions about the case or parties to a proceeding in order to identify those jurors displaying bias or prejudice.

QUICK COURSE OUTLINE

CRIMINAL PROCEDURE

CRIMINAL PROCEDURE

Bill of Rights: First eight Amendments to the Constitution of the United States. The states are bound to follow these rules based on the Due Process Clause of the Fourteenth Amendment.

Two exceptions:

1. Right to indictment by a grand jury.
2. Right to reasonable bail.

EXCLUSIONARY RULE

IN GENERAL

The exclusionary rule prohibits introduction of evidence obtained in violation of a defendant's Fourth, Fifth, and/or Sixth Amendment rights. Illegally obtained evidence is inadmissible at trial. Evidence so obtained, however, may be used for impeachment purposes.

"FRUIT OF THE POISONOUS TREE"

All evidence ("fruit of the poisonous tree") obtained from the exploitation of illegally obtained evidence must also be inadmissible at trial. *Wong Sun v. United States*, 371 U.S. 471 (1963).

Exceptions to the "fruit of the poisonous tree" doctrine:

1. Evidence obtained from an independent source.
2. An intervening act of free will by the defendant.
3. Inevitable discovery.

LIMITATIONS ON THE EXCLUSIONARY RULE

1. Inapplicable to grand juries (unless in violation of the federal wiretapping statute), civil proceedings, internal agency rules, and parole revocation proceedings.
2. Good faith reliance on law, defective search warrant, or clerical error.
3. Impeachment purposes.
4. *Miranda* violations. *United States v. Leon*, 468 U.S. 897 (1984).

HARMLESS ERROR TEST

If illegal evidence is admitted, a resulting conviction should be overturned on appeal unless the government can show beyond a reasonable doubt that the error was harmless.

OTHER CONCERNS

The admissibility of evidence or a confession is determined by a judge outside the hearing of a jury. The government bears the burden of establishing the admissibility of the evidence by preponderance of the evidence.

FOURTH AMENDMENT

FOURTH AMENDMENT

"The right of the people to be secure in their persons, houses, papers, and effects, against unreasonable searches and seizures, shall not be violated, and no Warrants shall issue, but upon probable cause, supported by Oath or affirmation, and particularly describing the place to be searched, and the persons or things to be seized."

REASONABLENESS

1. The Fourth Amendment provides that people should be free from unreasonable searches and seizures. Governmental seizures of persons, including arrests, are seizures within the scope of the Fourth Amendment and so must be reasonable.
2. The Fourth Amendment protects the privacy interests of people, not places. *Katz v. United States*, 389 U.S. 347 (1967).

AUTOMOBILE STOPS

Police may not randomly stop a single automobile for license and registration checks. *Delaware v. Prouse*, 440 U.S. 648 (1979).

SEARCH

An important factor in determining the legality of a search under the Fourth Amendment is ascertaining the reasonable expectation of privacy by the person being subjected to that search. *Bond v. United States*, 529 U.S. 334 (2000).

INCORPORATION OF THE "BILL OF RIGHTS"

The Fourteenth Amendment incorporates many of the rights in the Bill of Rights to apply not only to the federal government but also to the states rights.

1. These rights include the following:
   a. Fourth Amendment—prohibition against unreasonable searches and seizures and the exclusionary rule;
   b. Fifth Amendment—prohibition against compulsory self-incrimination;
   c. Sixth Amendment—right to a speedy trial, a public trial, and a trial by jury, to confront witnesses, to a compulsory process, to the assistance of counsel;
   d. Eighth Amendment—prohibition against cruel and unusual punishment.
2. The rights do not include:
   a. Right to grand jury indictment; or
   b. Eighth Amendment prohibition against excessive bail.

PROBABLE CAUSE

Probable cause is the existence of trustworthy facts or knowledge sufficient for a reasonable person to believe that the suspect has committed or is committing a crime.

1. "Stop and Frisk": If police have a reasonable suspicion of criminal activity or involvement in a completed crime, supported by articulable facts, they may detain a person for investigative purposes. *Terry v. Ohio*, 392 U.S. 1 (1968).
2. If the police have reasonable suspicion that the detainee is armed and dangerous, they may frisk the detainee for weapons.
   a. Duration: The detention must be no longer than necessary to conduct a limited investigation to verify the suspicion. If during the detention, probable cause arises, the detention becomes an arrest.

SEIZURE

1. Arrests: An arrest occurs when the police take a person into custody against his will for purposes of criminal prosecution.
   a. An arrest must be based on probable cause. *California v. Hodari D.*, 499 U.S. 621 (1991).
   b. An arrest warrant is generally NOT required for arresting a suspect in a public place.
   c. An arrest warrant is required for a non-emergency arrest of a person in his home.

EVIDENTIARY SEARCH AND SEIZURE

IN GENERAL

1. A proper search requires a valid warrant under the Fourth Amendment, unless the search is one of the valid warrantless searches.
2. Reasonable Expectation of Privacy: In order to contest a search, the person being searched must establish standing. Standing is established through the person showing that he had a legitimate expectation of privacy and that there was governmental conduct involved.
   a. Legitimate Expectation of Privacy.
      i. A right to possession of the place searched.
      ii. The place searched was his home whether or not he owned or had a right to possession of it.
      iii. He was an overnight guest of the owner of the place searched.
   b. Governmental Conduct: Constitutional guidelines for a reasonable search and seizure are limited to actions taken by a government agent. If a non-government agent enacted the search without state authority, a Fourth Amendment challenge cannot be made.
      i. If the crime is induced by governmental conduct that "shocks the conscience," it violates due process.

Evidentiary Search and Seizure continues on page 2

TWO TYPICAL SEARCHES

1. Searches conducted pursuant to a warrant.
2. Valid warrantless searches. *Illinois v. Rodriguez*, 497 U.S. 177 (1990).

1. SEARCHES CONDUCTED PURSUANT TO A WARRANT

1. Warrant must show probable cause [see Probable Cause box on page 1].
   a. Use of informers: "Totality of the circumstances" test.
   b. Going "behind the face" of the affidavit.
2. A search warrant will be held invalid if it meets all prongs of the following three-pronged test:
   a. A false statement was included in the affidavit by the affiant (officer applying for warrant);
   b. Affiant intentionally or recklessly included the false statement; and
   c. The false statement was material to the finding of probable cause.

2. WARRANTLESS SEARCHES: Valid Exceptions to the Warrant Requirement

1. Search Incident to an Arrest.
2. "Automobile" Exception.
3. Plain View.
4. Consent.
5. Stop and Frisk.
6. Hot Pursuit.
7. Administrative Searches.

"SHOCKS THE CONSCIENCE" TEST

1. "Shocks the conscience" test: Due process requires evidence to be obtained in a manner that does not offend one's "sense of justice." *Rochin v. California*, 342 U.S. 165 (1952).
2. Body searches invoke privacy rights and their "reasonableness" requires a balancing between the public's need for the evidence against the gravity of the invasions.

SEARCH INCIDENT TO AN ARREST

1. Incident to a lawful arrest, the police may search the person (or an area within the arm span of the person) to obtain weapons. *Chimel v. California*, 395 U.S. 752 (1969).
2. If person being searched is in an automobile, the search incident to an arrest may include the entire passenger compartment of car (including glove compartment, but not the trunk or any containers).
3. Search must be contemporaneous in time and place with an arrest.
4. Note that if the underlying arrest was not lawful, the subsequent evidence found may be suppressed based on Fourth Amendment issues.

Note: A police officer does not need probable cause to conduct a search incident to a lawful arrest. However, the police officer needs probable cause to seize any object he finds during the search.

"AUTOMOBILE" EXCEPTION

If the police have probable cause to believe that a vehicle contains evidence of a crime, they may search the entire vehicle or any container that might reasonably contain the item for which they had probable cause to search. (Contrast this to a search incident to an arrest.) *Chambers v. Maroney*, 399 U.S. 42 (1970).

However, the police are limited in their search by evidence for which they are looking. If the police have probable cause to believe that an ice chest in the trunk contains contraband, they may search only that ice chest, not the rest of the car. On the other hand, if the probable cause is fairly broad and calls for contraband that may be anywhere in the car, they may search the entire car.

PLAIN VIEW

The police may make a warrantless seizure of evidence in plain view (*Horton v. California*, 496 U.S. 128 (1990)) when they:

1. Are legitimately on the premises.
2. Discover contraband, evidence, fruits, or instrumentalities of crime.
3. See such evidence in plain view.
4. Have probable cause to believe that such item is an instrumentality of a crime or evidence of such.

CONSENT

1. The police may search a person or the premises under the authority of that person if given consent. This is the most popular method of a warrantless search by the police.
2. The consent given must be voluntary and intelligent. However, a voluntary and intelligent consent is not predicated on the person giving the consent knowing that he may withhold consent.
3. The scope of the search is limited by the scope of the consent.
4. Any person with an apparent equal right to use or occupy the property may consent to a search. Any evidence found in such a search may be used against others who reside at the premises or other owners. *Bumper v. North Carolina*, 391 U.S. 543 (1968).

STOP AND FRISK

A police officer may stop a person for arrest if he has a reasonable suspicion based on articulable facts. Stop equals detainment, but does not equal arrest. *Terry v. Ohio*, 392 U.S. 1 (1968).

HOT PURSUIT

Police in "hot pursuit" of a fleeing felon may make a warrantless search and seizure, and may also seize (without a warrant) evidence likely to disappear before a warrant can be obtained. While in pursuit, police may even pursue the suspect into a private dwelling, but must reasonably consider whether or not those inside the dwelling will be harmed.

ADMINISTRATIVE SEARCHES

Agencies may obtain warrants for searches of private residences and commercial buildings. The standard is much lower—a showing of a general and neutral enforcement plan will justify issuance of a warrant.

HABEAS CORPUS

COLLATERAL ATTACK

1. No right to counsel for indigents.
2. Preponderance of evidence standard to show an unlawful detention.
3. State may appeal if the writ is granted.

SENTENCING AND PUNISHMENT

SENTENCING

1. Right to counsel.
2. Right to confrontation and cross-examination.
3. Re-sentencing and reconviction after appeal.
   a. If a harsher sentence is imposed, the reasons must be stated on the record.
   b. Exceptions:
      i. Trial de novo.
      ii. Jury sentencing.

PUNISHMENT

The Eighth Amendment prohibits "cruel and unusual" punishment.

1. Punishment grossly disproportionate to the offense.
2. Death penalty: Not in itself cruel and unusual; however, the judge or jury must have reasonable discretion, full information regarding defendants, and guidance.
   a. May not be imposed for rape of an adult woman.
   b. May not be imposed for felony murder, unless defendant acted with reckless indifference to human life.

SIXTH AMENDMENT

RIGHT TO COUNSEL

Attaches when adversarial judicial proceedings begin. *Powell v. Alabama*, 287 U.S. 45 (1932).

Examples: Formal charge, preliminary hearing, indictment, or arraignment.

"CRITICAL STAGE"

The state does not have to provide an attorney throughout the criminal process, only at a "critical stage" of the proceedings. *Coleman v. Alabama*, 399 U.S. 1 (1970).

FIFTH AMENDMENT

PRIVILEGE AGAINST SELF-INCRIMINATION

"A person shall not be compelled in any criminal case to be a witness against himself."

CONFESSIONS

An accused's Fifth Amendment's rights are violated when prosecution uses at trial evidence of the accused's own incriminating words that were "deliberately elicited" after commencement of adversarial proceedings in the absence of the defendant's counsel.

CUSTODIAL INTERROGATION

"Custodial interrogation" refers to questioning initiated by law enforcement officers after the person has been taken into custody or otherwise deprived of his freedom in a significant way.

1. Custody: The standard is whether, based upon the totality of the circumstances, and assessed objectively, there was a formal arrest or restraint of freedom of movement of the degree associated with a formal arrest. Objective indicia of custody include, but are not limited to:
   a. Formal arrest.
   b. Prolonged detention.
   c. Demeanor of police officers (e.g., confrontational questioning) and the ratio of officers to suspects. *Thompson v. Keohane*, 516 U.S. 99 (1995).
2. Interrogation: Interrogation is any direct or express questioning about the crime being investigated. *Illinois v. Perkins*, 496 U.S. 292 (1990).

INTERROGATIONS

Miranda v. Arizona, 384 U.S. 436 (1966).

Rule: Any statement, whether inculpatory or exculpatory, made by a suspect as the result of custodial interrogation may not be used against the suspect in a criminal trial, unless it is shown that the police provided procedural safeguards to secure the suspectís Fifth Amendment privilege against self-incrimination.

EXCLUSIONARY RULE

1. Impeachment of defendant: Statements obtained in violation of *Miranda* may be used nonetheless to impeach defendant at trial if he testifies inconsistently with the custodial statement.
2. The "fruit of the poisonous tree" doctrine does not apply to *Miranda* violations.

COERCED CONFESSIONS

1. Rule: A statement obtained by police from a suspect as the result of coercion is inadmissible at trial in violation of the Due Process Clause and the Fifth Amendment privilege against self-incrimination.
2. State action is required (i.e., a government agent, such as police, must be coercing the confession).
3. Factors in determining voluntariness:
   a. Use or threatened use of force;
   b. Use of psychological pressure;
   c. Promise of leniency in exchange for a confession; and
   d. Use of deception to secure a confession. *Spano v. N.Y.*, 360 U.S. 315 (1959).

MIRANDA WARNINGS

1. *Miranda v. Arizona*, 384 U.S. 436 (1966): For a confession to be admissible under the Fifth Amendment privilege against self-incrimination, a person in custody must, prior to interrogation, be informed in substance, that:
   a. He has the right to remain silent;
   b. Anything he says can and will be used against him in court;
   c. He has the right to the presence of an attorney; and
   d. If he cannot afford an attorney, one will be appointed for him if he so desires.
2. The above warning must be given:
   a. When anyone is in custody by a government agent and accused of a crime; and
   b. Prior to an interrogation by the police.

USE OF CONFESSION

Use of confession for impeachment: Statements obtained in violation of the *Miranda* warnings may be used to impeach the defendant's trial testimony but may not be used as evidence of guilt. Subsequent confessions are valid.

WAIVER

1. Waiver: Accused may waive the privilege against self-incrimination and/or right to counsel. Waiver must be:
   a. Voluntary;
   b. Knowing; and
   c. Intelligent. *Moran v. Burbine*, 475 U.S. 412 (1986).
2. Waiver may occur only after the full *Miranda* warnings have been given.
3. Prosecution must prove the validity of a waiver by a preponderance of the evidence.
4. Waiver must be expressly stated or implied by the accused's words or conduct. Exceptions: *Oregon v. Elstad*, 470 U.S. 298 (1985).
   a. Public safety: Need not be given in a situation where there is a threat to public safety.
   b. Covert interrogation: Not required when the suspect is unaware that he is speaking with a law enforcement officer.
   c. Booking questions: Need not be given prior to routine booking questions.

CONFESSIONS

1. Fourth Amendment: "Harmless error test"—voluntariness.
2. Fifth Amendment: Privilege against Compelled Self-Incrimination.
3. Sixth Amendment: Right to Counsel.

RIGHT TO SILENCE

Suspect may enforce this right in any manner and at any time prior to or during questioning by indicating that he wishes to remain silent. Interrogation must then cease. The invocation of this right after receiving Miranda warnings may not be used against the defendant at trial (e.g., prosecution cannot argue that defendant must be guilty because he remained silent during questioning). *Doyle v. Ohio*, 426 U.S. 610 (1976); but see *Fletcher v. Weir*, 455 U.S. 603 (1982).

RIGHT TO ASSISTANCE OF COUNSEL

1. If the accused indicates that he wishes to consult an attorney at any time prior to or during questioning, interrogation must cease.
2. Police may not reinstate communication unless the accused's counsel is present.
3. The cease-interrogation rule does not apply:
   a. Unless the accused's request for an attorney is unambiguous; or
   b. If the accused's request for counsel cannot be reasonably construed as an expression of a desire for assistance in dealing with the custodial interrogation.

GOVERNMENT AGENT

1. A waiver is not applicable in the case of secret interrogations, i.e., the use of an undercover agent to elicit incriminating information.
2. The government must demonstrate the intentional relinquishment or abandonment of a known right or privilege.
3. Once right to counsel attaches, if defendant requests assistance of counsel, deliberate elicitation must cease until the defendant talks with his lawyer or initiates communication.

DELIBERATE ELICITATION

"Deliberate elicitation" occurs when the police: *Massiah v. United States*, 377 U.S. 201 (1964).

1. Intentionally seek to obtain incriminating information from the accused either via formal interrogation or use of an undercover agent;
2. Intentionally create a situation likely to induce the accused to make incriminating statements; or
3. Knowingly exploit an opportunity to confront the accused without counsel present.

DOUBLE JEOPARDY

IN GENERAL

- Under the Fifth Amendment, a person may not be retried for the same criminal offense once jeopardy has attached.
- Jeopardy attaches in a jury trial at the empaneling and swearing in of the jury.
- In bench trials, jeopardy attaches when the first witness is sworn in.

Double Jeopardy continues on page 4

SEPARATE SOVEREIGNS

The constitutional prohibition against double jeopardy does not apply to trials by separate sovereigns. Thus, one may be tried for the same conduct by both state and federal government or even by two states. However, municipalities are not considered a separate sovereign for the purposes of double jeopardy analysis. *Heath v. Alabama*, 474 U.S. 82 (1985).

Example: A woman is falsely charged with the murder of her husband in the state of Washington. The woman is subsequently convicted of that charge by a vindictive jury. In time, however, she finds out that her husband is alive and well in Louisiana. Based on erroneous legal advice given by a disbarred fellow prisoner, the convicted murderer escapes to Louisiana and kills her husband. The woman is brought to trial in Louisiana. She raises the defense of double jeopardy. Her defense will fail because two sovereigns, in this case, Washington and Louisiana, may try and convict her of the same crime—murder of her husband.

REPROSECUTION

1. After mistrial: *United States v. Perez*, 22 U.S. 579 (1824); *United States v. Dinitz*, 424 U.S. 600 (1976).
   a. Definition: A mistrial is a judicial determination of a trial before a verdict is reached; it is granted on the motion of either party or on the court's own motion that a new trial be held.
   b. Mistrial over the defendant's objection bars prosecution unless there is a "manifest necessity."
   c. Verdict of conviction could be reached but would have to be reversed on appeal due to an obvious procedural error.
   d. Mistrial with defendant's consent: Defendant may not object to re-prosecution.
   e. Exception: the Double Jeopardy Clause bars re-prosecution after a mistrial is declared if the prosecutor or judge intended to provoke the mistrial motion.
2. After acquittal: *Ball v. United States*, 163 U.S. 662 (1896); *Green v. United States*, 355 U.S. 184 (1957).
   a. Definition: Verdict of not guilty by judge or jury or any ruling by a judge that represents a resolution in the defendant's favor of some or all of the factual elements charged.
   b. Rule: Defendant may not be re-prosecuted.
3. After dismissal: *United States v. Scott*, 437 U.S. 82 (1978).
   a. Definition: Judicial termination of a trial before a verdict is reached, but does not involve a resolution of any factual element of the offense charged.
   b. Rule: Re-prosecution after dismissal made on defendant's motion or without objection therefrom is not barred.
4. After conviction: *United States v. Tateo*, 377 U.S. 463 (1964).
   a. Rule: Re-prosecution of a defendant who successfully appeals his conviction on the basis of prejudicial error is not barred.
      i. Exception: Reversal of a conviction obtained on the sole ground that the evidence was insufficient to sustain the guilty verdict.
   b. Multiple punishment: The government is not barred from convicting and imposing punishment on a person in a single proceeding for violation of separate statutory provisions that constitute the same offense if the legislature so permits.
   c. Collateral estoppel: Prosecutor may not re-litigate an issue of ultimate fact in a second prosecution if it has once been determined by a valid and final judgment in the defendant's favor. Test is whether a rational jury could have based its verdict upon an issue other than that which the prosecutor seeks to foreclose from consideration.

ENTRAPMENT

IN GENERAL

1. Entrapment applies when a government agents acts improperly with respect to the defendant. It can be raised either as a defense at trial or as a pretrial motion thereby barring prosecution of the entrapped party. *United States v. Russell*, 411 U.S. 423 (1973).
2. Conduct may be so outrageous in some circumstances to constitute a violation of due process. Jurisdictions employ either a subjective or an objective test.
   a. Subjective test: entrapment is proved if a government agent implants in the mind of an innocent person the disposition to commit the offense and induces its commission so that the government may prosecute. *Sherman v. United States*, 356 U.S. 369 (1958).
   b. Objective test: Entrapment is proved if police conduct falls below commonly accepted standards for the proper use of government power.

TRIAL

RIGHT TO FAIR TRIAL

1. Right to trial by jury. *Duncan v. Louisiana*, 391 U.S. 145 (1968).
   a. Only for "serious" offenses, i.e., those with the possibility of imprisonment for more than 6 months.
   b. No jury trial required for civil contempt. Where no penalty is authorized, if the actual sentence is more than 6 months, the right to a jury trial arises.
   c. No constitutional right to 12 jurors, but there must be at least 6.
   d. No right that the jury verdict be unanimous if there are 12 jurors; for 6-person juries, decision must be unanimous.
   e. Right to have the jury selected from a cross-section of the community
      i. Defendant may contest the fact that a significant segment of the community has been omitted, even if he is not a member of such segment.
      ii. Applies only to venire: there is no right to proportional cross-section of community on the defendant's particular jury.
   f. Prosecution may not use peremptory challenges to exclude potential jurors solely because of race or gender. *Batson v. Kentucky*, 476 U.S. 79 (1986).

RIGHT TO CONFRONT WITNESS

1. Defendant has the right to confront witnesses in a criminal prosecution. This right is not absolute:
   a. Defendant may be removed if he is disruptive.
   b. Defendant is not deprived of his right if he voluntarily leaves the courtroom during the proceedings.
2. Confessions of co-defendants are inadmissible, unless:
   a. References to the defendant can be removed;
   b. The co-conspirator is a witness; or
   c. It is used in rebuttal of defendant's allegation that his own confession was the result of coercion.
3. Statements made at prior judicial proceedings may be admitted if:
   a. Witness is unavailable following a good-faith effort on the part of the prosecution; and
   b. Defendant had an opportunity to cross-examine.

RIGHT TO COUNSEL

1. Right to Appointed Counsel at Trial: "In all criminal prosecutions, the accused shall enjoy the right to…have the assistance of counsel for his defense."
   a. Indigents: Right to counsel does NOT apply in all criminal prosecutions.
   b. Felonies: Defendant has right to counsel in felony criminal trials; the accused is entitled to court-appointed attorney if he cannot afford one.
   c. Misdemeanors: An indigent is entitled to the assistance of counsel in any trial in which a sentence of imprisonment may be imposed.
2. Right of Self-Representation: Must be asserted in a timely fashion or it is LOST; Court may appoint "standby counsel" to take over during trial if necessary.
3. Right to Appointed Counsel on Appeal: The Sixth Amendment is limited to prosecutions. The defendant is entitled to the assistance of counsel under the Fourteenth Amendment Due Process and Equal Protection Clauses for a first appeal but not for subsequent appeals. *Douglas v. California*, 372 U.S. 353 (1963).
4. Right to Effective Representation of Counsel: The Sixth Amendment also requires that counsel provide effective representation of the client. *Strickland v. Washington*, 466 U.S. 668 (1984).
   a. Representation is ineffective if counsel's conduct "so undermines the proper functioning of the adversarial process that the trial cannot be relied on as having produced a just result."
   b. Test:
      i. Deficient representation: Defendant must identify acts or omissions depriving him of effective assistance, based on objective, prevailing norms.
      ii. Prejudice: Defendant must show a reasonable probability that but for such acts or omissions the result would have been different.